Mysticism without Bounds

Mysticism without Bounds

Essays from the
International Conference on Mysticism
-Human Transcendence,
Economic Life, Medical Materialism-

Editor
Dr. Kurian Kachappilly CMI

Christian World Imprints™

First Published in 2015 by

Christian World Imprints(TM)
Christian Publishing & Books from India
H-12 Bali Nagar, **New Delhi-110015**
info@christianworldimprints.com
www.ChristianWorldImprints.com
Phone: +91 11 25465925

ISBN-13: 978-93-5148-064-8 ISBN-10: 93-5148-064-X

Cataloging in Publication Data--DK
Courtesy: D.K. Agencies (P) Ltd. <docinfo@dkagencies.com>

Mysticism without Bounds (Conference) (2011 : Bangalore, India)
Mysticism without bounds : essays from the International Conference on Mysticism : human transcendence, economic life, medical materialism / editor, Dr. Kurian Kachappilly, CMI.
pages ; cm
Includes index.
ISBN 9789351480648
ISBN 935148064X

1. Mysticism--Congresses. 2. Transcendental logic--Congresses. 3. Economic life of fixed assets--Congresses. 4. Economics--Religious aspects--Congresses. 5. Biomedical materials--Congresses. I. Kachappilly, Kurian, editor. II. Title.

DDC 204.22 23

Printed at Replika Press Pvt. Ltd.

Dedicated
To

Mr. Joseph Kurian Kachappilly
and
Mrs. Annam Joseph Kachappilly
-My beloved parents-
who instilled in me
a quest for the glimpse of the 'Beyond'
revealed in the history of the humanity.

The Book

"*Mysticism without Bounds*" explores the interdisciplinarity as a way of naming the phenomenon of crossing-over boundaries that mysticism makes possible. Scientists and rescarchers reveal that certain common grounds do exist among the various forms of consciousness, scattered among the world's religions, theologies, sciences, philosophies, and art forms. The discovery of such points of convergence among religions, sciences, and philosophies on 'mysticism' is intellectually very exciting and it holds out the possibility of creating a new worldview in which these disciplines would be seen as distinct yet complementary ways of exploring the same underlying reality. The present volume ignites an awareness about 'Mysticism' embracing various realms of human thought, like -- Timelessness with Time, Everyday Spirituality, Human Transcendence, Economic Life, Medical Materialism, Yogic Interpretation, Mystical Enthusiasm, Psychology, Contemporary Scientific Views, and Theology.

The book is a collection of keynote/research papers presented at the International Conference "Mysticism without Bounds" (MwB) with the sole motive to create awareness of the essential unity of humanity irrespective of any social barrier. The author hopes that they will help the inquisitive readers and lovers of truth in discovering this essential unity so as to work for the good of the humanity.

The Editor

Dr. Kurian Kachappilly is the Professor of Philosophy and Religion at the DVK, Bangalore, India; and Associate Director, Research Centre, Christ University, Bangalore, India. Hc holds Master's Degrees in English Literature and Psychology, and a Licentiate and Doctorate in Philosophy from the Katholieke Universiteit Leuven, Belgium. He is a Visiting Fellow at the Bangalore University, Bangalore; Katholieke Universiteit Leuven (KUL), Belgium; Fakultät für Informatik & Wirtschaftsinformatik, Würzburg, Germany; the University of Santo Tomas, Manila, the Philippines; and other institutions.

Dr. Kachappilly is a prolific writer with several books and many scientific articles to his credit. Some of the books include *God of Love Revisited* (1998), *Between Partners* (1999), *Word of God Retold* (2001), *God of Love: A Neoclassical Inquiry* (2002), *God-Talk Reconstructed: An Introduction to Philosophy of God* (2006), *Process: Implications and Applications* (2006), *Mystic Musings in Art and Poetry : Thematic Essays from the International Conference 'Mysticism without Bounds'* (2013), *Mystic Musings in Religions: Selected Papers from the International Conference 'Mysticism without Bounds'* (2013), etc. His major areas of research are 'Indian Roots of Process Philosophy', 'Whitehead and Philosophical Doctrines of Buddhism', 'Innovative Experiments in Pedagogy', 'Religion vis a vis Society', 'Inquiry into Religious Experience' and 'Corporate Social Responsibility'.

Contents

1. Introduction 1
Dr. Kurian Kachappilly CMI

2. Mysticism Yesterday, Today, Tomorrow: The Intersection of the Timeless with Time 13
Dr. Bernard McGinn

3. Economic Life and Human Transcendence: A Paradigm for Everyday Spirituality 31
Dr. Antoon Vandevelde and Dr. Roy Varghese Palatty

4. The Sacred in Creation and the God-intoxicated Celt? 57
Dr. Una Agnew

5. Distress and Joy in love of the Absolute: Understanding the Mystic's Love Affair with God 75
Dr. Paul Moyaert

6. Between Mysticism and Medical Materialism: The Relevance of William James and John Dewey for the Question of Neurotheology 99
Dr. Jonathan Weidenbaum

7. Sobering Up To the Other: Levinas' Paradoxical View on Mystical Enthusiasm 113
Dr. Roger Burggraeve

8. "I Live, Not I; It is Christ Who Lives in Me" (Gal 2:20): A Yogic Interpretation of Paul's Religious Experience....... 141
Dr. Joseph Pathrapankal CMI

9 Mysticism without Bounds: Jacob Boehme, William Blake and Jung's Psychology 153
Dr. Patrick Menneteau

10. 'Cosmo-theandric' Mysticism: Contemporary Scientific Views.................................. 179
Dr. Thomas Manikkam CMI

11. Mysticism and Apophaticism without or within Bounds?: Four Contemporary Challenges for Christian Theology in a Western Context.............................. 201
Dr. Lieven Boeve

12. The Mystical Strategies of St Teresa of Avila.............. 221
Dr. Peter Mark Tyler

13. Presence and Mysticis: Retrieval of Pseudo-Dionysius in Deconstruction and Theology........................... 245
Dr. Sebastian Madathummuriyil

14. Contributors.................................. 267

15. Index of Subjects.............................. 273

16. Index of Authors 283

1

Introduction
'Mysticism without Bounds'

Dr. Kurian Kachappilly CMI
Christ University, Bengaluru, India

'Mysticism' (from the Greek *mystikos*) is "the pursuit of communion with, identity with, or conscious awareness of an ultimate reality, divinity, spiritual truth, or God, through direct experience, intuition or insight."[1] In fact, there is no single definition or common description of mysticism, for mysticism is a trans-cultural phenomenon, found in all different religions. Strictly speaking, mysticism is not to be connected with religions per se, for its scope is very wide, embracing all realms of human thought. Hence, in "Mysticism without Bounds" (MwB2011), an attempt is made to explore the "mystical consciousness" from different disciplines, like religions (Hinduism, Judaism, Christianity, Islam, Buddhism, Taoism, etc), sciences (biology, new physics, neuroscience, and logic), humanities (philosophy, theology, spirituality, psychology, etc.), and art forms (poetry, music, dance, visual arts and rituals).

The MwB2011 – jointly organized by Christ University and the DVK, under the aegis of Dharmaram College - was attended by over 320 delegates from thirty countries like Australia, Belgium, Canada, China, Congo, Germany, Korea, Japan, Nigeria, Philippines, South Africa, Sweden, Thailand, UK and USA. There were about 200 Indian delegates from different universities, faculties, institutes and centres

[1] http://en.wikipedia.org/wiki/Mysticism

across the Indian Subcontinent. There were also representatives from various Indian Associations like ACPI (Association of Christian Philosophers of India), BAP (Bangalore Academy of Philosophers), KPC (Kerala Philosophical Congress), ILAAM (Indian Leuven Alumni Association Meeting), etc. About 150 scholarly papers were presented in five parallel sessions, chaired by delegates, participants and invited guests, in addition to the key-note papers. Some of the highlights of the MwB2011 include (i) Inauguration by Dr. Jose Panthaplamthottiyil, (ii) Presidential Address by Swami Veda Bharati, (iii) Key-note papers by Dr. Bernard McGinn (USA), Dr. Paul Moyaert (Belgium), Dr. Peter Tyler (UK), Dr. Reimund Bieringer (Belgium), Dr. Una Agnew (Ireland) and Dr. Francis Vineeth (India).

May I place on record my heartfelt thanks and appreciation to all the delegates, presenters, participants, event partners, who have extended their wholehearted support toward the successful organization of the MwB2011, especially to all the heads of the institutions: Dr. Augustine Thottakara (Rector, Dharmaram College), Dr. Thomas C. Mathew (Vice Chancellor, Christ University) and Dr. Francis Thonippara (President, DVK); Dr. Lieven Boeve (Dean, Faculty of Theology, KUL, Belgium); Dr. Antoon Vandevelde (Dean, Institute of Philosophy, KUL, Belgium); and Dr. Annette Meuthrath (Asia Desk, Institute of Missiology Missio, Aachen, Germany). In a special way, I do acknowledge with thanks my great indebtedness to the administration and office-bearers of the Institute of Missiology Missio, Aachen, Germany, for their generous contribution and support toward the organization of the International Conference, 'Mysticism without Bounds' (MwB2011), from January 05 – 08, 2011.

Part I

Some of the philosophical questions concerning mystical consciousness are: (i) What is its cognitive value, its potential reality-revealing function, if it has one? (ii) How to evaluate mystical consciousness 'within' a tradition? (iii) How to evaluate mystical consciousness independent of ('without') a particular tradition?[2]

[2] Here I gratefully acknowledge my indebtedness to my Professor Dr. Greg Moses (who was a visiting fellow at the Institute of Philosophy, K.U. Leuven, Belgium) for

It is fairly clear that mystic quests, as traditionally conceived, are 'salvation' trips rather than 'truth' trips. The last thing a mystic himself/herself would want to do is to prove his/her faith/experience, in the sense a scientist would understand the word 'proof'. The well-known epithet of Kierkegaard 'Let all the proofs go!'[3] probably alludes to this conviction of mystics. Mysticism doesn't just happen inside a (religious) tradition; rather it tries to bring a tradition to perfection in the interior dimension of people and in their lives as a whole. As Gimello points out, the function of Buddhist meditation is to induce an experiential realization of the truths of Buddhism: this is enlightenment, liberation, or *Nirvāṇa*.[4] The mystical quest, thus, functions as a privileged test of valuational and empirical adequacy of a (religious) tradition in which it takes place. Mystics 'prove' a religious tradition, not with logical and empirical arguments, but by showing what happens when it is put into practice in a radical way in the inner person. According to Carl Albrecht, genuine mysticism often is accompanied by gratuitous love, which is the goal of all knowledge. This love serves as the only unmistakable criterion for the authenticity of mystical experiences.[5]

Such criteria do work well 'within' the religious traditions and they would help us to establish the validity of such mystical experiences. But, it seems that the determination of the evidential value of mystical experiences requires some ways of evaluating the complex phenomenon of mysticism independent of ('without') religious traditions. Perhaps the most straight forward and the most common way of positing the question is: Can the mystical experience be justified, or grounded? We can approach this question from different perspectives.

First of all, there are philosophers, like Huxley and Clifford, who hold the view that the 'ethics of belief' compels one to withhold acceptance of belief, unless all the evidence points to its truth. For example, Clifford, in his book *Lectures and Essays*, states that "it is wrong

---

the conception and development of this section. Cf. http://members.optusnet.com.au/~gjmoses/relxp4fr.htm.

[3] Cf. S. Kierkegaard, *Philosophical Fragments*, trans. David F. Swenson, Princeton: Princeton University Press, 1936, 31-33.

[4] Gimello, *An Introduction to Zen Buddhism*, cited in C. Humphreys, *Zen Buddhism*, London: Unwin, 1961, 154.

[5] See, H.M.E. Lassalle, Zen Meditation for Christians, Illinois: Open Court, 1974, 51.

always, everywhere, and for anyone to believe anything upon insufficient evidence."[6] Although scientific methodology requires objectivity, we do not apply Clifford's 'ethics of belief' to every aspect of our own lives. There are times in our lives when we allow what we hope and fear to influence what we choose to believe rather than insisting on rigorous proofs. Moreover, it seems meaningless to evaluate mystical experience on the plain of rationality. As William Alston suggests, people who fail to acknowledge the difference between religious experience and sense perception are guilty of "epistemic chauvinism" – treating criteria developed in one practice as relevant for another different practice.[7]

Secondly, there are other theologians and philosophers, like Schleiermacher and Pascal, who argue that religion is purely an affair of the 'heart' and not of the 'mind'. Schleiermacher, for instance, holds the view that God is reached through the experience, or "feeling of absolute dependence,"[8] which is not at all an aspect of reason. The consciousness of being absolutely dependent, for him, is the same as "being in relation with God," which, he believes, is an absolute irreducible feature of religion. In fact, Schleiermacher has had great influence on the philosophy of religion. More and more people have become convinced that religion has nothing to do with reason, but only with experiences. Such an attitude is devastating and dangerous for various reasons. (i) It bifurcates reason from other human faculties, which otherwise cannot be conceived as watertight compartments; rather any human response (such as mystic experience) should be a total response, involving the cognitive, conative and affective aspects/dimensions of human person. (ii) Religion becomes a totally subjective affair, in which 'anything goes'; that is to say, religion becomes 'a matter of taste', not different from liking or disliking, for instance, a person or thing.

Thirdly, there are scientists, philosophers and theologians, who like to shun both 'epistemic chauvinism' and 'religious subjectivism' as extreme views, and emphasize complementarity between science and religion. Science and religion are conceived as two faces of one project:

---

[6] Clifford, *Lectures and Essays*, New York: Macmillan, 1901, 176.

[7] William Alston, "The autonomy of religious experience," *IJPR*, 1992, 67.

[8] Schleiermacher, *The Christian Faith*, ed. H.R. Mackintosh, Philadelphia: Fortress Press, 1928, 18.

"Science without religion is lame, religion without science is blind."[9] As two faces of one project, science and religion are indeed complementary, and both are necessary and dependent on each other in many ways. Religion depends on science in order to know the ever changing factual scenario of which it has to make sense; whereas science depends on the conceptual models of religion or view of life in order to determine its own meaning. The necessity of interdependence and complementarity is amply brought out by Galileo: "The Bible shows the way to go to Heaven, not the way the heavens go,"[10] and Bruemmer: "Science shows us the way the heavens go, but not the way to go to Heaven."[11] "Mysticism without Bounds" thus explores this interdisciplinarity- as a way of crossing-over boundaries - that mysticism makes possible and concrete; and helps us to discover those points of convergence that exist among the various forms of consciousness, scattered among the world's religions, theologies, sciences, philosophies, and various art forms.

In fact, different religious and theological traditions have described this fundamental mystical experience in various ways. However, at the core of all the major religions and theologies, there exists a current of mystical teachings which, when compared to one another, exhibit a startling degree of cross-cultural agreement. Consider some of the mystical utterances: *Puruṣa eva idam sarvam* (Ṛgveda); "*Sarvam khalu idam Brahma*" (Ch. Upaniṣad); "Flight of the Alone to the Alone" (Plotinus); "*Nos totaliter convertimur in Deum*" (Meister Eckhart); "It is the vision of the One" (Henry Suso). All these mystical hymns/songs express the intuitive vision or direct experience of the 'One' as the inner reality of all – an ego-transcending and world-transcending experience.

Sciences and mysticism appear antithetical, but we find in mysticism a type of spirituality which has close epistemological parallels to science. Studies in several areas of science address the same issues that concern the mystics, and while science, like quantum physics, does not 'prove' mystical teachings, the fundamental reality which it describes is not

---

[9] Albert Einstein, *Out of My Later Years*, New York: Philosophical Library, 1950, 51.

[10] Cf. Perry M. Rogers, *Aspects of Western Civilization*, New Jersey: Prentice Hall, 1998, 44.

[11] Vincent Bruemmer, "Science, Religion and Agency of God," ed. Andre Cloots & Santiago Sia, *Framing a Vision of the World*, Leuven: Leuven University Press, 1999, 19.

incompatible with the fundamental reality testified to by the mystics. Apart from some branches of science, various philosophical disciplines, such as ontology (which is concerned with the nature of reality), epistemology (which deals with the nature, acquisition and limitations of knowledge) and phenomenology (which insists on the first-person, experiential stance that mystics try to achieve) would appear to relate to various aspects of mystical consciousness, although they have not yet been correlated in a systematic way.

Many art forms are not only ways for mystics to communicate what they are trying to teach, but they have also helped shape the minds and imaginations of the mystics. Poetry, music, dance, visual arts and rituals have emerged as fascinating ways to connect the undifferentiated states of oneness, non-duality, and the differentiated states of diversity and multiplicity. Gerardus Van der Leeuw, for instance, explains how music helps us overcome all boundaries: "Music leads into the depths of life, there where the boundaries flee away."[12] Similarly, art's function to represent reality as matter-spirit continuum, human icons as sacred stories, music as an agent of transcendence, poetry as symbolic and suggestive method of communication and communion with the divine, and sacraments as ways of uniting humanity with God are some of the major themes in the New Age Spirituality.

The discovery of such points of convergence among religions, sciences, philosophies and arts on 'mysticism' is intellectually very exciting; and it holds out the possibility of creating 'a new worldview' in which these disciplines would be seen as distinct yet complementary ways of exploring the same underlying reality.[13] This new worldview can create an awareness of the essential unity of humanity, and work for the welfare of all, irrespective of social, political and religious differences.

Part II

True to the spirit of interdisciplinarity, which the phenomenon of mysticism makes possible, this work contains eight original and scholarly papers from different streams of thought. Prof. Dr. Bernard

---

[12] Gerardus Van der Leeuw, *Sacred and Profane Beauty*, New York: Holt, Rinehart and Winston, 1963, 257.

[13] Cf. www.centerforsacredsciences.org, 4 Dec 2011.

McGinn, in his "Mysticism: Yesterday, Today, Tomorrow" highlights the way in which mysticism both as a phenomenon *within* religion and as an aspect *of* religion always has had a temporal dimension, and has served to revitalize tradition - to challenge and renew rather than reject. With regard to history, the essay investigates how mysticism as an aspect *of* religion has enjoyed a surprising historical development - a before, a now, and a future. Even as a phenomenon *within* religion, some forms of mysticism may aim for an escape from time, but, as Dr. McGinn argues, the realization of this goal is itself realized only *through* time, that is to say, it is a temporal process, involving a long period of preparation, a moment of realization, and finally an often lifelong commitment to make the encounter(s) with God effective in the life of the mystic and those whom he or she encounters.

Dr. Antoon Vandevelde and Roy Varghese Palatty, in "Economic Life and Human Transcendence: A Paradigm for Everyday Spirituality" make explicit the spiritual aspects of economic activities, which involves three dimensions. First of all, spirituality involves a certain relation to oneself; and it is argued that this is also required by sensible economic action. Secondly, spirituality is utterly important in our relations with others, for instance, on the work floor. Finally, spirituality has a macro dimension, which entails an acute awareness of the gift dimension of life and a sense of connectedness to the universe.

Dr. Una Agnew, in her "The Sacred in Creation and the God-intoxicated Celt" examines the phenomenon of what Macquarrie calls 'the God-intoxication' of the Celt and investigates something of its mystical influence in some aspects of Celtic Christianity. Inspired by a foundational Creation Myth, Sean Ó Duinn refers to *nert*, a primordial sacredness that invades the universe with fecundity and dynamic energy. Beginning in time as an initial undifferentiated source of power, this energy becomes personalized in the form of gods and goddesses, and these gods or goddesses become Christianized so that their kingdoms persist as 'thin places' permeable to transcendent deity. A Christian prayer to the One true God of all the elements demonstrates a conversion from a deep rooted reverence of pagan energy to a fully personalized Christian God. Since, similar prayer formulae are found in Hindu Scriptures and the Celtic *lorica,* she draws an interesting parallel, which would form the basis for challenging Hindu-Celtic discussion and dialogue.

Based on the autobiographical works of Teresa of Avila, Dr. Paul Moyaert, in his "Distress and Joy in loving the Absolute," argues that mystic love has to be understood from the perspective of a passionate love in which desire is dominating love. However, mystic love, it is argued, doesn't fall together with the burning flame of desire. For, mystic love, which is a journey through the desert, consists in a painful transformation of a passionate love of desire into a love without desire, called in Christian mysticism, 'the marriage with God'.

The main objectives of Dr. Jonathan Weidenbaum's paper "Between Mysticism and Medical Materialism" are (i) to outline the relevance of James and Dewey for the increasingly popular strategy of identifying the numinous with the neurological; and (ii) to examine a more far-reaching question: 'If mystical experiences cannot be fully accounted for through brain science, can they be employed as further evidence for the existence of God, or some other version of the divine'? In his paper Dr. Weidenbaum seeks to demonstrate that a re-discovery of the reflections of James and Dewey on these topics not only contributes to one of the most vital and contemporary debates in the philosophy of religion, but serves to illuminate the very nature of spirituality.

Dwelling on the thoughts of Levinas, Dr. Roger Burggraeve, in his "Sobering Up To the Other: Levinas' Paradoxical View on Mystical Enthusiasm," discovers a double, apparently contradictory, approach to mystical enthusiasm. Upon closer inspection, the author maintains, they do not annul each other but on the contrary need each other. Illustrating his stand, the author further argues that in his first major work, *Totality and Infinity*, Levinas is quite disapproving of 'mystical enthusiasm;' but in his second major work *Otherwise than Being or Beyond Essence*, the idea of enthusiasm appears once again. Especially Levinas' movement of 'trans Descendence', he concludes, offers possibilities for a Christian 'thorough reflection' on mysticism, starting from Spirit-theology.

Dr. Joseph Pathrapankal, in his article "I Live, Not I; It is Christ Who Lives in Me,"analyzes Paul's mystic experience of a union between himself and Christ, an experience which lies at the very basis of his life and mission. This analysis is carried out from a Yogic perspective in the hope that this attempt would contribute towards an Indian interpretation of a biblical text. Yoga is a method by which an individual may become united with God, and to achieve such a union with God is the perfect yoga, which in Christian language is often called mystic union. Paul is a model for everyone who wants to get into a close relationship with Christ and he invites everyone to have this experience of oneness and togetherness with Christ, which we can call a *yogic* experience.

In his paper, "William Blake's Mystical Visions and the Science of Psychology," Dr. Patrick Menneteau presents the components of the mystical visions of the eighteenth-century English poet William Blake as they can be empirically observed in his poetry and illustrations, in the light of Carl Gustav Jung's hypothesis of the collective subconscious, which is characterized as interdisciplinary: empiricism, phenomenology, mythology, occultism, mysticism, and alchemy as parts of his psychological research. Dr. Menneteau takes up this study and research along the following lines: (i) some parallels between Jung and mysticism, (ii) mysticism without bounds: a possibility or a danger: the psychological dimension of mysticism and (iii) the mystical dimension of psychology, 'mysticism unbound'.

"Contemporary Sciences offer Insights for 'Cosmo-theandric' Mysticism" is indeed a grand 'offer' of late Dr. Thomas Manikkam to the MwB2011 International Conference. Based on the scientific observations of Edwin Hubble and supported by Albert Einstein, Stephen Hawking and others, Dr. Manikkam welcomes the scientific cosmology of the "Expanding Universe" and interprets this expanse of the universe as set in motion by a 'designer' God who governs it with immanently interacting laws of rhythmic motions, and as such this universe indicates intrinsic values for all subsystems, including our planet Earth together with all its living and non-living components. This interpretation of the universe is also corroborated, on the one hand, by the findings of biological and ecological world views emerging from Quantum physics and, on the other, by psychologists like G. Bateson, who read our mental process as always a sequence of interactions between the various elements of reflection and awareness, what is generally called "Human Consciousness," leading to the Upanishadic understanding of Energy, as Consciousness of God, or the unbroken Ultimate Reality; from that One is born life, mind and the worlds.

From a western cultural-theological perspective, Christian mystical experience and the accompanying negative theology face challenges from (i) the philosophical engagement with negative theology, (ii) cultural encounters with religion and spirituality, (iii) scientific challenges to mystical experiences, and (iv) interreligious comparative accounts of mysticism. In his "Mysticism and Apophaticism without or within Bounds?", Dr. Lieven Boeve argues that the attempt of most of these approaches to understand Christian mysticism from underlying generic patterns, thus reducing the very particularity and narrativity of Christianity to these structures, misses, from a Christian theological perspective mystical experience (and the negative theology, from which it arises), what is fundamentally unique about the Christian mystical tradition.

Dr. Peter Tyler in "The Mystical Strategies of St. Teresa of Avila," argues that the context of Avila's circumstances, especially inquisitorial pressure, as a result of traces of *alumbradismo*, her status as a woman and her interest in mystical prayer, means that her texts have to employ a particular 'mystical strategy', termed the *theologia mystica*. This strategy, inherited from the medieval Dionysian tradition emphasizes both *affective* and *deconstructive* approaches to mystical writing. Here the author concentrates on the six 'strategies of unknowing': direction of locution, contradiction, humility, disorientation, humour and ordinary speech. By employing these strategies, Teresa of Avila shows herself to be a true master of 'mystical strategy' in preserving the importance of personal affective prayer in times of great institutional pressure against these forms of prayer.

In harmony with postmodern sensibilities, Dr. Sebastian Madathummuriyil in "Mysticism in Postmodern Theology" explores Jean-Luc Marion's theological and phenomenological projects to liberate theology's God (and phenomenology's phenomenon) from the limits and preconditions of human thought and language. Employing the Dionysian notion of God as beyond both affirmation (metaphysics of presence) and negation (negative theology), the possibility of a "third way" is opened up, in which the author argues that the retrieval of Dionysius' theology in the phenomenological and theological projects of Marion embodies the re-emergence of mysticism in postmodern theology by re-imagining God's insistent and abiding presence, paradoxically, in terms of apparent withdrawal, distance, or absence.

To conclude, let these scholarly and challenging papers from different streams of thought create an awareness among the inquisitive readers of the need of overcoming the 'boundaries' and discovering the 'unity' of self, which the international conference 'Mysticism without Bounds' aims at: "One who knows only the differentiated experience [...] comes to know an undifferentiated experience," the experience of "the primal self, *das Urselbst*."[14] The unity of self is often conceived and interpreted in terms of 'God-experience' with its basis within non-phenomenal self, and a unity that promises the unity of all experiences within the phenomenal world.

[14] Cf. Phil Huston, *Martin Buber's Journey to Presence*, New York: Fordham University Press, 2007, 68.

2

Mysticism Yesterday, Today, Tomorrow
The Intersection of the Timeless with Time

Dr. Bernard McGinn
University of Chicago, Chicago, USA

In his *Four Quartets*, the greatest mystical poem of the twentieth century, T. S. Eliot has these well-known lines:

> But, to apprehend
> The point of intersection of the timeless
> With time, is an occupation for the saint-
> No occupation either, but something given
> And taken, in a lifetime's death in love
> Ardour and selflessness and self-surrender![1]

This paper will be a meditation on these lines, more specifically a consideration of how mysticism involves the intersection of the timeless with time, as well as the simultaneity of the point and infinity. These intersections, I believe, are defining marks of mysticism - yesterday, today, and tomorrow.

---

[1] T. S. Eliot, "The Dry Salvages," in *Four Quartets,* London: Faber & Faber, 1959, 44. For studies, Paul Murray, *T. S. Eliot and Mysticism: The Secret History of "Four Quartets,"* New York: St. Martin's Press, 1991; Michael Spencer, "Mysticism in T. S. Eliot's *Four Quartets*," *Studies in Spirituality* 9 (1999), 230-66; and Kenneth Paul Kramer, *Redeeming Time: T. S. Eliot's Four Quartets*, Lanham, MD: Cowley Publications, 2006.

Mysticism is a modern term created by Western scholars of religion, though with roots in Christian use of the qualifier *mustikos* (hidden) in such phrases as *sensus mysticus*, *contemplatio mystica*, and *theologia mystica*.[2] Nevertheless, many faith traditions have been willing to use the word mysticism as a way of pointing to the importance of deeper consciousness of the divine presence as a life-transforming process, however differently this is conceived across traditions. Some students of mysticism have seen mysticism as essentially a way to escape from the constraints of quotidian life and the temporal process in order to encounter God in the timeless now of divine eternity. Mysticism, therefore, has been viewed as the core of religion, a union with God that is essentially the same across all faiths, however varied its expressions. On the other hand, other scholars have emphasized that mysticism is contextual and has always constituted a threat, implicit or explicit, to the established temporal structures of religions - earned, legal, and institutional.

All three of these views have elements of truth, but if taken in isolation none of them captures the full meaning of the phenomenon. Mysticism is a complex and contentious phenomenon that resists single-minded reductions. In this talk, I will touch on only one issue, examining mysticism, or what I prefer to call "the mystical element of religion,"[3] as containing a temporal and an eternal dimension, as well as a particular and universal aspect.

Mysticism as a phenomenon *within* a particular religion and as an aspect *of* religion in general always has a temporal dimension. Within any religious tradition we can say that however much some mystics and forms of mysticism may aim for an escape from time, the attainment of this goal is itself realized only *through* time, that is, as part of a temporal process involving, most often, long periods of preparation, some form of attainment of the desired goal of finding God, as well as a return

---

[2] For a brief history of the term, see Louis Bouyer, "Mysticism. An Essay on the History of the Word," in *Understanding Mysticism*, ed. Richard Woods, Garden City: Doubleday, 1980, 42-55.

[3] For an argument supporting the language of "the mystical element of religion" (an expression I take over from Friedrich von Hügel), see Bernard McGinn, *The Foundations of Mysticism: Origins to the Fifth Century*, New York: Crossroad, 1991, xvi.

to temporality and a commitment to live in a way that manifests the effects of the encounter with God or the Ultimate. This is why most mystics have sought to spread their message to others. The historical dimension of the mystical process, as well as the temporal dimension of the impact the mystics have had is what makes it possible to write histories of Hindu mysticism, Buddhist mysticism, Jewish mysticism, Christian mysticism, or Islamic mysticism.

Different traditions approach the importance of this historical dimension in diverse ways that I hope may become part of our discussions at this conference. Here, I will restrict my remarks to my own tradition, that is, to some considerations on the intersection of the timeless with time in the history of Christian mysticism. In Christian belief, human beings have no power to attain the higher, eternal world on their own. What makes contact with God possible is God's initiative of coming into time, particularity, and corporality. Christians believe that God became human in Jesus Christ, entering human history both in his short life in Palestine two millennia ago, as well as in his continuing temporal existence in the church.[4] Hence, within Christianity mysticism cannot, by definition, be a historical or static reality, but must be an evolving phenomenon helping to complete the Body of Christ, as the great twentieth-century mystic Pierre Teilhard de Chardin realized so well. The historical evolution of mysticism, no less than the development of doctrine, issues a strong challenge to those who try to view Christianity as an unchanging, ideal reality without serious mutation and change. Within the context of what the late Ewert Cousins called the emergence of "world spirituality,"[5] the changes to come in Christian mysticism as it interacts in ever more complex fashion with other traditions during the twenty-first century, will probably be even greater than those of the past. But, what does it mean for Christian mysticism to have evolved and developed and how does this involve the intersection of the timeless with time?

---

[4] For interesting modern reflections on the Incarnation and the spatio-temporal world, see Thomas Torrance, *Space, Time and Incarnation*, Oxford: Oxford University Press, 1969, especially 74-76.

[5] See Ewert H. Cousins, *Global Spirituality: Toward the Meeting of Mystical Paths*, Madras: Radhakrishnan Institute of the University of Madras, 1985.

My reflections on this issue come from my own attempt over several decades to write a history of Christian mysticism,[6] as well as a consideration of some specific themes developed by mystical authors. For me studying and writing about the evolution of Christian mysticism has been a process, both reassuring and surprising. When I first conceived of writing a history of Christian mysticism, I had a number of convictions, perhaps better surmises, about the shape and intent of the project. Some of these have been confirmed in the actual process of writing. Among these was my sense that no form of Christian mysticism should ever be considered as final or normative—all the vibrant mystics and groups of mystics, especially when seen in their contexts, are historical instantiations of the supreme core of Christian mysticism, the prime intersection of the timeless and time in the life of Christ.[7] A major structural motif of my approach from the outset, however, has proven richer and more surprising than I originally thought.

My initial supposition about the development of Christian mysticism was that it could be structured according to three great layers, sediments, or strata—a kind of geological model. Over the foundation set down in scripture and the faith of the church (itself never static), the first major level of the mystical tradition was what can be termed as monastic mysticism, in the sense that it found its first formal expression in the thought of Origen of Alexandria, the great proto-monastic exegete and theologian of the third century. Monastic mysticism found its institutional matrix in the development of the form of life we call "monasticism" in the fourth century. This assured it a location in society and an historical situation and continuity that allowed its proliferation in East and West. In Western Christianity, the twelfth century, known as the era of the birth of Scholastic theology, is now equally famous as being the golden age of monastic theology and mysticism.

Something extraordinary happened around the year 1200 in the West. Social, cultural, and religious forces suddenly helped in initating a new layer of mysticism, novel forms of encountering God characterized

---

[6] Bernard McGinn, *The Presence of God: A History of Western Christian Mysticism*, New York: Crossroad-Herder, 1991- 4 vols.

[7] See Hans Urs von Balthasar, "Spirituality," in *Explorations in Theology I: The Word Made Flesh*, San Francisco: Ignatius Press, 1989, 211-26.

by democratization (being expressly open to all believers), secularization (capable of being realized outside the cloister), and vernacularization (expressed in the expanding vernacular literatures). This new layer, or sediment, was birthed within the context of experiments in religious life, especially the mendicants and the beguines, and was noteworthy because, for the first time in Christian history, women played a preponderant part. It also witnessed the creation (sometimes also the resuscitation) of mystical themes and forms of language not found in traditional monastic mysticism, a prime example being the possibility of attaining a deep union of identity with God, at least on some level. A less happy consequence was the beginning of tensions between mystical teachers and the institutional guardians of orthodoxy, a topic of great complexity that I can only mention here.[8] This layer of what I have called "The New Mysticism" formed the second major stage in the story of Western Christian mysticism, one that bridged the gap of the split of Western Christendom into the mutually-contending worlds of Roman Catholicism and Protestantism in the sixteenth century.

Nevertheless, it also seemed clear to me from the beginning of my work that Western Christian mysticism has undergone a third major shift in the Early Modern period. This level, which I've referred to as the "Crisis of Mysticism," is still with us, though developments in the twentieth century begin to suggest that we can speak of it as a stratum of both crisis and renewal. Battered by internal forces, especially the papal condemnation of "Quietistism," the primary form of late seventeenth-century mysticism, and undercut from without by the rise of the Enlightenment rationalistic view of human nature and destiny, mysticism as a living intellectual force collapsed in the eighteenth and nineteenth centuries. This was, however, a vibrant time for Eastern Christian mysticism in Russia. It was not until around 1900 that new (often non-theological) interest in mysticism opened up the possibility for a rebirth, one that has continued to grow in the past century due to three sources. The first was the emergence of important mystical teachers, both within and without the formal religious world ("unchurched mysticism"); the

---

[8] For more on this, Bernard McGinn, "'Evil-Sounding, Rash, and Suspect of Heresy': Tensions between Mysticism and Magisterium in the History of the Church," *Catholic Historical Review* 90 (2004), 193-212.

second was the flowering of the study of mysticism in many disciplines (theology, philosophy, psychology, etc.); the third was the emergence of interreligious dialogue on mysticism, which, despite considerable input from adherents of many traditions, may said to be still in its infancy.[9]

What a deepening awareness of the nature of this three-layered model has revealed to me is the extent of the interactive nature of the levels. In the mystical tradition, because the teachings of the mystics deal with attempts to find the hidden God and to express this ineffable contact to others, we see an ongoing intersection of the timeless with time. All the writings, sayings, and practices of the mystics are temporal and cultural constructions that can be looked on as evidence for the study of past societies and religions. Yet there is more. Because the various mystics and forms of mysticism represent attempts, impossible but necessary, to speak of what lies beyond human time and space, they contain core insights that both challenge and instruct current believers who are drawn by the same desire to find deeper contact with the divine. Mystical teaching has a presentiality that is different in nature from the doctrinal and legal pronouncements of the past.

Though every religion depends on the process of the handing on of truths and practices--what Christians call tradition--the mystical tradition seems to have a special form of tradition. This is visible in the way in which past and present have interacted in the formation of the various layers and types of mysticism. The three great layers that I have pointed to were to some extent successive, but it is more important to note that they have always interacted, both in the past and in the present. For example, the New Mysticism that began about 1200 did not cancel out the importance of the monastic mysticism that preceded it—it grew out of it and continued to feed upon it for its own vitality. Meister Eckhart, one of the most original of Christian mystics, for all his freshness, is not fully comprehensible without understanding how he used the mysticism of Pseudo-Dionysius to find ways of expressing the union of God's ground and the soul's ground. Other fourteenth-century mystics, such as the English canon Walter Hilton, nourished themselves

---

[9] For some reflections on this new development and its possible future, Bernard McGinn, "The Venture of Mysticism in the New Millennium," *New Theology Review* 21 (2008), 70-79.

on the riches of the twelfth-century Cistercian and Victorine mystics in order to give shape and order to the mystical teaching of the late Middle Ages. In mid-twentieth-century Christianity it was a monastic mystic, Thomas Merton, who did more than anyone to help spread the message of the importance of contemplation to a broad audience. In short, what has continued to surprise me is how the temporal unfolding of Christian mysticism provides a richer and richer symphonic whole precisely because each of the major levels can still provide living resources for what has come after. Theologically, the source of this ongoing vitality lies in the way in which the great mystics have come into contact with timeless Truth and been able to convey something of this in their writings. The great scholar of Jewish mysticism, Gershom Scholem, recognized this when he said that the mystic not only hands on a religious tradition, but also claims to have had direct contact with the source of the tradition, which is why Scholem argued that for the most part mystics have revitalized the religious traditions in which they stand, rather than challenging or seeking to overturn them.[10]

The Christian mystics provide intriguing insights into the mystery of the intersection of the timeless and time and of the concrete here and the infinite there. Here, I will concentrate on how some late medieval mystics used terms and images regarding limits, or limit situations, specifically "point," "rim," and "atom," to express the intersection of the human and divine realms. These terms, to be sure, have different valences, but they all can be used to express insights about the temporal and the spatial aspects of the meeting of Creation and the Creator. A more detailed study of such words and their use would reveal further observations on this perhaps overlooked aspect of the history of mysticism. Let me start with two great mystics who were almost exact contemporaries, Dante Alighieri (1261-1321) and Meister Eckhart (ca. 1260-1328).

Dante's *Commedia*, composed from about 1308 to 1320, is many things, not least a mystical poem, especially the *Paradiso*. The poem is a journey through time and space, both in the personal sense of recounting the story of Dante the pilgrim, and in the universal sense of containing an entire cosmology and a history of salvation, beginning

[10] Gershom Scholem, "Mysticism and Society," *Diogenes* 58 (1967), 1-24.

from the pilgrim's lostness in sin, *nel mezzo di cammin di nostra vita* (Inf. 1.1), through the circles of hell, purgatory, and heaven, finally to fruition in the vision of the eternal *l'amor che move il sole e l'altre stelle* (*Par*. 33.145).[11] Contrary to some recent critics who want to make Dante into a deconstructionist *avant le lettre*, I think that we need to take the poet's acceptance of medieval belief seriously, not least his claims that he actually knows whereof he speaks when he says he went to heaven. In his letter to Can Grande della Scala, Dante claims, like Paul in 2 Corinthians 12:2-4, to have journeyed to heaven. Speaking of himself in the third person (again like Paul), he says that "the author" "[…] saw certain things which the one who descends from there [i.e., heaven] is powerless to relate," because "[…] 'the intellect plunges itself to such a depth' in its very longing, which is for God, 'that memory cannot follow'." Thus, "memory fails, since it has transcended the range of human faculty."[12] Similar claims to be like Paul are found throughout the *Paradiso*. The point of such claims is not to debate whether or not Dante the author did indeed assert he had gone to heaven, but to realize that the theological and mystical intent of the poem is to show the readers how they should see their lives partaking of the same journey toward eternity as Dante the pilgrim. Again, the letter to Can Grande says, "[…] the purpose of the whole [poem] and the part [*Paradiso*] is to separate those living in this life from the state of misery and to lead them to the state of heavenly joy."[13] Or, in the words of Par. 1.70-72, although "passing beyond humanity (*trasumanar*) may not be set forth in words, therefore, let the example suffice for any for whom grace reserves that experience." The *Commedia* is a true fiction in the sense that it presents the true meaning of an individual life as an exemplification of the destiny of humanity realized through the Incarnation. The poem not only contains mystical teaching; it embodies *theologia mystica* in its intricate web of positive and negative language about God designed to

[11] For a text and translation, see *Dante Aligheri: The Divine Comedy*, trans. by Charles S. Singleton, Princeton: Princeton University Press, 1982.

[12] Dante's *Epistola XIII* to Can Grande della Scala can be found in Paget Toynbee, ed., *Dante Aligheris Epistolae: The Letters of Dante*, Oxford: Clarendon Press, 1966, where the letter, however, is numbered as X. This passage is from X. 28 (ed., 189-90; trans., 208-09). The poet is commenting on and citing *Par*. 1.7-9.

[13] Ep. X.15 (ed., 178).

lead the reader beyond the temporal and the local world into the eternal and the infinite realm.

Some key themes in the *Paradiso* are of particular importance for showing how Dante understood the intersection of the timeless and time. Here, I only have time to look at one, the notion of the *punto* (point), the infinitesmal spot or place where the finite creation crosses over into infinity, which is also where time yields to eternity. In his upward movement through space and time, as well as the sempiternal *aevum* that mediates between time and eternity, Dante finally reaches the *primum mobile*, the first created sphere that provides motion to all the lower spheres. Gazing at the rapidly-revolving *primum mobile* in *Paradiso* 28.16-18, he says, "I saw a point which radiated a light so keen that the eye on which it blazes needs must close because of its great keenness." As Christian Moevs has shown, this *punto* is God in the sense of "the indivisible irreducible unity, a measure of space and time reduced to infinity, to the dimensionless," and therefore the *punto* represents "the nexus between the world and its ground of being, between the multiplicity of creation and the self-subsistent reality in which it consists."[14] (This is why Dante also associates the *punto* with the Incarnate Word.) Later, in the *canto* Dante goes on to say "[...] from that *punto* [...] depends heaven and all nature" (*Par.* 28.41-42), and he describes how the choirs of heaven sing "to that fixed point (*punto fisso*) which holds and shall ever hold them to the 'where' (*ubi*) in which they have ever been" (*Par.* 28.95-96). This point is God, but not God in God's trinitarian nature, something that the pilgrim will not see until he has passed over into the eternal heavenly *empyreum* in *Cantos* 30-33. The *punto* is God as the intersection of time and eternity, the paradoxical coincidence of the dimensionless point and the universe that depends upon it (see *Par.* 29.1-18). As Dante summarizes in *Canto* 30.11-12: "Not otherwise the triumph which always plays around the point that overcame me (*al punto che mi vinse*), seeming to be embraced by that which it embraces."

---

[14] Christian Moevs, "Il puno che mi vinse: Incarnation, Revelations, and Self-Knowledge in Dante's *Commedia*," in *Dante's 'Commedia': Theology as Poetry*, ed. Vittorio Montemaggi and Matthew Treherne, Notre Dame: University of Notre Dame, 2010, 267-76 (quotations at 267, and 270), as well as Moevs's *The Metaphysics of Dante's "Commedia,"* Cambridge: Cambridge University Press, 2005, Chap. 5.

Dante's German contemporary, the Dominican Meister Eckhart, can be read as preaching a message of fleeing time, space, and all particularity in order to plunge into *das einic ein*, the "Single/Only One" of the ground in which God and the soul are identical. The Eckhartian poem called the *Granum sinapis*, for example, commands the reader: "Drive away all something, all nothing/ Leave place, leave time, avoid images too [...]/ Sink all my something into God's nothing, / Sink in the bottomless flood!"[15] The friar's full message, however, is deeper and more complex, not a final simple flight *from* time and multiplicity, but a dialectic of detaching and regaining, a willingness to surrender all things in order to find them in a new way.

Eckhart's imperative of detachment and divesting oneself of all things, even self-identity, holds out a promise that total detachment (*abgescheidenheit*) and letting-go (*gelassenheit*) make it possible to fulfill the Pauline command of realizing in our own lives Christ's coming "in the fullness of time" (Gal. 4:4). In German Sermon 38, for example, Eckhart interprets Paul's fullness of time (*plenitudo temporis*) not only as the soul's essential independence from time, but also as the gathering up of the whole of history into the present moment, that is, into the "now of eternity in which the soul knows all things in God new and fresh and present and joyous as I have now at present."[16] Thus, Eckhart reminds his hearers that, like Christ, they possess the fullness of time within the eternity present in their ground, if only they can come to recognize this and live their lives on the basis of this truth. What it means to realize the "fullness of time" within daily existence is, I think, made clear by the Dominican's notion of learning to "live without a why" (*sonder/ âne warumbe*), that is, to live like God, who has no "why."[17] This is to live in time from the perspective of eternity. The person who lives "without a why," like God, is no longer constrained by the whys and wherefores of doing things for any external purpose, but only acts out of

[15] I use my translation found in *The Essential Writings of Christian Mysticism*, New York: Random House, 2006, 295.

[16] Meister Eckhart, Pr. 38 (DW 2:231-32). The same interpretation of Gal. 4:4 is found in Prr. 4, 11, and 24 (DW 1:74, 177-78, 422-23), and in the Latin works in *In Io.* n. 293 (LW 3:245).

[17] On living "without a why," see Bernard McGinn, *The Mystical Thought of Meister Eckhart*, New York: Crossroad, 2001, 147-61.

an expression of inner joy and overflowing goodness. Living "without a why" helps us understand why Eckhart's mysticism, though it insists that separation from time and the world is necessary, can also be accurately, if paradoxically, described as a "this-worldly mysticism."[18]

These reflections on the relation of time and eternity in Eckhart lead to the consideration of another aspect of his preaching that has long been a puzzle. German Sermon 86 has been seen as one of Eckhart's most profound homilies, but has also been a problem due to its obscurity and differences in vocabulary (and sometimes themes) from his other preaching.[19] In this sermon the preacher exegetes the story of Mary and Martha from Luke 10. Traditionally, the account had been read as teaching the superiority of the contemplative life, as represented by Mary, but Eckhart argues for the superiority of the life that combines active, practical service and contemplative desire as figured in Martha. The preacher mounts numerous arguments, exegetical and theological, for the superiority of Martha's role. Among these is Eckhart's analysis of why Jesus called out Martha's name twice (Lk 10:41). According to Eckhart, the first "Martha" referred to her "perfection in temporal works," while the second indicated that she did not lack anything necessary for eternal happiness. Eckhart praises Martha by saying that she stands in the midst of things but they do not reside in her. Therefore, she is one of the "unimpeded people" (*âne hundernisse*), who "stand in the midst of things but not in things." Eckhart continues, "They stand very near and yet do not have any less of it than if they stood up there, at the rim of eternity" (*umberinge der êwichkeit*). Therefore, Martha is also said to have "redeemed the times" (Eph. 5:16), "by continually ascending by means of the mind to God; not according to different images, but by means of living intellectual truth." Although this ascent might seem to abstract her from time and space, its goal is described as "standing above all things, yet under God, on the rim of eternity."

[18] Reiner Schürmann, *Meister Eckhart. Mystic and Philosopher*, Bloomington: Indiana University Press, 1978, 47, 109-10.

[19] Pr. 86 can be found in DW 3:481-92. I use the translation of Frank Tobin in *Meister Eckhart, Teacher and Preacher*, ed. Bernard McGinn, New York: Paulist Press, 1986, 338-45. There is an extensive commentary on this sermon; see especially Dietmar Mieth, *Der Einheit von Vita Activa und Vita Passiva in den deutschen Predigten und Traktaten Meister Eckharts und bei Johannes Tauler*, Regensburg: Pustet, 1969.

What is this mysterious "rim of eternity"? The sermon tries to explain by distinguishing three modes of attaining God: first, seeking God through creatures; second, a "pathless path [...] beyond self and all things, beyond will and images"; and finally, "a path that is yet a being-at-home. It is to see God is his ownness" (*sînesheit*), as Christ did when he said "I am the way, the truth, and the life" (Jn. 14:6).[20] The sermon identifies the "rim of eternity" with the second mode, a direct contact with God that is nevertheless lower than the unmediated vision of the divine *sînesheit*, not unlike Dante seeing the divine *punto* that is not yet the vision of the Trinity. The "rim of eternity," then, might be said to be another way of expressing where time and eternity intersect.[21] If the *umberinge der êwichkeit* can serve as a spatio-temporal metaphor for this encounter, it is important to remember that for Eckhart, as for all Christian mystics, it is always the Incarnate Word who effects this coincidence of opposites. In German Sermon 91 he says, "God brings eternity into time and with himself brings time into eternity. This takes place in the Son, when the Son pours himself out in eternity, then all creatures are poured out with him."[22]

Two English mystics from the end of the fourteenth century provide us with more insight on how mystical authors struggled to find words to express the convergence of the domains of time and eternity. The anonymous author of the *Cloud of Unknowing* wrote in the last decade of the fourteenth century. The visionary Julian of Norwich was given her showings in 1363, wrote them down not long afterwards as *A Vision showed to a Devout Woman*, and, after many years reflecting on the theological meaning of the visions, completed the Long Version of her text, entitled *A Revelation of Love*, in the early fifteenth century. Both mystics sought to convey what it means to find eternity in the midst of time.

The author of *The Cloud of Unknowing* introduces his special exercise of "lifting up the heart to God with a humble impulse of

---

[20] These passages are taken from Pr. 86 (DW 3:485-87; trans. 340-41). The expression *umberinge der êwichkeit*, found five times here, does not occur elsewhere in Eckhart's corpus.

[21] Eckhart's "rim of eternity" is so obscure that little comment has been given it.

[22] Pr. 91 (DW 4:96).

love" in Chapters 3-6 of the treatise.[23] His teaching about how to put a "cloud of unknowing" between oneself and created reality and to strike against the divine cloud of darkness and unknowing "with a sharp dart of longing love" (Chap. 6) is well known. Less studied is how these chapters contain a profound doctrine on the role of time in the exercise of seeking God. The prayer exercise he teaches, according to the author, "does not need a long time before it can be done, as some men seem to think." Rather, "It is the shortest possible exercise that men can imagine. It is neither longer not shorter than an atom (*athomus*)," which, according to the "good philosophers in the science of astronomy, is the smallest particle of time. It is so little that, because of its littleness, it is indivisible and almost inconceivable" (*undepartable and neighonde incomprehensible*).[24] Echoing Anselm's *Meditations*, the author says that God will ask us to give an account of all our time, and that such an account "is neither longer nor shorter but exactly equal to each single stirring that is in the chief working power of your soul, that is, the will." Each impulse of love that seeks to attain God is therefore no more nor less than an atom of time. God gives the soul its time atom-by-atom and it is within this "indivisible and almost inconceivable" instant that we either find God or forget him by a direct, vertical relationship. Human weakness cannot expect to be attentive to all these instants (22,560 atoms per hour in medieval reckoning!). Therefore, the only way to be assured of finding God in each atom of time is "for the love of Jesus." The intersection of time and eternity is once again Christological: "So love Jesus and everything that he has is yours. By his Godhead he is the maker and giver of time. By his manhood he is truly the keeper of time. And by his Godhead and manhood together he is the truest judge and accountant of the spending of time."[25]

The *Cloud* author's contemporary, the anchoress Julian of Norwich, also reflected on how God intersects with space and time. In the account of the third revelation at the beginning of Chapter 11 of the Long Version

[23] For an edition, *The Cloud of Unknowing and Related Treatises on Contemplative Prayer*, ed. Phyllis Hodgson, Exeter: Catholic Records Press, 1982. I use the translation in *The Cloud of Unknowing*, ed. James Walsh, New York: Paulist Press, 1981.

[24] *Cloud*, Ch. 4 (ed., 10; trans. adapted, 121-22).

[25] Ch. 4 (ed., 12; trans., 125).

she says: "And after this I saw God in a point—that is to say in my understanding—by which sight I saw that he is in all things. I beheld attentively seeing and knowing in that sight that he does all that is done. I marveled in that sight with a soft dread and thought, 'What is sin?"[26] The point in which Julian sees God is spatial and seems to have some relationship to her earlier vision of the world as a small hazelnut (Chap. 5. 7-13; ed. p. 139), but her meditation on the meaning of the vision moves on to a temporal plane—the difference between God's seeing of all things simultaneously in eternity and our temporal existence in which things seem to happen by chance. She says, "For the things that are in the foreseeing wisdom of God from without beginning, which rightfully and with dignity and continually he leads to the best end as they come about, fall upon us suddenly, ourselves unknowing."[27] She concludes this first section of her analysis of the vision by insisting that she sees God, but not in God's self apart from creation: "For in this time the working of creatures was not showed, but of our Lord God in the creature. For he is in the mid-point of all things, and all he does, and I was sure that he does no sin" (Chap. 11.15-17). In other words, Julian is seeing God in creatures, though from God's perspective *in a pointe*. Roland Maissoneuve summarizes: "For her the point represents the central point of a reality and of all the elements of the reality: man in his nothingness and infinity; the created in its minuteness and immensity; God in his immanence and transcendence."[28]

One of the most influential, though today forgotten, books in the history of Christian philosophical theology is the mysterious Hermetic treatise called the *Book of the Twenty-Four Philosophers*, a collection of definitions of God supposedly composed by a colloquium of unnamed philosophers that circulated along with two commentaries. The book first

---

[26] The edition of Julian used here is *The Writings of Julian of Norwich*, ed. Nicholas Watson and Jacqueline Jenkins, University Park: Pennsylvania State University, 2006, Chap. 11.1-4 (ed., 163). I have made my own translations.

[27] Chap. 11.7-10. In Chap. 64.19-23 (ed., 325) Julian has reflections on the temporal *poynt* or instant of time in which we are called to judgment that echo those of the *Cloud* author about the *athomus*.

[28] Roland Maisonneuve, "Julian of Norwich and the Prison of Existence," *Studia Mystica* 3 (1980), 26-32 (quotation at 32). See also Carmel Brendon Davis, *Mysticism and Space*,Washington, DC: Catholic University Press, 2008, 127-36.

appeared in the twelfth century and includes much ancient lore, though I doubt the claims that it goes back to late antiquity.[29] The most famous of the enigmatic definitions given is the second: "God is the infinite sphere whose center is everywhere and whose circumference is nowhere."[30] This geometico-theological definition gave birth to much cogitation and comment, being discussed by Alan of Lille, Thomas Aquinas, Eckhart, and Nicholas of Cusa, to name but a few.[31] Dante also seems to have known the definition. Whoever first hit upon this pregnant attempt to "define" God seems to have been inspired by the same imperative that drove the mystics surveyed here—as well as many others—that is, to find some way of putting into words through the transformation of spatial and temporal terms the intersection of the timeless and time that is at the essence of what we call mysticism.

References

1. Bouyer, Louis, "Mysticism: An Essay on the History of the Word," in *Understanding Mysticism*, ed. Richard Woods, Garden City: Doubleday, 1980, 42-55.
2. Cousins, Ewert H., *Global Spirituality: Toward the Meeting of Mystical Paths*, Madras: Radhakrishnan Institute of the University of Madras, 1985.
3. Dante Aligheri, *The Divine Comedy*, 4 vols. trans. by Charles S. Singleton, Princeton: Princeton University Press, 1982.
4. Dante's *Epistola XIII* to Can Grande della Scala can be found in Paget Toynbee, ed., *Dante Aligheris Epistolae: The Letters of Dante*, Oxford: Clarendon Press, 1966, where the letter, however, is numbered as X. This passage is from X. 28 (ed., 189-90; trans., 208-09).
5. Davis, Carmel Brendon, *Mysticism and Space*,Washington, DC: Catholic University Press, 2008.
6. Eliot, T.S., "The Dry Salvages," in *Four Quartets*, London: Faber & Faber, 1959.

---

[29] Claims for a late antique Greek original are advanced in the "Introduction" to the critical edition of Françoise Hudry, *Liber Viginti Quattuor Philosophorum*, Turnhoult: Brepols, 1997, CCCM 143A.

[30] *Deus est sphaera infinita* [some versions read: *intelligibilis*] *cuius centrum est ubique, circumferentia nusquam*. For the axiom and the two commentaries on it, see Hudry, 7-8, and 37-39.

[31] There is a large literature on the axiom. The most detailed history, though now outdated, is that of Dietrich Mahnke, *Unendliche Sphäre und Allmittelpunkt: Beiträge zur Geschichte der mathematischen Mystik*, Halle: Niemeyer, 1937.

7. Hudry, Françoise, *Liber Viginti Quattuor Philosophorum*, Turnhoult: Brepols, 1997, CCCM 143A.
8. Kramer, Kenneth Paul, *Redeeming Time: T. S. Eliot's Four Quartets*, Lanham, MD: Cowley Publications, 2006.
9. Mahnke, Dietrich, *Unendliche Sphäre und Allmittelpunkt: Beiträge zur Geschichte der mathematischen Mystik*, Halle: Niemeyer, 1937.
10. Maisonneuve, Roland, "Julian of Norwich and the Prison of Existence," *Studia Mystica* 3 (1980), 26-32.
11. McGinn, Bernard, "'Evil-Sounding, Rash, and Suspect of Heresy': Tensions between Mysticism and Magisterium in the History of the Church," *Catholic Historical Review* 90 (2004), 193-212.
12. McGinn, Bernard, "The Venture of Mysticism in the New Millennium," *New Theology Review* 21 (2008), 70-79.
13. McGinn, Bernard, *The Foundations of Mysticism: Origins to the Fifth Century*, New York: Crossroad, 1991.
14. McGinn, Bernard, *The Mystical Thought of Meister Eckhart*, New York: Crossroad, 2001.
15. McGinn, Bernard, *The Presence of God: A History of Western Christian Mysticism*, New York: Crossroad-Herder, 1991-.4 vols. to date.
16. Meister Eckhart, Pr. 38 (DW 2:231-32). The same interpretation of Gal. 4:4 is found in Prr. 4, 11, and 24 (DW 1:74, 177-78, 422-23), and in the Latin works in *In Io.* n. 293 (LW 3:245).
17. Mieth, Dietmar, *Der Einheit von Vita Activa und Vita Passiva in den deutschen Predigten und Traktaten Meister Eckharts und bei Johannes Tauler*, Regensburg: Pustet, 1969.
18. Moevs, Christian, "Il puno che mi vinse: Incarnation, Revelations, and Self-Knowledge in Dante's *Commedia*," in *Dante's 'Commedia': Theology as Poetry*, ed. Vittorio Montemaggi and Matthew Treherne, Notre Dame: University of Notre Dame, 2010.
19. Moevs, Christian, *The Metaphysics of Dante's "Commedia,"* Cambridge: Cambridge University Press, 2005.
20. Murray, Paul, *T. S. Eliot and Mysticism: The Secret History of "Four Quartet,"* New York: St. Martin's Press, 1991.
21. Scholem, Gershom, "Mysticism and Society," *Diogenes* 58 (1967), 1-24.
22. Schürmann, Reiner, *Meister Eckhart: Mystic and Philosopher*, Bloomington: Indiana University Press, 1978.
23. Spencer, Michael, "Mysticism in T. S. Eliot's *Four Quartets*," *Studies in Spirituality* 9 (1999), 230-66.
24. *The Cloud of Unknowing*, ed. James Walsh, New York: Paulist Press, 1981.
25. *The Essential Writings of Christian Mysticism*, New York: Random House, 2006.
26. *The Writings of Julian of Norwich*, ed. Nicholas Watson and Jacqueline Jenkins, University Park: Pennsylvania State University, 2006.

27. Tobin, Frank, in *Meister Eckhart:Teacher and Preacher*, ed. Bernard McGinn, New York: Paulist Press, 1986.
28. Torrance, Thoas, *Space, Time and Incarnation*, Oxford: Oxford University Press, 1969.
29. Urs von Balthasar, Hans, "Spirituality," in *Explorations in Theology I: The Word Made Flesh*, San Francisco: Ignatius Press, 1989.

3

Economic Life and Human Transcendence
A Paradigm for Everyday Spirituality

Dr. Antoon Vandevelde
&
Dr. Roy Varghese Palatty
Institute of Philosophy
Katholieke Universiteit Leuven, Leuven, Belgium

Introduction

In a pluralized society, spirituality has a special role to play. A society lacking spiritual capital, the capacity to form social capital, remains deeply impoverished, whatever level of consumption it achieves.[1] The wealth of a community is not decided by money alone, but on how this money is allocated effectively to improve the overall development of the person-in-community. We do not subscribe to the Hobbesian dogma that human beings are basically selfish and violent. They have other motivations also. Spirituality does not have to be brought into economic life from without. It is not something that is to be imposed; it is to be found out in everyone. Like the infinite potential within all people, spirituality needs to be uncovered, rekindled and encouraged. It is not to convert the 'corporate cannibals into economic vegetarians.' We try to make explicit the spiritual aspect that is potentially already there. This paper is divided

[1] Philip Goodchild, *Theology of Money*, Durham: Duke University Press, 2009, 158-63.

into four sections: first, we argue that the domain of spirituality is not in a cloistered life but in the midst of economic life; second, the re-reading of the self-interest based interpretation of economic life helps us to see that it can be a starting point for other motivations; third, we analyse how economic motivation and spiritual interest work together both in East and West. Here, we explore the spiritual dimensions of wealth and sharing and we put into perspective the macro-dimensional view of life. Finally, we propose three new paradigms for business spirituality – corporate ashram, care-holder approach, and *oikonomia* & *okologics* for solid ecumenism.

1. Economic Life and the Domain of Spirituality

For a long time, within a Platonising tradition of Christianity, this life was considered to be no more than a bridge towards real life, life after death in the glory of God. However, there have been other traditions within Christianity. According to the Benedictine motto, '*Ora et Labora*' - 'pray and work', the normal and ordinary aspects of life are as important as longing for the divine. Work is worship. To make oneself useful for others, this is the core of a meaningful life. Our karma decides our destiny. When we say man is the crown of creation, it means primarily that he is skilled and capable of hard work. Honest and committed work is a sincere prayer. Experiencing the celestial in the midst of the earthly, the extraordinary in the midst of the ordinary, the exceptional in the midst of the normal, the mystical and sacred in the midst of the mundane and profane is vital. In *Gitanjali*, the Indian mystic poet Rabindranath Tagore says about the divine experience: "He is there where the tiller is tilling the hard ground and the path-maker is breaking stones. He is with them in sun and in shower, and his garment is covered with dust."[2] Indeed, a restless mind and a meaningless heart can find peaceful equanimity and meaningful existence when it changes activity with spiritual life.

Within the Platonic tradition, spirituality has been explained in terms of detachment from the "real world." It would aim at the construction of another real world with extended bonding, responsibility

[2] Rabindranath Tagore, *Gitanjali*, London: Macmillian and Co., 1938, 11. Tagore received Nobel Prize in literature in 1913 for a selection of his poetry, *Gitanjali*.

and attachment. However, it is possible to re-discover the innate spiritual character of human life and the inseparable connection of every person with nature and community. Everyday spirituality is not a flight from the world but a different way of looking at the world and enjoying it. The Zen way to affluence teaches us that we should rather limit our desires than try to expand the means to fulfil them. Happiness supposes some wealth, but not maximal wealth. Beyond a certain – rather low – threshold there is hardly any connection between happiness and income. Here, the rational arguments in favour of 'frugality' can go together with a deeper sense of spirituality. Frugality is both a way of life and a public good. It is, on the one hand, a spiritual attitude of detachment and asceticism which renounces the ruthless pursuit of self-interest and directs the gaze to higher things; and, on the other hand, it refers to a number of social and economic problems related to the responsible use of resources in order to bring about sustainable development and well-being.[3] Hence, a self-interested or ego-centric principle of utility should eventually transform to one of mutual solidarity. We have to deal prudently and frugally with the environment so as to satisfy the needs of the present generation and the future as well. A spiritual outlook always considers the invisible Other – the people, the planet and the Highest Good. Moreover, spirituality calls for a reinterpretation of economic exchange. Instead of an endeavour to maximize self-interest, exchange should aim at achieving a mutual benefit: I profit from our interaction, but I want it to be beneficial for you too. This is the secret of engaging into long term cooperation.

Every human person experiences an immense longing for a higher form of happiness that contains within itself the seeds of mysticism. The "everyday mystic" is a man with immense longing. Our longing for higher things makes us spiritual and mystical. "The heart is a lonely hunter" because it is restless until it rests in ultimate happiness. Our perseverance and longing for higher goals is something amazing and spiritual. Human solidarity is the mark of everyday mysticism. This

[3] Luk Bouckaert, "Spirituality as a Public Affair," *Ethical Perspectives*, 10 (2003), 106-117. Bouckaert explains the possibility of sustainable development in the contemporary business field by following an attitude of frugality. Both the popularly called rational, and the spiritual attitudes co-exist in the idea of frugality.

experience normally appears in the greyness and banality of daily life, in contrast to the psychologically dramatic way the mysticism of the great saints is normally portrayed. The mystic dimension is not merely something different added to our temporal life. Similarly, every joy and success points toward the eternal light and everlasting life. According to Karl Rahner, the Catholic German theologian,

> Where an ultimate responsibility is assumed in obedience to a person's conscience, where ultimate selfless love and fidelity are given, where an ultimate selfless obedience to truth regardless of self is lived out, at this point there is really in our life something that is infinitely precious ... that is able to fill out an eternity.[4]

Rahner calls mysticism of everyday life a "mysticism in ordinary dress," or a "mysticism of the masses."[5] In the Indian religious and philosophical traditions, work is considered as *Yajna* or a sacrifice. Your karma purifies the mind, which is an essential pre-requisite to any spiritual pursuit. One must do one's karma to the best of one's ability. We cannot neglect material dharma in favour of retreating to a hermitage just as we cannot neglect spiritual dharma or our responsibility to God and the collective good in favour of greed and other destructive forms of materialism.[6] The domain of spirituality manifests itself as a complex phenomenon in the spheres of intellectual activism, emotional encounters, and moral activities.

A Spirit-centered person or a Wisdom-leader can lead his firm in an exceptionally enlightened way. We have examples in both the Eastern and the Western traditions. In India, for example, leaders are called

---

[4] Karl Rahner, "Eternity from Time," *Theological Investigations, Vol. XIX*, trans. Edward Quinn, London: Darton, Longman and Todd, 1984, 177.

[5] Karl Rahner, "Religious Enthusiasm and the Experience of Grace," *Theological Investigations XVI*, trans. Edward Quinn, New York: Seabury Press, 1979, 35-51. For a brief discussion on this topic, see Harvey D. Egan, *Karl Rahner: Mystic of Everyday Life*, New York: The Crossroad Publishing, 1998.

[6] For the recent and elaborate discussion on the Eastern vision of business spirituality, see Sharda S. Nandram and Margot Esther Borden, eds., *Spirituality and Business: Exploring Possibilities for a New Management Paradigm*, New York: Springer, 2010.

Rajarshi – king and sage. They are not opposite. A brief narrative of the mythological story of the life of King Janaka (hailed as the archetypal rajarshi leader in the Indian tradition) might be useful to convey the meaning of a spirit-led leadership process. When Janaka felt tired of managing the affairs of his kingdom, he called his ministers to the capital city of Mithila and told them that he would like to delegate the duties of running the kingdom to them, and that he would go for a retreat. On that day, in the stillness of midnight, Janaka shed all his regalia, and walked out of the palace, wrapped in a single cloth, bare-footed and bare-headed. He was alone, walking out of the city-gates, towards the ever-deepening forests. He walked the whole night, struggling in his mind with deep existential questions: What have I been doing these years? What is the true purpose of my life? Who am I really? What will happen when I am no more in this body? At daybreak he spotted a hermitage and saw there a sage absorbed in meditation. Janaka sat on the ground, patiently waiting for the sage to return to external consciousness. The sage asked: What brings you here? Janaka asked for instruction and guidance. The sage took him under his tutelage, but asked him to become involved in the everyday activities of the hermitage for a week. Activities included collecting firewood, milking the cow, cooking the food, cleaning the hut and so on. Janaka actively involved himself in all of this. On the eighth day, the sage said, 'now I will answer all your questions, and give you practical lessons.' Janaka got enlightened and returned to Mithila with a full heart and soul. So he could resume his duties as the monarch.[7] Against the task-shooting mechanical routine activities, spirit-led conscious involvement makes us happy and spiritual. Similarly, the idea of a philosopher-king in the Greek tradition reflects not only an aristocratic, hierarchical and authoritarian tradition, but also the idea of inner enlightenment. This spirituality does not just involve our interiority, but has also a meaning for everyday life. Everyone has spirituality, just as everyone has physicality. It is all about our actions and choices; it is where spirit is given flesh, where intention becomes action. This leads

[7] Cited in S. K. Chakraborty, "Spirit-Centered, Rajarshi Leadership," in *Spirituality and Ethics in Management*, ed. Laszlo Zsolnai, Boston: Kluwer Academic Publishers, 2004, 33-49.

to an effective utilization of resources, together with a re-discovery of the innate spiritual character of human life. As Sri Aurobindo says:

> Spirituality is in its essence an awakening to the inner reality of our being, to a spirit, self, soul which is other than our mind, life and body, an inner aspiration to know, to feel, to be that, to enter into contact with the greater reality beyond and pervading the universe which inhabits also our own being, to be in communication with It and union with It, and a turning, a conversion, a transformation of our whole being as a result of the aspiration, the contact, the union, a growth or waking into a new becoming or new being, a new self, a new nature.[8]

2. The Economics of Spirituality and Self-interest

What drives economic man? In the *Metaphysics*, Aristotle distinguishes between 'praxis' and 'poiesis,' between action in the narrow sense of the word and 'productive activities.' Praxis or action is intrinsically valuable, i.e., the end is in the activity itself. Seeing, thinking, living, loving, politics, practicing philosophy are Aristotle's privileged examples. In these cases there is no exteriority between the action and its result. Love, friendship, wisdom, the political debate that is constitutive for communal life: these are all goals in itself. They do not serve any further goal. 'Poietic' activities involve the making of something. This category encompasses instrumental and strategic activities. An artisan tries to make beautiful or useful objects. These serve us in our daily purposes. Generally speaking, Aristotle privileges praxis above poiesis. What is an end in itself is higher than what is merely a means for something else. However, it is important to see that work has a practical ('praxis') dimension, as well as an instrumental value. Work produces a good or service, but at the same time it displays the quality of the artisan. He derives social prestige and pride from his work. Hence, work is not only instrumentally valuable in that it provides the worker with an income or with valuable objects, but it is also intrinsically valuable. Intrinsic value can be discovered in three aspects: (1) work structures our time,

---

[8] Sri Aurobindo, *The Supramental Manifestation upon the Earth*, Pondicherry: Sri Aurobindo Ashram Press, 2005, 17.

(2) it integrates us in social relations where human beings need each other's cooperation, and (3) it is a source of appreciation, and hence of self-respect. Maybe economic action starts from self-interest, but, mostly, it becomes indistinguishably service to the others, as well as source of self fulfilment. By rendering service to the others, unwittingly, we contribute to our own self-realisation.

Strategic intelligence is indispensable for leaders and managers. Yet, this strategic rationality may result in counter-productivity if it overlooks the value-based and spiritually motivated trust amongst the affected agents. Unfettered strategic rationality can jeopardise the common good of an organization. There are many examples of managers that have ruined their firm because they were driven by short term profit motives. Very often these were engendered by perverse remuneration systems, such as huge bonuses and stock options. The general justification for unleashing the motivation of self-interest is that it increases economic growth and social wealth. Especially in the eighteenth century, at the dawn of the science of economics, when ecological limits to growth were not already clearly recognised, this was considered to be a good in itself. Moreover, economic growth was supposed to make conflict settlement and peace keeping easier, by creating the opportunity for win-win-situations. Hence, there is a turning upside down of the whole hierarchy of values at that time. Every factor that fosters economic growth was considered to be good. Even ethical values were made instrumental for this goal.

The invisible hand mechanism states that vanity, the pursuit of self-interest, the flourishing of private vices leads indirectly to the common good for the whole of society. According to this argument, the economy must act according to its own principles, and not by the moral considerations imposed on it from without. In other words, moral actions contradict market rules and drive the moralizing entrepreneur out of the game.[9] This argument is based on the presupposition that

[9] For example, economists from Albert Carr to Milton Friedman argue that people responsible for decisions and actions in business should not exercise social responsibility in their capacity as company executives but concentrate on increasing profits for their companies. Eventually they could engage in philanthropic activities in their private life, but not in business life. This point of view has been criticised by the defenders of the stakeholder's conception of the firm. Business life can only be sustainable if firms

market and morality, economic life and spiritual motivations may not go together. However, this is wrong. Markets without morality degenerate into war of all against all. What works well is moderate self-interest, selfishness corrected by honesty.

Adam Smith knew perfectly well that the invisible hand works only when all or most actors on the market mitigate the pursuit of their self-interest, i.e., when they respect some moral rules. His *Inquiry into the Origin and Nature of the Wealth of Nations* is preceded by a *Theory of Moral Sentiments*. In this book, on moral philosophy, Adam Smith explains that human beings are not only motivated by self-interest: they also desire the sympathy of others. We want others to look at us and to approve our actions and our general way of life. As we know that people rarely ever sympathise with extreme sentiments and gut reactions, they will be inclined to moderate their emotions and the corresponding actions. Self-command attracts and enhances the sympathy of the bystanders. Hence, our passions are governed by an inner logic that moderates them. A sensible concern for one's own interests is not bad in itself. It only becomes an evil if it degenerates into free-rider conduct, selfishness, opportunism, the ruthless pursuit of self-interest, even at the cost of other human beings or ethical values. Self-interest has to pass the sympathy test in order to be able to fuel the invisible hand. Hence, moral considerations should not be imposed on them from without, but they are potentially already there, although we are not always aware of them. As Pope Benedict XVI says, "It is becoming ever so clear that the development of the world economy has also to do with the development of the world community and with the universal family of man, and that the development of spiritual powers of mankind is essential in the development of world community. The spiritual powers are themselves a factor in economy: the market rules function only when a moral consensus exists and sustains them."[10]

---

take into account the interests of all those who are affected by the activities of the firm. Moreover the tendency to turn public goods into private ones is most harmful for the poorest members of society.

[10] Joseph Cardinal Ratzinger, "Church and Economy: Responsibility for the Future of Economy," *Communio*, 13 (1986), 200.

Economic man bases his actions on instrumental rationality and self-interest. This is not necessarily a bad thing. At a very basic level, even when one wants to help other people, one has first of all to take care of oneself. Moreover, self-interest does not necessarily exclude altruism. Many people integrate to a certain measure the interests of their children, friends and colleagues in their self-interest. Yet, they have to decide what kind of self it is that an economic man wants to serve. Reflexive rationality precedes instrumental rationality: What kind of person do I want to be? This question inevitably leads us to return to the spiritual self. A sensible egoist should try to develop a rich personality. This is more than just self-conservation. According to Aristotle, a human being aims not just at mere survival but also at 'a good life'. This means that we should in some way connect our limited existence to some transcendent aim, I mean to something we consider to be greater than ourselves. Mostly transcendence is interpreted in a religious sense, but there are also non-religious forms of transcendence. Some people live for their children, or for their beloved, others put their life to the service of a particular value, an NGO, a community, an association, a Church. Eventually, they are even willing to sacrifice their life for a good, something they consider to be utterly important. Of course this involves a risk. We all know of political militants who have been working half a life for a party that in the end deceives them cruelly. Some people have so discover that the person they have loved above everything has betrayed him or her. Our children often do other things than what we dreamed of. However, refusing all commitments in life would lead to an impoverished and flat existence. One can try to avoid disillusions and frustration by never falling in love, by refusing to get children, or by avoiding all external commitments, but in the end this leads to a life that is dull and unattractive.

A sensible egoist would not only develop a rich personality. He should also cultivate personal integrity. Integrity refers to one's inner unity and wholeness, which is the result of the integration of one's self.[11] The integrated-self characterizes an agent's relation to herself – to her desires, to her character, and to her agency. It is true that integrity is

[11] Etymologically, the term 'integrity' is related to 'integer,' which means a whole number or the unification of parts into a whole.

not merely a personal virtue.[12] There are two fundamental intuitions on integrity: first, integrity refers to a formal relation to oneself, or between parts or aspects of oneself; and second, integrity is connected in an important way to acting morally. We should not develop a fragmented personality. A person may be subjected to many conflicting desires. Someone acting at each moment out of the strongest immediate desire, with no deliberation or discrimination between more or less worthwhile desires, clearly acts without integrity. Harry Frankfurt calls such a person a 'wanton'.[13] Wantonness seems everywhere, but an integrated person has to decide what he or she wants to be. One has to discriminate between various desires in order to act on self-fulfilling desires. The self-deceived person is unable to perceive what actually motivates him. He acts out of external motivations. "Wholeheartedness - the consistency of and non ambivalence about one's various endorsements – is really a necessary condition for having integrity."[14] Self-determination and resolving conflicts on the level of the self is the first step toward developing an integrated self, and thus toward discovering the spiritual self. Many a time we fall into idolatry. We treat the part as the whole, which is not the whole as such. The reduction of wholeness into parts, and accepting parts as a whole, is idolatry. Integrity is not a matter of material wealth and income. It is on the level of 'being,' rather than 'having.'

3. Human Transcendence and the Economy of Spirituality

Turning to the self in no way means self-centredness or defining one's self in a way that excludes others. Human beings are not atomistic individuals. Aristotle introduces the question in the *Nicomachean Ethics*: what is the nature of the human good or happiness (*eudaimonia*)? He examines three ways of life: hedonism, politics and contemplation.[15] He rejects the hedonistic way of life as infra-human, 'a life fit only for cattle,' unworthy of a human being. Also, Aristotle argues that money

---

[12] Cheshire Calhoun, "Standing for Something," *Journal of Philosophy*, 92, 5 (1995), 235-60.

[13] Harry Frankfurt, "Freedom of the Will and the Concept of a Person," *Journal of Philosophy*, 68, 1 (1971), 5-20.

[14] Frankfurt, "Freedom of the Will and the Concept of a Person," 18.

[15] Aristotle, *Nicomachean Ethics*, ed. D. Ross, Oxford: Oxford University Press, 1980, Book I, 5, 6-7.

and wealth are not a proper goal for human endeavour, but merely instrumental to other goods that really matter. For a successful life we need some wealth, but not too much. Economic activities are necessary for developing 'higher' interests, but we should not become slaves of our desire to have more (than the others). Someone choosing a political life participates fully to public debates and is willing to set aside his self-interest for the common good. The highest form of life consists of contemplation. It is the life of a philosopher seeking truth. However, this is not the only important thing in life. In our political and economic activities we reach out to our neighbours, to persons who are in need. In contemplation we transcend to the other – the one who is the Highest Good.

Human happiness encompasses various dimensions. Our self-interest involves taking interest in the others. This includes various forms of familial, social and political relationship. Aristotle argues: "self-sufficiency applies not to a person on his own, living a solitary life, but to a person living alongside his parents, children, wife, friends and fellow-citizens generally, since the human being is by nature a social animal."[16] The same applies to the corporate world. It is the not the self of an individual alone, but the self of all that counts. Quite often, we can distinguish a 'corporate self' within firms. A strongly individualistic, self-assertive view of the organization, based on so-called atomistic individualism, could explain the organization as a temporary nexus of contracts and 'calculative' ties and bonds. However, this is not a very plausible image of a firm. Indeed it is opposed to the corporate values, goals, visions, and to the organizational consciousness of the firm that stresses very clearly its inevitable collective dimension – 'a collective self.' Hence, individual identity in contemporary highly differentiated society is multilayered: individuals accept their role in collective entities, yet keeping their personal identity.

There is no inherent conflict between spirituality and involvement in business. From time immemorial, the great aims of human endeavour (*purushārthas*) have been classified into four in the Indian tradition – wealth (*artha*), aesthetic pleasures (*kāma*), righteousness/ethical living/ harmony with the global environment (*dharma*), and blissfulness

[16] Aristotle, *Nicomachean Ethics*, Book, I, 7, 1097b, 11.

(*moksha*). Material prosperity has never been treated as something bad in this tradition. It believes that a strong, stable and sustainable personal embeddedness in organizational life is indispensable for attaining spiritual values. According to this tradition, money definitely is wealth, but also health, education and skills can be treated as wealth, since their importance transcends mere market value. All human endeavours are interdependent and should be pursued equally. Excessive importance given to one over other dimensions of human flourishing brings negative consequences. Kautilya, the author of ancient Indian economy and political science (*Arthasāsthra*) however, says wealth (*artha* – economics) is most important; for dharma and aesthetic pleasures (*kāma*) are both dependent on it.[17] Similarly, Buddhist economics sees no conflict between religious values and economic progress. Spiritual health and material well-being are not enemies. They are natural allies. The Buddhist view of work, as E. F. Schumacher explains, functions on at least three levels: "to give a man a chance to utilize and develop his faculties; to enable him to overcome his ego-centeredness by joining with other people in a common task; and to bring forth the goods and services needed for a becoming existence."[18]

The unity of self-development and transcendence is not paradoxical, although the former has egoistic connotations and the latter suggests self-abandonment. Transcending oneself amounts to accepting external values, which means submitting to inter-subjective standards.[19] This is quite important for the managerial function of a business corporation. A manager has to participate to the inter-subjective zones of his organization. He has to integrate into a collective entity. In other words, "to exist as a self is for management to be situated in the spiritual and moral space of the organization."[20] This situation points to the equivocal and multidimensional engagement of managers endowed with varied motivations. While using their authority managers shall

[17] Kautilya *The Arthashastra*, trans. L. N. Ranganathan, New Delhi: Penguin Books, 1992, 122.

[18] E.F. Schumacher, *Small is Beautiful: A Study of Economics as if People Mattered*, London: Blond and Briggs, 1973, 49.

[19] Alpar Losoncz, "Spiritual Motivation in Management," in *Spirituality and Ethics in Management*, ed. Laszlo Zsolani. Boston: Kluwer Academic Publishers, 2004, 81-82.

[20] Losoncz, "Spiritual Motivation in Management," 81.

make judgements on the basis of their own system of ethics, emotions, aesthetics and ecological commitments. The popular stakeholder theory[21] has recognized the structure of this *ex ante* social responsibility and the importance of taking into account the interests of all stakeholders. A good leader with long-term planning has to concentrate on people, planet and profit (3 'P's). One's spiritual needs are fulfilled by the recognition and acceptance of individual responsibility for the common good, by understanding the interconnectedness of all of our lives, and by serving humanity and planet.

This insight may be an innovation within economics; it is immemorial wisdom in the traditional teachings of world religions and philosophies. As Buddhism teaches, we have to work with true love for all beings, in a spirit of benevolence, not only for human beings but also for all kinds of beings on the planet earth. Extreme utilization of resources, by way of production and consumption, is fundamentally problematic. Buddhist ethics contributes to the exploration of a new system of ecological economy.[22] It leads us to transform our inner values in the direction of saving our planet from crisis. Both at the micro and macro levels, corporations have to transcend their limited short-term goals in order to attain higher values of life. The spiritual dimension of wealth-seeking, the economy of sharing and the macro-dimensional view of life may help us to understand this better.

3.1. The Spirituality of Money and Wealth

In everyday life a conversation amongst a couple on the possibility of earning more money is not unusual. But, having access to such a conversation in the eighth century BCE is quite revealing. In the *Brihadāranyaka Upanishad* we find a conversation between a woman named Maitreyee and her husband, Yajnavalkya. "How far would wealth help us to get what we want?"[23] is the question. Maitreyee wonders:

[21] A stakeholder is any individual, group or organization who has a stake in the performance of the organization.

[22] Simplicity and non-violence are the most important principles of this economy. Ecological economics tries to maximise a broad conception of well-being. Human fulfilment and development of character are inevitable parts of this economy. See, Schumacher, *Small is Beautiful*, 48-68.

[23] *Brihadāranyaka Upanishad*, Part 4, 5, 57.

if "the whole earth, full of wealth" were to belong just to you, could you achieve immortality through it? "No," responds Yajnavalkya, "like the life of rich people, so also will be your life. There is no hope of immortality by getting more wealth." Maitreyee asks, "What should I do with that by which I do not become immortal?" Maitreyee's rhetorical question has been cited again and again in Indian religious philosophy to illustrate the human predicament and the limitations of the world. However, we can read it in a different and positive way. This conversation points to the intrinsic and extrinsic motivation of the wealth one obtains. On the workplace, for example, if I do a better job because my employer offers me a bonus, I have been externally motivated. If I do a better job because it makes me proud of myself and gives some inner joy, I have been internally motivated. Intrinsic motivation brings passion for work. A good leader must be a passionate leader to evoke the intrinsic motivation of the co-workers. Passion is more important than finance.

As Aristotle notes in the very beginning of the *Nicomachean Ethics* (echoing the conversation between Maitreyee and Yajnavalkya about 3000 miles away), "wealth is evidently not the good we are seeking; for it is merely useful and for the sake of something else."[24] Indeed, we are not looking for wealth as such, but for something more. Yet we cannot denounce the value of wealth and ignore its mediating function. The usefulness of wealth lies in the important things that it allows us to do.[25] Wealth is a means that helps us to improve the quality of our life and to reach our transcendent ends. Man cannot be trapped in the quest for material means forgetting the ends of his existence. Wealth has individual, social and transcendent purposes.

The nature of money explains exchange. But, the nature of exchange does not explain money. How do we understand the function of money? Adam Smith famously describes money as, the "great wheel of circulation:" "The great wheel of circulation is altogether different from the goods which are circulated by means of it. The revenue of

[24] Aristotle, *The Nicomachean Ethics*, Book I, 5, 7.

[25] Amartya Sen, *Development as Freedom*, Oxford: Oxford University Press, 2000, 14. Sen quotes Aristotle to explain the basis of the capability approach that explains the usefulness of wealth in order to achieve substantive freedom. Indeed, freedom is the basis for aiming at transcendence.

society consists altogether in those goods, not in the wheel which circulates them."[26] As a mere vehicle or means of exchange, money contributes nothing to the overall output of society. As Aristotle reminds, king Midas died from hunger, because everything he touched turned into gold. Money is not wealth or value. It is a mere token of value. According to Aristotle money is good in as far as it functions as a measure of value and as a mere means of circulation. However, its very logic goes far beyond these evident functions. Money can also serve to store value and so it becomes desirable in itself. What should be a mere instrument becomes the supreme goal for many people. They tend to sell everything, even their soul for money. The Achilles' heel of the current financial system is that all actors involved tend to confuse mere signs of value with value itself, signs of wealth with wealth itself. 2500 years ago, Aristotle already denounced this confusion. He distrusted the ambivalence of money. It helps to achieve need fulfilment in the most efficient way, but it also tends to pervert all genuine commitment to values. Nowadays, we could add that it became also a means for transferring inequality from one to the following generation.

The power of money is spiritual. Money is based on trust and the excessive longing for money is a quasi-religious form of belief. Hence, it should not come as a surprise that religion is the only surviving barrier to consumerism. As Philip Goodchild remarks, "the theology of money, with its promises, its narcissistic self-positing as the supreme standard and measure of value, its speculative detachment from current conditions, and its despotic power expressed in debt, can be transformed only by a stronger spiritual power."[27] God or the mammon: this is the basic choice the Bible evokes to us. There is nothing wrong with sound entrepreneurship or with selling the products of one's creativity, but money-making is not a proper goal in life.

Indeed, wealth has a social function and therefore it needs to circulate and to be distributed more or less evenly. Gandhi tried to explain this by an example: "The circulation of wealth among people resembles the circulation of blood in the body. The concentration of blood at one spot is harmful to the body, and similarly, concentration of

[26] Smith, *Wealth of Nations*, 385.

[27] Goodchild, *Theology of Money,* 129.

wealth at one place proves to be a nation's undoing."[28] The more evenly social wealth is distributed, the better it serves society. Peter Drucker, one of the fathers of modern management, concludes his book entitled *Landmarks of Tomorrow* with a question as old as human existence: "what is the meaning of human existence and of human spirit?"[29] This question boils down to another, more precise one: What are we looking for if not for wealth and power? This will, he argues, inevitably take you to the spiritual values, a return to the transcendent: "mankind needs the return to spiritual values. It needs the deep experience that the Thou and the I are one, which all higher religions share." "The individual also needs spiritual values. He can survive in the present human situation only by re-affirming that man is not just a biological and psychological being but also a spiritual being, that is creature, and existing for the purposes of his Creator and subject to Him."[30] The rich are the trustees of the wealth they have. Their responsibility is 'beyond the walls' of their organizations.

3.2. The Economy of Sharing

We live in a community in which we share most of the public goods. Sharing makes our life meaningful. Over-reliance on narrow economic rationality has serious repercussions, like instrumentalizing the affected agents, using hidden agendas, practicing fraud in relation to rivals and explicitly or implicitly using zero-sum tactics to destroy rivals.[31] Hence, a good leader should share his money and strength in order to empower his colleagues in the firm.

This can be explained by the story of an Indian corporate idol, N. R. Narayana Murthy, the Founder-Chairman of Infosys Technologies. He responds to his friends when they asked him what he wanted to do with his business: "I want this [Infosys] to be the most respected software service in the world." He continues, "If you seek respect, you will not short-change your customers, you will be fair to your colleagues in the company, you will be transparent with your investors, you will treat

---

[28] M.K. Gandhi, *Collected Works*, New Delhi: Government of India, 1958-94, 8: 303.

[29] Peter F. Drucker, *The Landmarks of Tomorrow*, London: Heinemann, 1959, 200.

[30] Drucker, *The Landmarks of Tomorrow*, 200-01.

[31] Losoncz, "Spiritual Motivation in Management," 84.

your vendor partners with care and understanding, you will not violate the laws of the land in whichever country you operate, and you will live in harmony in whichever society you operate in [...]."[32] The corporation develops and believes in three value-based maxims. First, 'the softest pillow is a clear conscience'; second, 'a plausible impossibility is better than a convincing possibility'; third, and the most important is, 'In God we trust, everybody else brings data to the table.' His ideal of corporation is a spirit-led one. This brings, he believes, trustworthiness, integrity, courage, openness and fairness. This leads to develop an inclusive environment, where every member in the institution gets involved in the integral development of the firm. Two important factors strongly contribute to the economy of sharing: recognition and self-esteem of the different parties in business and a spirit-led life.

First, self-esteem is a great motivator for human beings.[33] A good manager should always create a climate in which self-esteem and collaborative action for the common good can flourish. This helps employees to deal with their fellow colleagues with respect, dignity and affection. Now, social recognition by peers and colleagues is an almost indispensable precondition for self-esteem. According to Adam Smith the desire for recognition more than love of ease and pleasure is the most powerful psychological motive for business activity. For modern man, recognition is the greatest good, while public humiliation is the greatest evil.[34] Anonymity is more dreadful than disgrace. Infosys uses the adage: "praise in public, criticize in private." Secondly a spirit-led life induces sharing. This is not only true for individuals. It is also important that a firm be inspired by values, by a common ethos, a spirit that infuses the whole of the interactions within the firm and the relations with outsiders. A clearly definable synergy and a shared vision help the partners of business to make a difference in all aspects of their existence. Moreover, trust in God helps us to trust in fellow-workers

[32] N. R. Narayana Murthy,*A Better India, A Better World*, New Delhi: Penguin Books, 2009, 159. *The Economist* ranked Narayana Murthy among the ten most-admired global business leaders in 2005. He is one of the India's most powerful CEOs. Today Infosys operates in thirty-eight countries with fifty thousand people from forty-five nationalities.

[33] Maslow's theory explains different levels of motivations in human behavior.

[34] Smith, *Theory of Moral Sentiments*, 13.

and in the other partners in business. Someone who uses the pillow of conscience can never harm the public good. Similarly, believing in the Ultimate helps us to look for 'plausible impossibilities' and gives us the imagination to start their realization.

A good business man has to be accountable not only to the firm he serves, but also to the general public. Here, philanthropy and volunteerism become integral parts of economic activities. It is not mere charity, but reaching out to the other for empowerment. One cannot empower the other with mere charity. We need responsible sharing. Yet, we can only share what we have or what we are.

3.3. Macro-dimensional View of Life

Our economic existence and spirituality also have a macro dimension. We are both guardians and guests on the earth. This means that we have no ownership of the earth, but just a mission: "to cultivate and to conserve it."[35] What we receive from Mother Earth, we have to return to the giver when we say good-bye to this given life. We cannot deplete in one generation natural resources that have been built up during thousands of years. This garden of earth is a gift that is given to everyone. It is important to recognise the gift dimension of life.[36] Indeed, human relations can never be based upon purely contractual agreements. An economic contract presupposes strict reciprocity: quid pro quo. At the moment when the contract is signed, ideally all rights and duties of both parties should be exactly determined. However, contracts are always incomplete. One can never specify precisely everything that is important for all parties in a contract. Take a labour contract. One can specify salary and general working conditions, but especially in a knowledge economy, more important is the quality of the work. Here, employers expect creativity, commitment and innovation. Now, this cannot be obtained from slaves, or on the basis of control.

---

[35] Genesis 2: 15.

[36] About the role of reciprocity in gift-giving, see, Antoon Vandevelde, ed. "Towards a Conceptual Map of Gift Practices," in *Gifts and Interests*, Belgium: Peeters, 2000, 1-20. By summarizing the famous essay of Marcel Mauss, *The Gift*, for example, Mary Douglas says that, "there should not be any free gifts," because charity wounds its beneficiaries. See, "No Free Gifts: Foreword" by Marcel Mauss, New York and London: W. W. Norton, 1990, vii.

This is the domain where the logic of the gift applies. This logic also encompasses reciprocity, but rather a loose type. When we give a gift to someone, there is an implicit expectance that something comes in return. However, when and in what form reciprocity takes place is not determined in advance. As there is no legal contract, there is also no guarantee that reciprocity will ever take place. The logic of the gift entails a risk. Within a firm, employers often pay more than the strict market clearing equilibrium wage. They organise from time to time a party for their collaborators. And they hope to be repaid with intrinsic motivation. Labour contracts are partly the result of bargaining, but also they are partial gift exchanges. Within economic life in general, the best illustration of the logic of the gift is the omnipresence of trust. Trust is not a commodity that can be 'produced'. An efficient legal system enforcing contracts can stimulate trust indirectly, but still, to trust someone is a wager. Even more generally, a newborn baby has no contract with its parents. Life is a gift, and we received from our parents much more than just life. They had to prepare a place for us, and moreover, they have provided us with language, education, material help, good advice, and so on. Similarly, we have received opportunities, public goods and a scientific and technological bequest from society. Finally, nature provides us with resources. A person endowed with spirituality is aware of this gift dimension of life and is grateful for it. It is the gift dimension that fundamentally links us to God and to the whole of universe.

It is impossible to quantify the gift dimension of life. The earth on which we live, the environment we enjoy or the relationships we experience are all saturated with gifts.[37] What we see at work here, is, as Paul Ricoeur says, a 'logic of superabundance' rather than a 'logic of equivalence.' As it is impossible to return this superabundance of gifts, we can only take our responsibility by passing on these gifts to others. We have a responsibility for our environment in the same way as a good ruler feels responsible towards his people or as a good steward who takes care of the goods that he has been entrusted with. Many a time, we are tempted to appropriate gifts, to turn them into private property rather

[37] Jean-Luc Marion, "The Saturated Phenomenon" in *Phenomenology and the Theological Turn: The French Debate*, trans. Bernard G. Prusak, New York: Fordham University Press, 2000, 185-89.

than to return it or to pass it on. This happens when we receive without gratitude or when we lose the sense of serviceability. A proper use of things involves a sense of ontological gratitude.

We all are guests in the sense that our presence on earth is not eternal.[38] Guests may come and go, but the house of earth will stand longer. What is given to us is for temporal use. We should receive with dignity, and not try to appropriate the common good. In other words, as I received hospitality from the other, I must also be hospitable to the other – to all living and non-living beings. All created things are at the disposal of the guest's freedom. It is important to note that working and using are two terms that are inseparably related. When we use something, we really work on it. This helps to bring out the potential of something. This can be done with respect or disrespect. Our instrumental rationality may tempt us to tyrannize our freedom, where we use the things of nature in order to exploit them.[39] Excessive instrumentalization entails a degradation of the potential qualities of resources. A fragmented world-view leads to "a reckless science and violent technology."[40] When we say that we work on some resources, this does not mean that we subdue things to mere usefulness. As Kant rightly says dignity cannot be cashed but it can only be valued.[41] Celebrating the aesthetic beauty of creatures helps us to look for higher goods. In his *Auguries of Innocence*, for example, the mystic poet William Blake celebrates this grand experience:

> To see a world in a grain of sand,
> And a heaven in a wild flower,
> Holy infinity in the palm of your hand,
> And eternity in an hour.[42]

[38] "I am a guest on earth for just a little while" (Psalm. 119: 9). There is a small handbook titled *We all are Guests on Earth: A Global Christian Vision for Climate Justice* by Christoph Stueckelberger, Bangalore: Dharmaram Publications, 2010.

[39] William Desmond, *Ethics and the Between*, New York: SUNY Press, 2001, 416-21.

[40] Schumacher, *Small is Beautiful*, 143.

[41] Immanuel Kant, *Groundwork of Metaphysics of Morals*, ed. Mary Gregor, Cambridge: Cambridge University Press, 1997, 42.

[42] William Blake, "Auguries of Innocence," http://www.online-literature.com/poe/612/ [accessed on 10th November, 2010].

To care for nature and every being in nature is very important in everyday life. We receive, in one or another way, from all beings. So, mutual hospitality and a caring attitude are essential for the common good of the society. Eco-spirituality or geo-economics is not something optional, but mandatory and they become ethical imperatives. This is evident in spiritual economics. One of the Cree Indian prophecies echoes Aristotle's story of King Midas: "Only after the last tree has been cut down; only after the last river has been poisoned; only after the last fish has been caught; only then will you find that money cannot be eaten."[43] We consume in order to survive. One does not survive in order to consume.

4. New Paradigms

Life is not, as Shakespeare's Macbeth says, "a tale told by an idiot, full of sound and fury signifying nothing." It has a purpose. Its purpose is not just material. Our linear thinking and binary logic is limited. Life is both black and white, material and spiritual, immanent and transcendent. The boundaries between here and there, now and then, secular and sacred, micro and macro get dissolved with the dawning of new awareness or enlightenment. This seems to be a coincidence of opposites. A soul-less corporation is dead. It has no higher purpose. Higher purposes give reasons for existence. If the purpose is lost, existence is lost. A well-founded purpose legitimates an institution. Here, we propose three new paradigms to find an integral vision for life in general and economic life in particular.

4.1. Towards a Corporate Ashram

The etymological meaning of the term *Mercurius* is related to *merx* (goods for sale), which means merchant or commerce. *Mecari*, meaning trade, is the source of words such as 'market' and 'merchandise.'[44] To our wonder, Mercury was not only the god of trade and tradesmen but also of the king of thieves. Hence, we sometimes see business leaders as exploiters of resources. But, business is a call. A business corporation

---

[43] Cree are one of the largest groups of indigenous peoples in North America, located mainly across Canada.

[44] http://en.wikipedia.org/wiki/Mercury_(mythology)

has to be an Ashram, where economics and ethics meet in a most sublime way. In a business ashram, the management has to take the stakeholders seriously and develop a proactive strategy. The relationship here is beyond pure reciprocity and contract. Here, we consider people and profit, planet and prosperity in a holistic manner. The other is recognized as a dignified person. No objectification, no extreme subjectification either. Hence, every economic problem is a spiritual problem as well. This promotes a profane or secular spirituality. The Homoo*economicus* model of functioning has been transformed into a homo *mysticus* model.

4.2. Towards a Care-holder Approach

The well-known statement according to which 'the business of business is business' ignores the fact that social issues are fundamental to business. Their neglect will affect the credibility and the very existence of business in the long-run. Gandhi identifies seven ills that afflict modern-day civilization: "politics without principles, science without humanity, commerce without morality, wealth without work, worship without sacrifice, pleasure without conscience, and knowledge without character."[45] Any development that disregards human worth is ultimately destined to end in disaster and disintegration. Our macro-dimensional view and an acute awareness of the gift dimension of life make us interconnected and care-holders of the other. A good leader leads and motivates his partners with care and concern. Then we feel that we are the custodians of our brother and sisters – the people and the planet. Our responsibility gives us more freedom.

4.3. Towards an ecological Oikonomia

Aristotle made an important distinction between '*oikonomia,*' and 'chrematistics'. *Oikonomia* is the use of wealth, while chrematistics is the provision, production or acquisition of wealth. *Oikonomia,* for Aristotle, is the art of using wealth, not just for mere survival (to *zên* – to live) but also for the Good Life (*eû zên*).[46] It is teleological. Chrematistics tends to simple money-making. It is short-termish, whereas *oikonomia*

---

[45] M.K. Gandhi, *Collected Works*, 8: 362.

[46] Aristotle, *Politics*, ed. Benjamin Jowett. New York: Cosimo Inc., 2008, I, 4, 24-25.

looks for the "management of the household so as to increase its use to all members of the household in the long-run."[47] This requires a way of bringing about a community and making it flourish. For this,land, resources, institutions, language, history and spirituality are needed. Herman Daly and John Cobb distinguish *oikonomia* from chrematistics on three levels: "First, it takes the long-run rather than the short-run view. Second, it considers costs and benefits to the whole community, not just to parties to the transaction. Third, it focuses on concrete use value and the limited accumulation thereof, rather than on abstract exchange value and its impetus toward unlimited accumulation."[48] *Oikonomia* views the market from the perspective of the total needs of the community.

The terms 'economy' and 'ecology'are closely connected. They refer to the management and the logic of the household. In our globalised world our *oikos* has become the whole world. More precisely, we belong to various communities, our family, our city, our work place, our country, and the whole of humanity. Hence, economic life cannot be divorced from ecological concerns. As Gandhi rightly says, "A human being is made of earth. His body springs from the earth and derives its sustenance from the various forms which earth takes."[49] We live in a complex network of living and non-living realities that surround us. As we are the children of Mother Earth, our life and economic activities must have a spiritual outlook by affirming responsible freedom and transcendent humanism. This requires a fresh understanding of our economic activities, i.e., an enlightened way of life.

Conclusion

In this paper, we have argued that spirituality does not have to be thought as otherworldliness. There is an important spiritual dimension in everyday life that has been conceptualised in the works of Gandhi, Tagore and Aurobindo, as well as in that of Aristotle, Smith and Kant. We have illustrated this thesis by reinterpreting the notion of economic

[47] Herman E. Daly and John B. Cobb, *For the Common Good: Redirecting the Economy toward Community, the Environment and a Sustainable Future*, Boston: Beacon Press, 1994, 138.

[48] Daly and Cobb, *For the Common Good*, 139.

[49] M.K. Gandhi, *Collected Works*, 28: 206.

exchange as aiming at mutual benefit, by broadening the category of self-interest, i.e., by amending instrumental rationality with a good dose of reflexive rationality, by showing the ambivalence of money and by highlighting the gift dimension of life.

References

1. Aristotle, *Nicomachean Ethics*, ed. D. Ross, Oxford: Oxford University Press, 1980.
2. Aristotle, *Politics*, ed. Benjamin Jowett, New York: Cosimo Inc., 2008.
3. Aurobindo, Sri, *The Supramental Manifestation upon the Earth*, Pondicherry: Sri Aurobindo Ashram Press, 2005.
4. Blake, William, "Auguries of Innocence." http://www.online-literature.com/poe/ 612/ [accessed on 10 November, 2010].
5. Bouckaert, Luk, "Spirituality as a Public Affair," *Ethical Perspectives*, 10 (2003), 106-17.
6. Calhoun, Cheshire, "Standing for Something," *Journal of Philosophy*, 92, 5 (1995), 235-60.
7. Chakraborty, S. K., "Spirit-Centred, Rajarshi Leadership," *Spirituality and Ethics in Management*, ed. Lazlo Zsolnai, Boston: Kluwer Academic Publishers, 2004, 33-49.
8. Daly, Herman E., and John B. Cobb, *For the Common Good: Redirecting the Economy toward Community, the Environment and a Sustainable Future,* second edition, Boston: Beacon Press, 1994.
9. Davies, Glyn, *A History of Money from Ancient Times to Present Day*, Cardiff: University of Wales Press, 2002.
10. Desmond, William, *Ethics and the Between*, New York: SUNY Press, 2001.
11. Douglas, Mary, "Foreword: No Free Gifts" in *The Gift* by Marcel Mauss, New York and London: W. W. Norton, 1990, vii-xxiii.
12. Drucker, Peter F., *The Landmarks of Tomorrow*, London: Heinemann, 1959.
13. Egan, Harvey D., *Karl Rahner: Mystic of Everyday Life*, New York: The Crossroad Publishing, 1998.
14. Frankfurt, Harry, "Freedom of the Will and the Concept of a Person," *Journal of Philosophy*, 68, 1(1971), 5-20.
15. Gandhi, M. K., *The Collected Works of Mahatma Gandhi*, vols. 8, 28, New Delhi: Government of India, 1958-1994.
16. Goodchild, Philip, *Theology of Money*, Durham: Duke University Press, 2009.
17. Kant, Immanuel, *Groundwork of Metaphysics of Morals*, ed. Mary Gregor, Cambridge: Cambridge University Press, 1997.
18. Kautilya, *The Arthashastra*, trans. L. N. Rangarajan, New Delhi: Penguin Books, 1992.
19. Losoncz, Alpar, "Spiritual Motivation in Management," in *Spirituality and Ethics in Management*, ed. Laszlo Zsolnai, Boston: Kluwer Academic Publishers, 2004, 75-86.

20. Marion, Jean-Luc, "The Saturated Phenomenon," in *Phenomenology and the Theological Turn: The French Debate*, ed. Dominique Janicaud and trans. Bernard G. Prusak, New York: Fordham University Press, 2000, 176-216.
21. Murthy, N. R., Narayana. *A Better India, A Better World*, New Delhi: Penguin Books, 2009.
22. Nandram, Sharda S. and Margot Esther Borden, eds., *Spirituality and Business: Exploring Possibilities for a New Management Paradigm,* New York: Springer, 2010.
23. Nikhilanda, Swami, *English Translation of Brihadaranyaka Upanishad.* http:// www.consciouslivingfoundation.org/ebooks/13/CLF-brihadaranyaka_upanishad.pdf [accessed on 10 September 2010]
24. Rahner, Karl, *Theological Investigations*, vol. XVI, trans. Edward Quinn, New York: Seabury Press, 1979.
25. Rahner, Karl, *Theological Investigations*, vol. XIX, trans. Edward Quinn, London: Darton, Longman and Todd, 1984.
26. Ratzinger, Joseph Cardinal, "Church and Economy: Responsibility for the Future of Economy," *Communio*, 13 (1986), 199-204.
27. Schumacher, E. F., *Small is Beautiful: A Study of Economic as if People Mattered*, London: Blond and Briggs, 1973.
28. Sen, Amartya, *On Ethics and Economics*, New Delhi: Oxford University Press, 1987.
29. Sen, Amartya, "Does Business Ethics Make Economic Sense," in *The Ethics of Business in a Global Economy*, ed. Paul M. Minus. Boston: Kluwer Academic Publishers, 1993, 53-66.
30. Sen, Amartya. *Development as Freedom*, Oxford: Oxford University Press, 2000.
31. Smith, Adam, *An Enquiry into the Nature and Causes of the Wealth of Nations*, ed. R. H. Campbell and A. S. Skinner, Indianapolis: Liberty Fund, 1981.
32. Smith, Adam, *The Theory of Moral Sentiments*, ed. A. L. Macfie and D. D. Raphael, Indianapolis: Liberty Fund, 1982.
33. Stueckelberger, Christoph, *We all are Guests on Earth: A Global Christian Vision for Climate Justice*, Bangalore: Dharmaram Publications, 2010.
34. Tagore, Rabindranath,*Gitanjali*. London: Macmillian and Co., 1938.
35. Vandevelde, Antoon, ed. *Gifts and Interests*. Belgium: Peeters, 2000.

4

The Sacred in Creation and the God-intoxicated Celt?

Dr. Una Agnew
Milltown Institute, Dublin, Ireland

The sense of an all-pervasive God, dynamically active in creation and involved in the everyday tasks of domestic life and work has come to be recognized as a dominant theme in Gaelic Christianity. I say Gaelic because the sources on which I lean most heavily are drawn primarily from Gaelic sources, which are of course Celtic in origin.[1] An acute sense of the nearness of God in everyday life especially among rural communities still survives in many places on the fringes of Western Europe.[2] 'God's help is nearer than the door' is a Gaelic saying used in common parlance, ['*is goire cabhair Dé ná andoras*']. This proverb used by Irish speaking people who live close to the land, though it may not be currently the catchword of Irish politicians and bankers who live on the brink of bankruptcy.

[1] Gaelic flourished as a spoken language in the outer Hebridies of Scotland and is still spoken on the Western and North-Western seaboards of Ireland; both of these countries spoke a similar branch of Gaelic: Q-Celtic while the Welsh language is derived from P- Celtic: both are drawn from the same Indo-European stock. Though the spoken language has diminished, Ireland still has a fully functioning Television station, *T na G* whose programmes are transmitted in Gaelic.

[2] J. Macquarrie, *Paths in Spirituality,* Oxford: Oxford University Press, 1972, 122-123. This Scottish theologian suggests that this renewed sense of God might be acquired through a renewed vision of the world and of human life itself such as that found in Celtic Christianity.

1. Daily round of Prayers

In order to understand what is still residual and attracting more and more attention today under the brand name of Celtic Spirituality, it is necessary to examine a genre of Christianity which practiced constant invocation of an immanent God with hints of mystical orientation. A number of ancient morning prayers which greeted God's presence in the new day, still live orally in the Gaelic language and have survived into the 21st century. These prayers have become popular today and are appearing in new translations and sung as hymns set in ancient musical tradition. These prayers originate from an ancient Gaelic oral tradition:

> I am bending my knee in the eye of the Father who created me
> In the eye of the Son who purchased me
> In the eye of the Spirit who cleansed me
> Love towards God
> The affection of God
> The smile of God
> The wisdom of God…
> And I'm asking the Three that my living shall be
> In the likeness of Jesus my Lord.

Focusing on the eye of God is not a peculiarly Irish phenomenon. But, this prayer shows an unmistakable sense of reverence under the eye of God, towards each person of the Trinity along with the desire to conform one's life 'in the likeness of Jesus' the Lord. The majestic eye of God is watchful while the smile and affection of God reassures. The God who sees is also the One, whose radiance endows all creation with blessedness. Traces of the same omni present immanent God, though always with a strong Trinitarian invocation, survive in an array of daily prayers that have been collected from the rural people of Ireland and Scotland.[3] These cover every aspect of a person's day, from the moment of rising, at the kindling of the fire:

---

[3] Alexander Carmichael, *Carmina Gadelica, Hymns and Incantations, with Illustrative Notes of Words, Rites and Customs, Dying and Obsolete,* Orally Collected in the Highlands and Islands of Scotland, 6 Vols, Edinburgh: The Scottish Academic Press, 1900-1954. See also Diarmuid Ó Laoghaire, SJ, *Ár bPaidreacha Dúchais,* Dublin: FÁS, 1975.

I will kindle my fire this morning
In the presence of the holy angels of heaven…
God kindle thou in my heart within
A flame of love to my neighbour
To my foe, to my friend, to my kindred all…

Similar prayers were said while milking, fishing, sowing, before eating, when greeting, journeying, spinning yarn, lighting the lamp, smooring the fire and going to rest. An everyday greeting in Gaelic is not 'Good Morning', 'Hi' or 'Hello' it is a prayer: 'May God and Mary bless you' *(Dia is Muire Dhuit)* which shows how far Christianity penetrated into the language and culture of a people. Scholars such as Alexander Carmichael and the Irish Jesuit, Diarmuid Ó Laoghaire SJ who collected these prayers in Gaelic, found them in abundance in the outer Hebridies of Scotland and on the Western and Northern seaboards of Ireland; both of these countries spoke a similar branch of Gaelic, Q-Celtic while the Welsh language is derived from 'P' Celtic: all are drawn from the same Indo-European stock. From these hundreds of prayers collected and written down, it is clear that each aspect of daily life, each physical feature of creation is seen and reverenced as an integral part of a God-filled universe:

Bless to me O God the moon that is above me
Bless to me O God the earth beneath my feet.
Bless to me O God my wife and my children
And bless to me O God myself who have care of them

The Scottish theologian John Macquarrie, summed up the Celtic people as 'God-intoxicated', possessed of a visionary sense of the Earth and retaining a holistic attitude toward Earth.[4]

The purpose of this article is to attempt to examine what John Macquarrie callsthe phenomenon of 'God-intoxication' present in Celtic Spirituality, and to trace its potential mystical influence in some

[4] John Macquarrie, *Paths in Spirituality,* Oxford: Oxford University Press, 1972, quoted by Sean Ó Duinn, Where Three Streams Meet: Celtic Spirituality, Dublin: The Columba Press, 2000, 7.

aspects of Celtic and Irish Christianity.[5] However, elusive these spiritual qualities may be today in the midst of Western materialism, it is clear that ancient Irish folklore was possessed of a sense of mystery and divine presence that is still never too far away from many rural Irish people. Difficult situations were often dealt with equanimity with the reassuring statement that: 'God is strong and has a goodmother'. St Brigid, above other Irish saints, was given pride of place in the home by being hailed 'Mary of the Gael'. She is the miracle worker in the home, protector of the household, often invoked in hearth prayers and in anything to do with child-birth, fertility and the health of domestic animals. Her distinctive crosses, still fashioned from rushes every year on the eve of her feast Feb 1st, are placed over doors and outhouses to solicit her protection.

In the earlier pagan dispensation, the elemental gods and goddesses of our pagan past, who ruled over mountains, rivers and seas, produced in people a fear of incurring their displeasure and a desire to bend to their demands. The fear could only be assuaged by incantations, charms and spells and constant watchfulness. This fear was carried over into Christian practice and produced both positive and negative effects. In some cases religiosity degenerated into an occultist belief in superstitious practices such as that of carrying an animal claw for protection or hanging a rag on a bush near a holy well for protection. Similar fetishes were coupled with the urge to manipulate 'secret wisdom' and sacred power by means of magical practices around totemic objects, places and gestures. We still have them around the festival of May 1st when people danced with a May bush to drawn down fertility on animals and land and on St Stephen's day when the wren was carried in triumph as a tribute to St. Stephen.[6] And so, side by side with authentic religious practice, there developed a culture of incantations, charms, spells and the concocting of magical potions to protect from danger or invite good

[5] Seán Ó Duinn, *Where Three Streams Meet: Celtic Spirituality,* Dublin: The Columba Press, 2000.

[6] Sylvie Muller, "Wren Ritual in Ireland", quoted in Ó Duinn, *Where Three Streams Meet*, 39.

fortune.[7] The witches in Shakespeare's play *Macbeth* could be seen to have been inspired by Celtic sources.

Prayers of protection are equally plentiful in the tradition since, as well as recognizing all creation as theophany, the Celt was also thoroughly aware of impending dangers that threatened from every direction. Threats to one's person, body and soul as well as one's land, family and community could come from pernicious sources. There is a strong urge to draw a shield around oneself as protection against "all cruel and merciless force / that may attack my body and my soul". It is interesting how traditions of penance in early Irish monasticism paid particular attention to evil inclinations which incurred practices of extraordinary asceticism such as standing up to one's neck in ice cold water and surrendering one's body to a bed of nettles.

The prayer entitled 'The Breastplace of St Patrick' or the Lorica of Patrick epitomizes perhaps, the central insight of Celtic Christianity which moves beyond, but does not lose sight of its pagan past. Timothy Joyce OSB sees it as a prayer 'alive with the power of God' [...] 'enmeshed in the Trinity' and in the immanence of a loving God. The goodness of creation is laced with the infinite power of God.[8]

Such prayers were intended for ritual repetition as if each piece of *lorica* draws the shield of Christ's protection, piece by piece around oneself.[9] If it were not firmly founded in early Irish Christianity, this prayer might have been mistaken as a spell for the donning of a magic cloak of protection. It is interesting how the Harry Potter series of books, conceived and written by A. K. Rowling, reverts to ancient religious practices to entrance the children of today.

---

[7] We have the well known folktale of Fionn McCool (the strong warrior of the Fianna) whose army of Fianna dug into the mountain, Sliabh Gullion, to obtain for him the magic potion destined to restore him to full vitality when an evil spell had been cast upon him by the wicked Hag of the mountain.

[8] Timothy Joyce OSB, *Celtic Christianity: A Sacred Tradition, A Vision of Hope* Maryknoll, New York: Orbis Books, 1998, 71.

[9] A *lorica* was a kind of protective corselet made up of separate pieces, sometimes of leather, sometimes metal or enamel and assembled and attached to one another to make a shield, by hooks or stitches. In French it was called *cuirasse.*

I gather to myself today
The strength of God to guide me
The power of God to uphold me
Wisdom of God to lead me
The eye of God to hear me
The word of God to speak for me
Hand of God to guard me

The full edition of this litany-like sequence represents a call on the omnipresence of Christ to act as shield, to protect and defend the traveler or the one faced with physical or moral danger. Ancient Gaelic sources refer to it as the prayer of the six directions.[10]

Christ be with me, Christ before me
Christ behind me, Christ within me
Christ beneath, Christ above
Christ on my right hand, Christ on my left
Christ in my sleeping, Christ in my rising
Christ in the heart of everyone who thinks of me….

Since, similar prayer formulae are found in Hindu Scriptures, the Celtic *lorica* makes an interesting parallel with aspects of Hindu spirituality. It is a prayer firmly rooted in the many powers of creation, yet invoking the incarnation of Christ and all who have achieved holiness in the new dispensation. The mystical power of this prayer so 'Christ-ian-ates' one's whole being that one can freely call on sun, moon, lightning, fire, wind, ocean, earth and rock as allies in Christian warfare against evil. There is a one-ing of self and community *through*, *with* and *in* Christ. It could be asserted that devout recitation of the *Deer's Cry* raises the soul beyond mystical boundaries by means of the illusive Celtic imagination which Deane says: "twists and turns through a sensuous spiritual energy, an asymmetrical symbolic language […] always anti-classical, anti-representational, anti-rational: All is flux and becoming."[11]

---

[10] Ó Duinn, *Where Three Streams Meet: Celtic Spirituality,* Dublin: Columba Press, 2000, 77-79

[11] John F.Deane, *The Work of Love: Incarnation, Ecology & Poetry*, Dublin: Columba Press, 2010, 21-27, 26.

What is significant in these early Celtic prayers is that they retained a holistic vision of life, which the rest of Europe was beginning to lose in the Middle Ages. Their sentiments held all things together under the caring eye of God and disposed the pray-er toward a more mystical prayer posture. The most famous exponent of this integrated vision of things must surely have been Don Scotus Eriugina (9th century Irish Christian philosopher and mystic), whose 'unified vision of reality' influenced many European thinkers and mystics of Medieval Europe though he himself came under the cosh in 855 AD.[12] The Celtic understanding of the world was imaginative, mystical and symbolic and had much in common with Asian and Eastern Churches. It often clashed with the Roman mindset which was literal, practical with leanings towards abstract conceptualization. Little wonder that Eriugena's integrated vision was dismissed as heretical and referred to as, 'Irish porridgc' since it attempted to include everything under God.

2. Nertor Neart

Macquarie's notion of 'The God-intoxicated Celt' seems to be based on the dynamism of an all-permeating energy that infused all things and toward which the Celt was particularly sensitive. This all pervasive energy that coursed through all things is given serious study by the Benedictine scholar of early and modern Irish, Dr. Seán Ó Duinn.[13] He points to the ancient Irish word *nert* which literally means 'energy' or 'power' and still exists in spoken Irish as *neart*.[14] This free flowing shape –shifting energy was strong in the consciousness of the pagan Celt and was seen to permeate all living things. It could magically change shape from animal to human and back again. Something of this flexibility of form making an intricate web of animated energy can be seen in ancient Irish manuscripts such as The Book of Kells and the Book of Armagh. This genre of colourful intricate Celtic design seems to indicate an Indo European influence.

---

[12] Timothy Joyce, *Celtic Christianity: A Sacred Tradition, a Vision of Hope,* Maryknoll, *New* York: Orbis Books, 1998, 57-61.

[13] '*Nert*' literally means 'energy' or 'strength' which is in its earliest pagan understanding is a dynamic power that permeates the whole earth for good and evil.

[14] *Ní neart go cur le chéile* is a proverb that says: 'real strength is united strength'.

The notion of *nert* is probably derived from a primordial Creation Myth which invests the universe with fecundity and divine energy. As pagans, the Celts were deeply religious in their veneration of an unknown source of power that inhabited the land. This undifferentiated religious sense emanating from 'a life-force that flowed through all things' was foundational to the earliest phase of Celtic religion.[15] Ó Duinn proceeds to trace two further stages of development before *nert* became fully Christianized in Celtic Christianity.[16]

One of the earliest poems written in the vernacular in Ireland was Amergin's ninth century incantation calling on divine power to calm the seas.[17] It evoked this first stage of *nert*: a sense of unity in all the elements ruled over by a divine power. Later this poem was interpreted by Christianity as speaking directly of a Christian God. Whatever God is evoked, it is clear that the combined energies of earth, air, fire and water are identified in the godhead which in turn suffuses all elements with divine *nert.* Divine power is all pervasive.

> I am the Wind that blows over the sea
> I am a Wave of the Ocean
> I am the Murmur of the billows
> I am a hawk on the high cliff edge

The second phase of the development of *nert* evolved into a personification of this energy, into a multitude of elemental gods and goddesses. The sun god Lugh was reverenced through the Celtic universe and gave its name to places as diverse as Lyons *(Lugudunum*) in France, London (Lughdenium) in Britain and County Louth (Co Lú) in Ireland. The pagan god Lugh also gives his name to the eight month *Lughnasa*, the harvest month which gave rise to dancing rituals such

---

[15] Quoted by Ó Duinn, *Where Three Streams Meet*, 2000, 85.

[16] This sense of a all–pervasive divine presence is not peculiarly Irish, it is present in most primitive cultures. It is found at Zuma Rock in Nigeria, West Africa where photography is forbidden and seen as a violation of a sacred place. Similarly, intuitions of the spirit that pervades Ayers Rock in Australia are strong and in India, of course, in a myriad of sacred shrines and in particular in the sacred mountain of Bodh Gaya.

[17] 'Amergin's Song', Thomas Kinsella, ed., *The New Oxford Book of Irish Verse,* London: Oxford University Press, 1986, 48, 395.

as those seen in a recent film based on a play by Brian Friel entitled: *Dancing at Lughnasa.*[18] Lugh also bestowed the fire of magic and artistic inspiration.[19] W. B. Yeats gives a modern rendition of this poetic fire in his 'Song of Wandering Aengus':[20]

> I went out to the hazel wood
> Because a fire was in my head

Traces of ancient elemental gods and goddesses have left their marks on many Irish placenames. The name of Éire itself, the official name of Ireland, derived from a goddess whose betrothal to the king of Ireland was a guarantee of fertility for the land.[21] Irish rivers' names are derived from goddesses: the Shannon, The Boyne, The Eirne while mountains and seas had their deities to whom sacrifice was offered. The river goddess of the Boyne River was central to sun-ceremonies surrounding the Neolithic passage tomb at Newgrange at the winter solstice. The first ray of winter sun entering the roof-box of this prehistoric tomb is a powerful reminder of a prehistoric belief in elemental gods who promised perennial triumph over death along with renewed fertility of the earth.

At a third stage of spiritual evolution, these gods/goddesses gave way before Patrician Christianization with its Trinitarian emphasis. The coming of Christianity to Ireland, as early as the third and fourth century and its continued success relied on a comprehensive conversion from a plethora of elemental gods that dominated the landscape, to the One

---

[18] First directed by Joe Dowling as a play in the Abbey Theatre Dublin, 1990 and later produced as a film in 1998 with Meryl Streep in the role of Kate Mundy and Pat O'Connor, Producer.

[19] Patrick Kavanagh,*The Green Fool,* London: Penguin Books, 1975, 201. The poet claimed that when poetically inspired, he was touched by a spark of the divine that impregnates the poet so as to bring forth immortal words. He is equally likely to say that in the act of writing, he is 'baptized by fire and by the Holy Ghost'.

[20] W. B.Yeats, "Song of Wandering Aengus" in *Collected Poems*, ed. Augustine Martin, London: Arena Books, 1990, 55-56.

[21] Lebor Gabála Érenn (The Book of Invasions) is the Middle Irish title of a collection of prose and poetry recounting the mythical origins and history of the Irish race from the beginning of the world down to the Middle Ages. It was compiled and edited by an anonymous 11th century scholar.

God who ruled over all the elements, the King of the Universe, given a new name in prayer and invoked poetically as *RínanDúl.* Patrician Christianity had the genius to use what was best in the old dispensation along with the people's natural reverence of natural beauty to become the cornerstone of the new religion. Christian prayers now, as we have seen above, celebrated a benevolent God who loved the world, was deeply in tune with all aspects of creation and thoroughly invested in everyday life. The Trinity become a strong feature of this era, since it suited the Celtic love of triads. Once see something of its survival today in the national symbol of the shamrock, although undoubtedly a later addition to Irish religiosity. Patrician spirituality coupled with the Celtic monastic movement seemed capable of integrating much of the riches of a pagan past into its spirituality. This explains the enormous success of Celtic Christianity and its missionary outreach.

What was the outcome of this radical transformation and did anything remain of the once ubiquitous religion? The kingdoms of these early elemental gods, mountains, rivers, islands and wells, retained their reputation as holy or 'thin places' the phenomenon called 'caol áit(acha)' dotted across the landscape, easily appropriating the names of Irish saints: Brigid, Patrick, Colmcille, Éanna, Finbar etc. all became places renowned for Christian pilgrimage and places of piety. Shrines once religious in the older dispensation became transformed into healing wells, sacred mountains, and holy islands. It is no longer Lúgh, or Manannan, (God of the Sea), Eithne, Méabh, Úna or Dana of the hills who command veneration, but a conscious awareness of these 'thin places' lived on commanding reverence and a desire for pilgrimage and penance. Celtic Christianity had no difficulty in embracing the notion of pilgrimage and penance: Croagh Patrick, Lough Derg, Clonmacnoise. Glendalough, Faughart and Guagán Barra and several Ladywells: these still testify to practices which have survived with or without the blessing of the official churches.

Prehistoric *Nert* has been finally transformed into a personal immanent God, and into a Christ who offers shield and protection for each day. The Celtic God is both 'beyond the beyonds' yet immanently present and fully engaged in daily life.

3. Poets are often Sensitive to Transcendent Energy

The power of 'nert' is still detectable in certain modern Irish poets, featuring certain poetic affirmation of radiance, epiphany, numinous presence emanating from creation. The patriot poet Joseph Mary Plunkett [1887-1916] senses the visible trace of God's beauty around him:

> I see his blood upon the rose
> And in the stars the glory of his eyes
> His body gleams amid eternal snows
> His tears fall from the skies. [22]

A later poet Patrick Kavanagh [1904-1967] in whose work is found, hints of a mystical imagination, expresses delight at God's beauty bursting out in backward places redolent with God's beauty. At another time, he sees God breathing his love in the riotous colours of a flowering bog:

> Green, blue, yellow and red
> God is down in the bogs and marshes…
> Beautiful, beautiful, beautiful God
> Is breathing his love by a cutaway bog [The One][23]

Nert seems to be alive and well in his work when, in his fictional alter-ego character Tarry Flynn, he exclaims that his spring landscape is alive with the Holy Spirit.[24] He may indeed be a good example of 'the God-intoxicated Celt' who, by his unorthodox behaviour, dismayed his farming neighbours and even his mother by the possibility that he might be half-mad.[25] We have already noted that W.B. Yeats considered poetic inspiration as 'a fire in the head' much as Kavanagh believes that his best work has within it 'a spark of divine energy', vestiges of Lugh

---

[22] "I see his Blood upon the Rose", *The Deer's Cry: A Treasury of Irish Religious Verse*, ed. Patrick Murray, Dublin: Four Courts Press, 1986, 195.

[23] Patrick Kavanagh, *The Complete Poems*, ed. Peter Kavanagh, Newbridge, Ireland: The Goldsmith Press, 1984, 291. Unless otherwise stated all quotations from this poet's work are taken from this edition of his works.

[24] Patrick Kavanagh *Tarry Flynn,* Middlesex, England: Penguin Books, 1978, 29-30

[25] Una Agnew, *The Mystical Imagination of Patrick Kavanagh: A Buttonhole in Heaven,* Dublin: The Columba Press, 1998 -1999, 187.

or Bel, the Celtic fire-gods. Lest we imagine that this unseen energy is always positive, Yeats senses the dark energy of defeat crossing the Irish landscape as 'a bitter black wind that blows from the left hand'.[26] And in a much more earthy way, in his 'Great Hunger' epic, Kavanagh saw an apocalypse of clay haunt every corner of the land. Kavanagh also saw the primitive all pervasive sacred pagan energy in the Celtic tradition suffused throughout the land.

4. 'Thin Places' or the phenomenon of the '*Caol Áit*'

The Celts had a strong belief in the after life.[27] At special places and times of the calendar year, when the veil between this world and the next was only barely drawn, these moments became designated as 'thin places'. Certain well defined landmarks like *Samhain* (Nov 1st) brought the summer season to a close and opened up the darker half of the year. At this transition time, the souls of the dead were understood to congregate with the living. A sense of spirit haunted the land. There is a strong hint of Celtic Underworld that permeates Irish consciousness at these times, so that family graves become places of veneration. At solstice and equinox times ancient Neolithic tombs became gathering places where people gathered to worship the sun's perennial triumph over darkness and its undying status as God of the earth. Similarly, *Bealtaine* (May 1st) closed the veil of winter and opened the new season with a procession of divine spirits and dance rituals around the new fire of the God Bel, author of new life and fertility. Thin places gave rise to further experiences of the 'god intoxication' to which Macquarrie referred, thereby opening up the boundaries of mysticism a little wider afield.

Celtic Christianity brought a similar sense of well-established semi-permeable soul-places such as: Iona in Scotland, Glendalough, Croagh Patrick and Lough Derg in Ireland. Since, Celtic civilization had married very well into the Brehon Law tradition, where the *tuath* was the unit of

[26] W.B.Yeats, "Red Hanrahan's Song about Ireland," in *Collected Poems*, ed. Augustine Martin, London: Arena Books, 1990, 77.

[27] Listening to his neighbours' appraisal of a newly built house, the writer Patrick Kavanagh concluded that Irish people never forget they must die since the main conversation indicated that the doorway was not sufficiently wide to allow for the passage of a coffin from its precincts and that exit through a window would be necessary.

land ruled over by a Celtic chieftain, the abbot of the monastery became the new *tuath* and spiritual leader of the community. In the golden age of Irish Christian monasticism, between the 5th and 8th centuries,the local abbot gathered monks around him so that monasteries became places of pilgrimage and holy learning under the saintly guidance of saints such as: Ciaran, Finian, Colmcille and Kevin. Holy places such as these developed into a whole series of 'thin places' renowned for holiness where the presence of God was palpably felt. Holy wells, High Crosses, holy mountains, ancient burial sites, lone bushes: all were treated with the utmost respect and reverence, hence the popularity still of pilgrimages to Lough Derg, Croagh Patrick, Clonmacnoise, Glendaloch. Iona in Scotland and Lindisfarne or Holy Island off the north east coast of England are all well established 'thin places'.

In postmodern times, now that the ancient aura of Ireland as the Island of Saints and Scholars is well and truly banished, the spirituality of the thin place or *caol ait* still persists. It can be recognized in the 'glimpse', 'the chink' or wisp of eternity that somehow escapes or emanates from what the poet Kavanagh calls 'the bits and pieces of everyday'.[28] Poetry often records these glimpses of eternity which ordinary mortals may dismiss as fanciful. Mark Patrick Hederman hails contemporary poetic and artistic expression as the 'underground cathedrals' being built in our culture. Rather boldly he declares:

> At this time the secret work of the Holy Spirit is not being done in most countries of Western Europe by politicians nor by church institutions. The people who are carrying the torch are not mostly artists…nor does it matter how much that work goes unrecognized… (since) that has been the profile of the Holy Spirit since the beginning of time.[29]

Irish people are beginning to recognize the prophetic role played by their poets. In his poem 'A Christmas Childhood' Kavanagh speaks of his glimpse of eternity set in the context of a humble haggard on a small farm: "The light between the ricks of hay and strawwas a hole in

[28] Patrick Kavanagh, "The Great Hunger,"in *The Complete Poems,* 79-104, 84

[29] Mark Patrick Hederman, *Underground Cathedrals,* Dublin: The Columba Press, 2010, 140-156, 141.

heaven's gable."[30] In a later poem he finds himself caught unaware in the stare of 'Fantastic light [that] looks through the eye of bridges'.[31] When Kavanagh asserts that 'revelation comes as an aside', he indicates that there are unbidden moments of knowledge and vision that are beyond reason.[32]

The Welsh poet R. S. Thomas (1913-2000) presents a classic example of the wisp of God in an out-of-the-blue glimpse of eternity caught in the poet's memory as 'the sun breaks through to illuminate a small field'. Recollecting the moment in tranquility afforded by his poetic skill, he likens it to 'turning aside like Moses to the miracle of the lit bush'. These are hints of mystical awareness which parallel the earlier more established experiences of 'thin places' where God's presence is near.[33]

The current Irish Nobel Laureate Seamus Heaney (1938-) shows he is not unaware of such moments of heighted sensibility when a sense of the powerful impact of nature is seen to have the effect of blowing open the heart that is caught 'off guard'. Such a moment hints of something beyond the ordinary; a moment of expanded consciousness which poet and mystic share.

> And sometime make the time to drive out west
> Into County Clare, along the Flaggy Shore
> In September or October, when the wind
> And light are working off each other...
> You are neither here nor there,
> A hurry through which known and strange things pass
> A big soft buffetings comes at the car sideways
> And catch the heart off guard and blow it open.[34]

Today these poetic glimpses may be all that remain of the ancient 'thin places' that brought people nearer their God.

---

[30] 'A Christmas Childhood' *The Complete Poems*, 143-144.

[31] *The Complete Poems,* 295.

[32] See also Patrick Kavanagh, "To Hell with Commonsense," in *The Complete Poems*, 288.

[33] R.S.Thomas, *Later Poems 1972-1982*, London: Macmillan, 1983, 81.

[34] Seamus Heaney, 'Postscript' in: *Spirit Level,* London: Faber and Fabler, 1996.

5. The Lios or Fairy Fort or Rath

Another influential spiritual and mythical phenomenon that consciously or unconsciously continues to permeate the Irish psyche is that of the predominance of the *lios* or ring-fort on the landscape. These are circular stone-walled spaces generally located on the tops of small hills or hillocks and scattered across the face of Ireland. They date from 1200 BC to 400 AD, remnants of a prehistoric farming people, most likely of Celtic origin. These are built with circular or oval shaped enclosure stone ditches to provide home and animals with a measure of protection against adverse forces from without. Inside, souterrains were dug as hiding places and as refrigeration for food preserved there throughout the year so that a kind of enclosed circle of life was lived at the heart of the lios with good look-out facilities over the neigbourhood. An estimated 30,000 of these ringforts with place names to match beginning with Rath or Lios, survive as conspicuous Irish landmarks today. It would not be an exaggeration to say that almost every farmer has a *lios* or *rath* somewhere on his farm.[35]

To further consolidate the *lios* as an otherworldly fairy place, an ancient mythical history of Ireland recounts the waging of war between two mythical tribes one human and one divine who strove to take ownership of the land. These two powerful tribes fought for possession and the end result was that the wizardly tribe, the Tuatha dé Danainn lost the upper hand and division of the land was imminent. In settling boundaries the fairy folk opted for the underground half of the land allocating to themselves the hollows of the hills and the megalithic sites and passage graves while the conquerors opted for the surface of the land. And so it was that the divine geniuses, the Tuatha dé Danainn, descendents of the gods appropriated the hollows of the hills but still retained a certain control over the fertility of the land.[36] A host of customs arose whereby sacrifices of corn, milk and butter were offered to the hidden *lucht si* who made their appearance at deaths, marriages and births and took their revenge on the crops when badly treated. So

[35] Hill forts were in use in many Celtic areas of central and Western Europe until the Roman conquest. Julius Caesar described the large late Iron Age hill forts he encountered during his campaigns in Gaul as oppida.

[36] Ó Duinn, *Where Three Streams Meet: Celtic Spirituality*, 55-61.

it was that a truce was made and the fairies or *lucht sí* agreed to live in peaceful coexistence with the conquerors provided certain sacrificial donations were duly made. And, so this multitude of lioses and raths throughout Ireland became known as fairy forts. People working on the land, learned to tread carefully on these ancient sites so that no one would dare disturb a lone bush or a fairy tree. There is still a strong taboo around these places and a belief it would bring bad luck to disturb their fairy tenants. Ironically, it now transpires that these clumps of fairy trees and lone bushes are ecological treasure for the pollination of crops.

Nuala Ní Dhómnaill, a contemporary Irish poet, insists that the *lios* is not only a physical landmark on the landscape but holds a space in the people's and in the poet's psyche.[37] This fairy-fort-within, houses the stuff of the gods and belongs to the sacred underworld. The poet is still obliged to be the messenger of Hermes, the winged god, and stay on the track of the gods who are being banished from the earth by materialism. The *lios* may be no more than a clump of trees on a hilltop; nevertheless it is symbolic of an inner place sacred to the gods. Stories and legends abound in relation to these fairy places. Ní Dhomhnaill believes that it is the poet or soothsayer who brings the stuff from that other world into the world of here and now so that the people are given access to its fairy or mystical power. 'When I write a poem', she says, 'I experience inspiration and a sense of being impregnated by the divine'. Many poets believe that the mystic and poet share moments of expanded consciousness that are similar.[38] What they do with these moments afterwards may differ, though not always.

6. Summary and Conclusion

When examined historically and in dialogue with well scrutinized ancient texts by scholars who are competent in the languages of these texts, it would appear that there is a long tradition in Ireland of celebrating earth astheophany. The Celts may not have built a political empire; instead

[37] Kimberly R. Myers, 'Nuala Ní Dhomhnaill and Women's Sensual Spirituality' in: *Things of the Spirit: Women Writers Constructing Spirituality,* ed. Kristina K.Groover, Notre Dame, Indiana: University of Notre Dame Press, 2001, 303-304.

[38] Doreen Gildroy, 'Poetry and Mysticism' in *The American Poetry Review,* (Mar/Apr 2009), 39.

they left behind them a spiritual legacy which emphasized hierophanies over dynasties. The marriage of Celtic nature worship with Christianity was most successful where it integrated the best of ancient beliefs with faith in a Triune God. In the golden era of Irish monasticism, a host of holy monks, men and women dedicated themselves to the study and illumination of God's word in manuscript as well asGod's word 'spoken' in creation and in the green church of the out-of-doors. The prayer practice of the ancestors left behind an oral legacy of holistic spirituality and a benediction of each moment of each day sufficiently robust to support mystical prayer. Could this be called 'God intoxication' probably not. Nevertheless, pockets of continuous prayer survived to demonstrate a strong sense of God attuned to all events and occasions, however commonplace. If 'God-intoxication' occurred it was because life was embraced on all sides as Divine mystery. These kinds of people, Mircea Eliade believed,saw themselves in a godlike role, tilling the soil in tandem with divinity. [39]

When sacrality is banished from the earth by consumerism and materialism, it is the poets who stay on the tracks of the fugitive gods.[40] Today it seems that the Holy Spirit works *incognito* among the poets and artists, mining the gold of 'thin places' and interior *lios*es which keep alive epiphanies of divine life as well as wisps of transcendence that might otherwise be lost. Even with the rapid arrival and departure of the so-called 'Celtic tiger'in Ireland and the threat that consumerist values would predominate, poets still show the way forward and help their audience retain a sense of transcendenceand a continuous acknowledgement of the sacramental dimension of creation. John O. Donohue showed himself to be a writer preeminent in allowing his consciousness to be seized by the numinosity of something in the landscape beyond himself. He experiencedfrequent sensations of blessedness or epiphany.[41] Thus, imagination, poetry and ascetical practice continue to consolidate in the psyche a strong religious sense.

---

[39] Mircea Eliade, "Earth Woman, Fertility," in *Patterns in Comparative Religions*, Nebraska: Bison Books, 1996, 263-69.

[40] Martin Heidegger, 'What are Poets for?' *Poetry, Language, Thought,* New York: Harper & Row, 1971, 71.

[41] John O Donohue, *Anam Chara: Spiritual Wisdom from the Celtic World,* London: Bantam Press, 1997, 44, 82.

I will conclude with a quotation from the poet Kavanagh who has already featured in this essay. Poetically he expresses the epiphany of a moment trapped in mystery. On a cold dismal March day, the sun breaks through so that a tree on the horizon becomes suddenly infused with aneternal radiance. The poet captures the moment, through the eyes of a simple farmer (probably himself) who is ploughing a field, in the inhospitable east wind. Everything seems cold, infertile, comfortless, and God-forsaken.Yet, in the twinkle of an eye, the poet finds himself caught up in a Trinitarian moment which binds together earth, tree, sky, the people and heaven.

> The pull is on the traces it is March
> And a cold black wind is blowing from Dundalk…
> Yet sometimes when the sun comes through a gap
> These men see God the Father in a tree
> The Holy Spirit is the rising sap
> And Christ will be the green leaves that comes
> At Easter from the sealed and guarded tomb. [The Great Hunger Stanza V]

Whatever this moment of expanded consciousness may be, it is a space which mystic and poet share, each in his or her own way. Intoxicating? Perhaps not, but heartwarming, yes!

5

Distress and Joy in Love of the Absolute

Understanding the Mystic's Love Affair with God

Dr. Paul Moyaert
Institute of Philosophy
Katholieke Universiteit Leuven, Leuven, Belgium

What is it that makes human nature sensitive to religion? Which aspects of the human condition might religion be able to benefit from? Philosophy and natural theology have put forward several faculties where religion could be seen as taking root. According to some, the desire for knowledge is the most important natural source of religion. Here, religion is seen to profit from man's intellectual curiosity and to appeal to his love for truth. Religious faith is understood as an expression of certain beliefs about the world that rest upon truth conditions in approximately the same way that other cosmological propositional beliefs do. A religious way of life is thus seen to consist in the practical application of the ideas and convictions belonging to a specific cosmological doctrine. Other philosophers argue, however, that the imagination is the strongest ally for religion. Instead of being seen as something akin to cosmological doctrines with scientific claims, religion is understood in relation to myths that strike the imagination and that deal with the more dramatic aspects of the human condition. According to philosophers such as Hume, Spinoza and Freud, for example, one must locate the strongest natural causes for religion in negative emotions such as anxiety, loneliness, helplessness and despair. For these thinkers, if religion is understood to take advantage of such negative existential experiences, this is because of the power that they possess to put our imagination into movement.

It is not very common amongst such philosophers to explain religious attitudes and ways of life as direct expressions of joy, or other positive affects. Instead, the force of the imagination is thought to depend upon the shock, or the momentous impact, of negative existential experiences. In contrast with these two approaches, I would like to understand religion in relation to another aspect of the human condition, namely our capacity for love and desire. The idea that love and desire can function as a fertile soil for religion, is of course, not a new one. For St. Augustine and many other Church Fathers, man's capacity to love and desire was thought to be an obvious and natural starting point for understanding the soul's relationship to God. In contemporary philosophical literature, however, this third approach has nevertheless lost the appeal it once had. There is one specific motivation for my interest in renewing this perspective, which I would like to draw attention straightaway: such an approach can contribute to a better understanding of mystical love.

One important implication of my approach here is that, no matter what spiritual heights mystical love may attain, it must derive some of its force from libidinal sources and psychic processes that are also found in more mundane and sensual forms of love. Some will likely object to this on the grounds that mystic love has nothing in common with less spiritual forms of love. There are two reasons why I feel that this argument is not philosophically attractive. Firstly, if we bar ourselves from any sort of comparison between mystic love and other, more mundane forms of love, it becomes particularly difficult to account for mystical love to outsiders, or the uninitiated. Secondly, the objection makes it even harder to account for the powerful attractive force that mystical love is capable of exerting on human nature. To put it differently, a mystical love affair with God has little chance of appealing to, or attracting an individual, if it is not rooted in the very nature of human love and desire. Like any form of love, mystical love requires natural dispositions in order to grip into and touch an individual's life. In my study here, I would thus like to raise the following question, which we shall consider in more detail below: In what sorts of less elevated expressions of love and desire is mystical love capable of finding a fertile ground? Before getting underway, it is important to point out that my perspective places a certain restriction on the complex and variegated domain of mysticism. This restriction should not pose any significant problems, however, for I shall be limiting my investigation to specifically Christian forms of mysticism, and though it is true that not all forms of Christian mysticism give expression to a love for the Absolute, it is nevertheless quite clear that love has exercised a great deal of inspiration in the lives of many Christian mystics. Indeed, in Christianity, love is one of the most essential definitions of God. I should also draw attention to a second limitation of my study here. I shall focus primarily on St. Teresa of Avila, whose story and spiritual doctrine is generally understood to constitute an important turning point in the history of Western mysticism. What is particularly interesting in the religious love story of St. Teresa is that, in writing about her prayers and the gifts she received from God, she deepened her account with a detailed introspective description of the effects that these prayers and gifts had on to the different faculties of her soul. This inward turn is rather novel and significant in the history of Christian mysticism. St. Teresa's perspective is consistent with Catholic theology, according to which God makes use of those faculties of human nature that are capable of being attracted by God and of being formed by his inspiration. Human nature and divine nature relate on each other. The shift towards an exploration of the inner, psychological aspects of the mystical experience, which is characteristic for most modern psychological approaches of mysticism, should nevertheless not be seen to amount to a reduction of mysticism to psychology. As we shall see, St. Teresa understands love not in terms of a subjective emotion, but in terms of a cognitive relation. Her spiritual doctrine works along the same lines as the common sense notion that to *love* someone is to *know* someone. Love is thus not an obstacle in knowing God, but rather a privileged means of coming to know him. To grow in love is therefore intimately related with obtaining a deeper insight into the nature of one's beloved.

A simple reference to the human capacity to love and desire is nevertheless far too vague to permit a better understanding of what is going on in mystical love. It is therefore important that we begin by distinguishing among different kinds of love; from here, we will be in a better position to examine the ordinary kind of love in which a love for the Absolute is rooted, or from which it draws its spiritual force.

Part I: Kinds of Love

1. Divine love and Parental love

To begin, let us consider *God's love* of creation (i.e. nature, animals and human beings). This is often compared with a *parent's love* for a child, even though the scope of the latter is clearly much more restricted than the former. The Biblical text itself suggests such a parallel. In neither case does this kind of love require any form of reciprocity. It is a love that precedes any sort of response on the side of the love-object. God loves his creatures before they are capable of understanding his love and responding to it. Similarly, parents love their children well before they are capable of understanding it and responding in kind. This form of love is a caring love, or *benevolentia*, i.e., a love in which you care about what is good for the other. Parents care for their child lovingly even when there is no possibility of the child ever becoming aware of it, such as is the case with children suffering from severe mental handicaps. The fact that this love precedes any sort of response in kind explains why it is deeply related to patience and long suffering. Since it does not originate in or necessitate a return of love, it is able to endure the lack of reciprocity. In this, parental love closely resembles the spontaneous and unconditional character of divine love. As asymmetrical as they might be at their origin, however, neither divine love nor parental love are divorced from a deep interest in reciprocity. Although God's love does not *depend* on its being returned, he sorrows over those who either ignore it or refuse to be touched by it. God is not indifferent to the response of his creatures. Though an absence of response on the part of his creatures may not leave God indifferent, his interest in reciprocity nevertheless does not radically affect his love's spontaneity. According to the well-known and classic metaphysical definition, 'God *is* love': love is not simply one of his attributes, but an expression of who he is. He must necessarily love, for love is his very nature. The point to which I would like to draw the attention, however, is the fact that neither generosity nor pure benevolence exclude, or preclude, a deep interest in reciprocation. To put it differently, divine love is not only deeply concerned with what is good for his creation, but also withmaintaining (or restoring) a *community* of love, i.e., a community in which his creatures are capable of personally recognizing his love and of acting in accordance with this recognition. Hence, he rejoices when community is restored with his creatures. In sum, though divine love is not *based* on reciprocity, it is nevertheless *closely* bound up with it. Similarly, though parental love is not based upon reciprocation, it does, on the one hand, deplore a child's lack of gratitude, and, on the other, welcome the child's return. We could also draw attention to another important similarity between parental and divine love: both forms of love are highly preferential, or biased, in nature, and hence never without an element of jealousy. In the Old Testament, for example, Yahweh explicitly acknowledges the ferocious jealousy of his love (Exodus 20:5; Deuteronomy 4:24). His jealous love erupts when his chosen people worship other divinities. In a similar way, we are not at all surprised to discover a tinge of jealousy in a father or mother whose child prefers the more lax, or indulgent, parents of other children.

2. Amor amicitiae

Both divine love and parental love must be distinguished from *amor amicitiae*, i.e., the love between friends and spouses. Love between friends and spouses cannot initially be brought about without reciprocity: just as one person cannot call another person a friend unless he or she does the same (or has, at least at one point in time, done the same), so also a husband cannot call a woman his wife unless she has never been capable of calling him her husband. Though it is true that *amor amicitiae* is capable, at least temporarily, of *tolerating* an interruption in reciprocity (such as in cases of infidelity or betrayal), it is important to point out that reciprocity nevertheless remains a hard-and-fast condition of this form of love. One friend may be able to love another friend even though the second party is no longer capable of doing the same, but, in contrast with divine and parental love, the love of friendship presupposes an initial reciprocity. In divine and parental love, the relation is the cause of love: God loves his creatures because they are his creatures, just as parents love their children because they are their children. In both cases, love is grounded on the basis of a pre-existing relation. The same is true both of the love between sister and brother and of the love an individual bears for his or her country. In *amor amicitiae*, on the other hand, love *creates* the relationship. Like divine love, *amor amicitiae* is also interested in maintaining and restoring reciprocity and community. It does not and cannot reduce to a pure benevolence. Benevolence is an altruistic love that finds its highest enjoyment in the existence and flourishing of the love-object. The love of friendship, in contrast, prefers the presence of the love-object over and above the latter's existence. Though it is true that the existence and the wellbeing of the friend (or spouse) are also irreducible sources of enjoyment, one cannot speak of friendship unless the presence of the other substantially increases the enjoyment one finds in his or her existence. To give a simple example, the sharing of an activity, such as going on a trip or watching a movie together, contributes a large part to what makes the activity more enjoyable. Moreover, in many cases, the presence of the friend (or spouse) functions as a condition of finding enjoyment in the activity in the first place. *Amor amicitiae* is thus not a mere joy in the beloved's existence. This observation provides us with an important point to consider: it is impossible to speak of *amor amicitiae* without one being pained by the separation (or absence) of one's friend or the spouse. In this type of love, therefore, distress and joy are clearly related to the presence and absence of the beloved. Equanimity before the absence, death, or loss of the love-object is, for this reason, not a morally adequate attitude. If such indifference is not first preceded by some degree of sadness, it is seen as a deficiency, rather than as a moral perfection. Though benevolence is also a decisive feature here, it cannot exist without a desire for the beloved's presence. One cannot call a person a friend if his/her presence or absence makes no difference. In this respect, it is important to see, more generally, how love both differs from and relates to desire. We are inclined to say that love, in itself, lacks nothing: it is a pure and simple joy in the wellbeing and existence of the beloved. What closer examination reveals, on the contrary, is that friendship and married love are inconceivable without some degree of desire for the loved one's presence.

3. Falling in love

There is a third type of love that requires our special attention, viz., the love in which, as we say, one *falls*. As we shall see, this is one of the most complicated kinds of love. One of its chief characteristic features immediately leaps out at us: one can fall in love with someone without being concerned with what is good for him or her. Philosophers who argue that benevolence is the very essence of love are liable to make use of this observation to claim that falling in love is not a genuine form of love. The most immediate source of enjoyment in falling in love, however, is the *desire for the beloved*; caring orbenevolent concerns do not express what falling in love is. There is a second reason why philosophy often hesitates to take falling in love as a genuine expression of love: love stands for a certain degree of permanence, whereas it is just as likely for one to fall in love as it is for one to fall right back out of it. Falling in love is far too fleeting a phenomenon to be a true manifestation of love. There is also another aspect of falling in love that is just as peculiar, and also merits our attention: falling in love is not necessarily interested in reciprocity. First and foremost, it is quite clear that falling in love can be, and many times is, a largely one-sided affair. One person can fall (or be) in love with another person without him or her even knowing it. Even beyond this, moreover, one may fall in love without any interest in having the beloved return one's feelings. In other words, this kind of love can be much more indifferent to the question of love being shared in common. What makes falling in love such a curious and fascinating phenomenon is that the inaccessibility of the beloved and the impossibility of reciprocity can, in some cases, function as a very *condition* of this kind of love. How are we to understand such a paradoxical phenomenon? In my mind, the complex relation of a lover to her beloved is conditioned upon her wanting two things at once, namely the *presence* of the beloved and the *desire* for the beloved. Distance, in this case, can function as a means for keeping the desire for the beloved alive. If desire for the beloved is preferred over the beloved's presence and acts as the final cause of the lover's enjoyment, the latter will, strangely enough, thrive upon the pain of distance and separation. What we come to see, then, is that a curious mixture of excitement and suffering characterizes falling in love.

4. Passionate Love

Let us now consider what happens when the desire for the beloved dominates love and is made absolute. We shall call this kind of love 'passionate love'. Just to be clear, though, I consider passionate love to be something quite different from a vehement desire for the beloved. The basic feature, I would argue, concerns not simply the strength of the desire, but the fact that the desire for the beloved is made absolute, or that it is preferred over and above the beloved's presence. Courtly love offers us an example of this. The lower-class knight desires a noblewoman knowing all the while that it will be absolutely impossible for him to find any real sexual satisfaction with her. He thus enjoys, thrives upon and cultivates the pain of an impossible mutual love relationship. In a similar way, romantic literature explores the infinite longing that animates passionate love. In this literary genre, the protagonist only enjoys the presence of the beloved if it is directly associated with the pain of an inevitable separation. The lover's infinite longing for his beloved both stimulates and conditions his excitation, which is enjoyable and painful at the same time. If satisfaction is understood to be the natural aim of human desire, a love in which desire is made absolute would seem to express something counter-natural in human eroticism. The fundamental aim of this kind of Eros is neither the wellbeing of the beloved nor a satisfaction with the beloved's presence, but rather a deep longing for him or her. It is not simply a mixture of love and desire that is too great to be satisfied, but, we should say, a love that is *deeply disinterested* in satisfaction. It is a love that finds no pleasure unless it is mingled with separation.

There are various kinds of circumstances that can make a reciprocal love-relation impossible: it can be either morally forbidden (e.g. due to a previous commitment) or physically impracticable (e.g. when one of the partners has to move overseas). In passionate love, at least as far as I understand it, the cause of this impossibility is not an accidental event. On the contrary, distance and impossibility are *required* for it to flourish. On the one hand, of course, I, as the lover, deplore the distance between myself and the beloved, doing everything in my power to overcome it. On the other hand, however, the pain of being separated from the beloved is also something I crave. Hence, in ordinary life, passionate love expresses itself in preferences for objects precisely insofar as they are impossible to obtain, such that the inaccessibility of the beloved is experienced simultaneously as a painful burden and as a source of one's fervent longing. The lover, therefore, neither wants the absence nor the presence of the beloved. Instead, I (awkwardly putting myself again in the lover's position) want the two things at once: distance when my beloved is present and proximity when she is absent. Hence, passionate love is not the sort of love that is strong enough to accept the fact that the love object might, unfortunately, be out of reach. Nor is it a love that is capable of waiting indefinitely for the beloved. Instead, it is a love in which, strangely enough, the lover demands the beloved *not* to answer his supplications. The aim of the love is the longing as such – distance is required to make the lover suffer. Distance is not what must be overcome, but rather that which must be created and cultivated at the very moment when the beloved is nearby.[1] This explains how the loving soul can weep in the presence of its beloved. This is also why neither the beloved nor the lover is able to understand the source of the love's fervent turmoil: as the beautiful French expression goes – *ni avec toi, ni sans toi*. A community founding reciprocity in which enjoyment is found in shared activities is thus not the truth of a passionate love. We have already seen how *amor amicitiae* too is not without desire, but as we saw, it is predominantly benevolent in nature, just like divine love and parental love. In other words, love, in this case, dominates desire. In passionate love, on the other hand, it is just the other way around: desire dominates love.

5. Amor concupiscientiae

St. Augustine establishes an important distinction between *amor concupiscientiae* and *amor amicitiae*. Is this distinction instructive for better understanding passionate love? At first sight, we note a strong similarity between passionate love and *amor concupiscientiae*, for in both cases we find a love dominated by the insatiable hunger of desire. However, I myself am inclined to avoid this Augustinian term when describing passionate love because, for St. Augustine, *concupiscientia* is understood to consist in an insatiable need for ever new and more intense sensuous desires and satisfactions. No satisfaction is enough to quell its gnawing hunger. Thus, while *concupiscientia* can clearly not be a reliable *basis* for love because love is understood to include benevolence

[1] D. de Rougemont, *L'amour et l'occident*, Paris: Collection 10/18, 1939.

and permanence, it is still not entirely at odds with benevolent aims either. Insofar as St. Augustine suggests that *concupiscientia* is an insatiable hunger for sensuous pleasures and satisfactions, the term, in my mind,is not appropriate to characterize passionate love. The true source of turbulence in passionate love is to be found, I would argue, in the infinite restlessness of its longing, and not an insatiable hunger for sensuousness and erotic novelty. In passionate love, the soul is not continually in search of ever newer satisfactions; it is, strangely enough, motivated by a desire that, in spite of desiring the beloved's presence, does not want to be satisfied. To put it differently, the double intentional object of passionate Eros cannot be understood in terms of a tension between love and lust. The desire as such is the source of a 'painful and enjoyable satisfaction'. Separation is preferred to the satisfaction offered in proximity.Even when one is capable of enjoying the beloved's presence, this enjoyment is conditioned by the idea that separation is ultimately unavoidable. When given expression outside of an appropriate context, this kind of love is capable of thoroughly exhausting and even destroying a person. The wonder of courtly love and romantic literature, on the other hand, lies precisely in the power they possess to create contexts in which this deeply suffering love is able to flourish.

One can thus understand why St. Augustine's distinction will not play a crucial role in my categorisation of the different kinds of love. Unlike my notion of passionate love, his conception of *amor concupiscientiae* seems to suggest that sensuous desires are essentially incompatible with benevolent love – in other words, that pleasure does not aim at what is good and does not spontaneously converge with benevolence. In this way, St. Augustine anticipates Freud, who argues that the incompatibility of lust and love is one of the most important causes of discontentment in the human condition. There is certainly some truth to the belief that pleasure and the good belong to two separate ontological orders. However, it is equally clear that they are not radically incompatible either. In a marriage, for example, *amicitia* and *concupiscientia* can exist side by side and mutually strengthen each other. In this case, sexual desires serve to create a new and more complex unity between the self and the other. Passionate love, in contrast, requires the desperation and suffering of separation: reciprocity and community are not its goal.

There is still one important kind of love that I have not yet discussed, namely *charitable love*. Our purposes do not require us to analyse this form of love in detail. It is sufficient to remark that St. Paul characterizes charitable love in terms of patience and long-suffering: it patiently bears the fact that communion between self and other cannot be restored. Charity thus bears the other's evil with long-suffering. In short, this love is also, unlike passionate love, deeply invested in community.[2]

6. Mystic love

To which kind of love is a mystical love affair most strongly related? I would argue that, at least *initially*, mystical love has everything in common with passionate love. It is a love that is consumed by desire. The mystical soul cannot find satisfaction in God, excluding, as it does, any form of reciprocity. The Absolute can only be present *in* the desire for it – hence, in the desire that itself is made absolute. However, there is second crucial element in my understanding of mystical love. Although it is deeply rooted in the paradoxes inherent to passionate love, it also involves a painful and often quite arduous transformation of these paradoxes. As we will see, mystical love develops from the turmoil and destructive passion of desire into a love purified from desire. Mystics such as St. Teresa make use of the metaphor of marriage in order to describe this transformed relation to God. Higher levels of prayer and more profound mystical experiences belong to the symbolic framework of a mystical marriage with God. Thomas Aquinas, in a similar way, links these higher manifestations of love for God with friendship. God is thus the mystical soul's companion. However, I would argue that linguistic expressions such as 'spiritual marriage with God' are somewhat misleading insofar as they attempt to reinsert mysticism under the heading of *amor amicitiae*; in my mind, an even more radical transformation takes place in the soul here, one that transfigures the soul into an expression of God's love. God expresses his love for the world through the love of the mystic's soul. The mystical soul is transformed

[2] P. Moyaert, "Barmhartigheid: transcendentie verdragen" in *Tijdschrift voor Filosofie*, 69, 4 (2007), 713-732.

into an instrument of a divine love that flows through it. This is what mystics come to understand as they grow closer to God. In the highest forms of mystical prayer and union, God is no longer an intentional object of a mystical Eros; instead, the soul loses its individuality and is transformed into an empty medium for God's love. As we saw, courtly love consists in a complex and highly ritualized love relation with an inaccessible Lady, such that Eros, as a combination of love and desire, can be cultivated in such a way that the lover does not succumb to its paradoxes. In a similar way, I would argue that religion offers another ritualized framework in which a desire made absolute is not only capable of being endured, but is also much more likely to be spiritually fertile. Without a religious context to impose rules and obligations upon the individual, passion for the Absolute is liable to become a rather dangerous and self-destructive love affair. Religion and, in particular, a strongly ritualized monastery life, can structure the infinite longing for Absolute.

Before going any further I would first like to comment both on the triadic structure of the mystical way and on the lower forms of prayer, i.e., those forms leading up to the ecstatic prayers in which the passionate soul is devoured by a desire for God. I will then give closer consideration to the paradoxes and dangers involved in such a passionate love affair. A few passages from the writings of St. Teresa of Avila and St. John of the Cross will help to illustrate my view. As I will show, the suffering of the "dark night of the soul" effectuates the painful transformation of passionate love into a love purified from desire and ecstatic infatuation. In the final section, I will then put forward an explanation of why this suffering plays a crucial role in deepening the soul's unification with God's love.

Part II: The transformation of mystic passion into an expression of God's love

1. The Triadic Structure of the Mystic Way

Mysticism has the structure of a path. The truth of the pilgrimage is not limited to its destination alone, for the journey itself is also a part of the truth, and this can only be discovered by making the journey. At the very beginning of the pilgrimage, the mystical soul does not know what it loves in God or about God. The soul is also incapable of explaining why God's attractive power is so much stronger than that of any other love-object. Certainly, the mystical soul responds to the Absolute by assenting to the desire that wells up spontaneously within it. However, it has no clear idea of the reality to which it assents. In spite of the images and ideas shaped by religious education, or stoked by a vivid imagination, the soul does not know what it is about God that attracts it. Instead, the soul attempts to evoke the virtual focus of its Eros with suggestive and expressive metaphors such as 'the hidden centre of all existence', 'the enduring source of life', the 'all-encompassing fulfilment', and so forth, but the soul itself does not understand the meaning of these tropes. And yet, from the outset, that which motivates the spiritually apt and educated soul is clear, viz., the pleasure found in prayer. The enjoyment that the soul finds in prayer inspires it to strive for greater perfection in this activity. To put it differently, instead of being drawn into prayer through a *contemptus mundi*, it is a particular pleasure connected with the activity of prayer as such that initially motivates the mystic soul. The better the soul is at praying, the more joy it finds in it. Pleasure, in this case, can be understood in the same way that Aristotle understands it, for what it gives expression to is the perfection of an activity.

Generally speaking, mystical love occurs in three phases. The first phase is known as the ascending movement of the soul and begins with the exercise of humble, meditative prayer. By achieving inner quietude, a transformation into the prayer of mystic union is brought about, the most spectacular manifestations of which are mystical rapture and ecstasy. In mystical ecstasy, the faculties of the soul are severed from the empirical world. This ascending movement is then followed by a second phase, namely the night of mystic suffering, which is characterized by a profound regression. As often happens in a melancholic depression, the mystic soul here loses all interest in what originally inspired it. It finds itself flooded by dark thoughts about its own sinfulness. Instead of transcending the empirical world and being filled by sublime visions of the divine, the soul collapses back in on itself and is persecuted by hallucinations of the devil. It loses all pleasure in praying. Whereas the ascending movement of the soul culminated in an ecstatic and euphoric self-forgetfulness in which it was filled with God's presence, in the mystic night, the soul is tortured by *acedia*, that is, by a hollow, barren apathy that gnaws away the soul and makes it profoundly restless. The soul has no option but to bear its suffering. To bear one's suffering is still an activity of the soul, of course, but it is an activity that is continually threatened by being swallowed up, or weighed down, by the apathetic inertia of *acedia*. Prayer no longer has the same meaning in the dark night as it did before; spiritual perfection too becomes an empty ideal. In the mystic night the soul's desires are emptied out as it loses interest in everything, even those things that once exalted it. Ultimately, the soul is painfully purified of every one of its desires. It no longer desires anything – not even God. Without the support of divine grace, the soul desperately struggles to survive this period of quasi-infinite suffering. Indeed, a significant number of mystics succumb to spiritual and physical exhaustion in the course of the dark night, while others find themselves 'purified' and are able, once again, to achieve higher forms of prayer. The higher forms of grace offered by God take root in the deep lassitude brought about by mystic suffering. Grace is what allows this indifference to develop into equanimity, which is a higher-order form of neutrality that, in contrast with the indifference of *acedia*, can be spiritually fertile. *Gelassenheit* prepares the soul for a deeper unification with God, a unification that no longer has anything in common with ecstatic trances.

2. From Meditation to Rapture

In conformity with the Christian art of prayer, as practised by the Carmelites, St. Teresa emphasizes that there is no better way to devote one's life to God and to divine contemplation than through humble, meditative prayer. In Christian mysticism, meditation is a rather disciplined form of prayer that requires the support of moral and spiritual education. It is grounded in the mind's captivation by the passion of Christ, and this alone must incite the soul to consider its sinfulness and to praise God for his infinite generosity. Devotional literature and spiritual guidance are required to ensure that one correctly understands the spiritual content of this meditation, such that it can become a fertile ground for what, in mystical literature, is called active purification, or moral perfection. This purification is said to be active in the sense that the mystical soul accomplishes it with the help of God's grace. Spiritual perfection is said to be passive, on the other hand, when it is brought about in spiteof one's efforts. We shall see precisely what is at stake in this distinction when we discuss the spiritual meaning of the mystic night. Meditation is only successful when the soul surrenders itself to it. As we have already seen, the subjective sign that the activity of prayer has reached some form of perfection is the enjoyment the soul derives from it. What the pleasure signals is the spontaneity of the activity of praying. The content of meditation, viz., the adoration of the Cross, explains why the soul can be touched, or excited, by this prayer. "Who is it," Teresa asks, "who sees the Lord covered with wounds and afflicted with persecutions, who will not embrace them, love them, desire them."[3] One of the spiritual fruits of this prayer is that it strengthens the believer's love for the suffering Christ, a love that expresses itself in the desire to become one with the Lord. In Christianity, to love God means to become one with him in the suffering of his son. There is thus no Christian mysticism that does not involve suffering.

The joy of meditation simplifies and eases the activity of prayer. From this point onwards, the soul's affectivity, or its capacity to be touched and moved, keeps it on track. More specifically, this affectivity keeps the soul in touch with the heartbeat of its libidinal Eros for the Absolute. The soul is able to float, no without some anxiety, upon waves of affect and joy because its emotions are disciplined according to the tenets of the Christian faith. Hence, the adoration of the cross, although it deeply moves the soul from within, never involves a pure and simple self-affection. "While the soul is seeking God in this way, it feels with the most marvellous and gentlest delight that everything is almost fading away through a kind of swoon in which breathing and all the bodily energies gradually fail".[4] This prayer is also called the prayer of confused contemplation, for the soul no longer requires the mental support of the imagination in order to be touched by God or to be moved by the desire to suffer as he did. Its contemplation is said to

[3] St. Teresa of Avila, *The Book of her Life* in *The Collected Works of* St. *Teresa of Avila*, Vol. I, trans. K. Kavanaugh and O. Rodriguez, Washington: ICS Publications, 1976, Chapter 26, §5, 173.

[4] St. Teresa of Avila, *The Book of her Life*, Chapter 18, §10, 120.

be confused simply because the soul has no clear idea, in its reflection on the Absolute, of the source of its joy. The joy found in affectively charged mystical prayer would thus be better described in terms of an ecstatic enthusiasm, which, of course, would be hardly compatible with the contemplative attitude, for the art of contemplation requires that one keeps one's distance from the world. Instead of evolving into contemplation, then, mystical meditation would seem to develop in the direction of infatuation.

> In loving, if it does love, it doesn't understand how or what it is it loves or what it would want. In sum, it is like one who in every respect had died to the world so as to live more completely in God. Thus, the death is a delightful one, an uprooting from the soul of all the operations it can have while being in the body. The death is a delightful one because in truth it seems that in order to dwell more perfectly in God the soul is so separated from the body that I don't even know if it has life enough to breathe.[5]

There is something quite remarkable in this kind of prayer. It is not simply a question of the soul's enthusiasm being so overwhelming that it completely absorbs the soul; what is so striking is how the benefits of this prayer do not directly or spontaneously flow back into the world. Instead, it is the soul's task, or moral duty, to make its prayers bear worldly fruit. It must therefore be morally disciplined in its adoration of the Absolute since ecstatic prayer neither strengthens its ties with the world nor incites it to search out God's presence in everyday life. Indeed, if one is not careful, one can find oneself cut off from the world by this kind of prayer. There are two reasons for this. Firstly, as mundane concerns are likely to hinder the soul's enjoyment of prayer, the believer is directly motivated to separate him/herself from them. Secondly, through this kind of prayer, the things and concerns of the world lose their importance relative to the believer's mystical infatuation, very much like when one falls in love. Eating, maintaining social contacts

[5] St. Teresa of Avila, *The Interior Castle* in *The Collected Works of St. Teresa of Avila*, Vol. II, trans. K. Kavanaugh and O. Rodriguez, Washington: ICS Publications, 1980, "The Fifth Dwelling Place," Chapter 1, §4, 336-337.

and other everyday sorts of activities are felt to distract one's attention from intense spiritual desire; the more mundane pleasures and activities of life thereby cease to have any appeal. For someone falling in love, the beloved comes to take on such a degree of all-consuming importance that the rest of the surrounding world seems to be emptied out and dried up, sapped of its very substance. In a similar way, the enjoyment found in ecstatic prayer is able to cut off one's ties with the outside world. To enjoy the Absolute means to become dead to the world. This explains why mystical love for the Absolute does not bear fruit in the world, for its enthusiasm is nothing like the peaceful enjoyment of God's hidden but all-embracing presence in the ordinary things of life. In this kind of prayer, God is only felt to exist in the mystical lover's desire, and never in the ordinary, day-to-day activities of the soul.This explains why we never find St. Teresa and St. John of the Cross speaking of *peacefully* enjoying the presence of their beloved. Instead, their testimonies bear witness to how the desire for an unreachable God replaces a steady, abiding love of God in the world. The passion of this love is therefore *wounded* more than ever by its desire for the unattainable. St. John of the Cross gives expression to this wounding in the following way:

> The wound effected by the cautery of love is incurable through medicine; for the very cautery that causes it, cures it, and by curing it, causes it. As often as the cautery of love touches the wound of love, it causes a deeper wound of love, and thus the more it wounds, the more it cures and heals.[6]

Elsewhere in *The Dark Night*, one can also read: "The spirit herein experiences an impassioned and intense love, because this spiritual inflaming engenders the passion of love."[7] Similarly, Richard of St. Victor speaks of the violence of love, Ruusbroec of love's rage, and Hadewijch of its fury. As in any passionate love, the mystic soul is so swallowed up by what it cannot attain that nothing is left over but an all-

[6] St. John of the Cross, *The Living Flame of Love* in *The Collected Works of St. John of the Cross*, trans. K. Kavanaugh and O. Rodriguez, Washington: ICS Publications, 1979, Stanza 2, 67, 597.

[7] St. John of the Cross, *The Dark Night* in *The Collected Works of St. John of the Cross*, Book 2, Chapter 11, §2, 353.

consuming desire for the beloved. This love can only quench its thirst by further intensifying its longing; the soul's enjoyment thus has nothing in common with peace, satisfaction or rest. Instead, it is a tortured and turbulent enjoyment, like that of a deep craving. If it is not tempered by moral discipline (i.e. active purification), desire for the Absolute is likely to drain the world of value and meaning, cutting the soul off from any appeal coming from the ordinary aspects of life. As the mystic soul is not concerned about its everyday health, its fellow brothers and sisters have to take over that function. The monastic life imposes its limits on a desire that has lost the inner sense of limits. The mystical soul is not even capable of rationally understanding its desire: just as the passionate lover can live neither with nor without its beloved, so the mystic's soul can live neither with nor without the Absolute.

> As for now the reasoning faculty is in such a condition that the soul is not the master of it, nor can the soul think of anything else than of why it is grieving, of how it is absent from its Good, and of why it should want to live. It feels a strange solitude because no creature in all the earth provides it company, nor do I believe would any heavenly creature, not being the One whom it loves; rather, everything torments it. But, the soul sees that it is like a person hanging, who cannot support himself on any earthly thing; nor can it ascend to heaven. On fire with this thirst, it cannot get to the water; and the thirst is not one that is endurable but already at such a point that nothing can take it away. Nor does the soul desire that the thirst be taken away save by the water of which our Lord spoke to the Samaritan woman. Yet no one gives such water to the soul.[8]

In mystical poetry, one can find many powerful metaphors describing this love as it teeters on the boundary between enjoyment and desolation, or between the living water of mystical ecstasy and the desert of the world. The lover wastes away in his or her restless, undying desire. If it is not disciplined by moral purification, by the rules of the cloister, or

[8] St. Teresa of Avila, *The Interior Castle*, "The Sixth Dwelling Place," Chapter 11, §5, 423-424.

by the ancient wisdom of spirituality, this love becomes void of content since things of the world can no longer sustain it. The more the soul is overwhelmed by its desire for the Absolute, the more it comes to see that it lives in abysmal emptiness. It is not difficult to anticipate the result of such a passion: the night of the mystic suffering is the price one pays for desiring the Absolute. The only things that are able to help one survive the nightmare of the mystic night are, as I mentioned, moral duties, spiritual wisdom, the ritualised movements of monastic life, and living together with caring brothers and sisters.

3. The Spiritual Meaning of the Mystical Night

It is not my concern to examine in detail the oppressive atmosphere of the mystic night of the soul. Instead, what I would like to understand is how mystics who manage to overcome their melancholic depression have attempted to explain the spiritual significance of the experience. Many mystics are somewhat spiritually *embarrassed* by the growing interest they take in their ecstatic prayers. They most often see the spectacular phenomena they experience in the uplifting movement of the soul as annoying by-products of their spirituality. St. John of the Cross is rather cynical, for example, about the mystic's belief that his or her ecstatic enthusiasm brings him or her in touch with God. All forms of intensive, affectively charged prayerare nothing more than the natural by-products of an overheated soul that reduce the Divine to subjective experiences. St. Teresa is milder in her judgment. According to her teaching, a spiritually educated soul need not eliminate or try to avoid such experiences of rapture; instead, it can accept these experiences as a gift of God's grace. In any event, one thing that mystics generally agree upon is that a true love of God can only be brought about by going through the mystic night, in which every desire for him is painfully extinguished. According to mystical teachings, *acedia* constitutes a trying but nevertheless very much necessary experience that the soul must undergo in order to become one with God. But, why is this so? Why is it impossible truly to unite with God without first going through this period of deep despair and loss?

The spiritual meaning of the mystic night must be understood in light of the paradoxes inherent to spiritual perfection. What spiritual perfection requires is more than an emptying of the soul of all its contents and ideas; beyond this, what it requires is that the soul must also be purified from all personal projects, hopes and desires. Secondary mystic literature often describes this self-mortification, or self-death, as the willingness to relinquish every expectation and representation one has of God, that is, everything by means of which the soul draws itself closer to God. These expectations and representations are too subjective for pure spirituality, springing up, as they do, from the weakness of human nature. The problem however is not that they are incorrect or false as representations, but that, ultimately, they only serve to fascinate and blind the mystic soul, thereby holding it back from true spiritual transformation. In order to receive these higher graces of spiritual perfection the soul must first be thoroughly emptied: it must give up *every* desire, *including* the desire for union with God.

This painful process of purification is clearly quite paradoxical, for it cannot be brought about by the soul alone. Why not? The giving up of every desire in order to attain higher spiritual perfection constitutes, itself, the aim of another desire. In other words, desire resurfaces at the very moment when the soul seeks most ardently to purify itself of desire. Admittedly, the giving up of every project is a rather unusual sort of life-goal; as strange at it seems, however, it is still a project of *some* sort, and as long as one has a project, one's life is structured by it. The content of the project might have changed, but the fact that one's life is still structured and oriented by it means that one is not yet capable of radical change and spiritual transformation. To *strive* to have no project is still to have a project. To give up every ideal is simply to pursue another ideal. The will, in short, cannot will itself away.

What is required for true spiritual purification is thus a *second-degree renunciation*, i.e., a renunciation that renounces the desire to renounce desire. The ideal of spiritual purification can therefore not be achieved by the soul alone, for in its very essence, the spiritual task is paradoxical and impossible in nature. What the soul is incapable of achieving on its own is nevertheless precisely what is (or can be) brought about *in* the soul during the mystic night. In the mystical night, spiritual purification happens *to* the soul, meaning that, instead of actively renouncing anything, the soul notices, with no small degree of suffering, how every interest and care that it once had cherished and clung to has since evaporated. The soul thus becomes one with its inner nothingness, we might say, such that even the project of making spiritual progress through suffering comes to lose its meaning. Unbeknownst to the soul, however, it is this emptiness that prepares it for a deeper unity with God.

St. Teresa gives an account of the moral and spiritual fruits of the soul's passive self-mortification. What radically changes here, in contrast with the stage of mystic adoration, is that now the soul's experience is marked by tranquillity. The soul is still capable of experiencing euphoric raptures, but these affects float in the utterly ethereal atmosphere of rest, peace and indifference: "And God has given me a kind of sleep in life, or it almost always seems to me that I am dreaming what I see. I am aware in myself of neither happiness nor pain, however great."[9] At the same time the soul is calmly aware that it is not acting autonomously. The soul knows that the life it lives is driven and sustained by something greater than itself, or by a larger reality. It knows that it does nothing on its own. "Here, in this dwelling place, these impulses are experienced most gently," Teresa writes, "but they do not proceed from the mind or the memory, nor do they come from anything that would make one think the soul did something on its own."[10]

The emptying of the soul of every desire is not the only transformation happening in the mystic night. The other one consists in the evaporation of the "ego". The ego is that part of the self that functions as a boomerang, i.e., as reality that always resurfaces time and again. The ego makes the subject interested in the meaning of its existence. "*Le moi est haïssable*", as Pascal puts it. The ego is always after love and recognition coming from the other; its highest goal is being loved, rewarded and being praiseworthy. This concern is not only deeply egocentric but is an inexhaustible source of personal trouble, unrest, hope and despair. In the mystic night the soul loses the interests of the ego. All her personal spiritual ideals vanish and disappear in a

[9] St. Teresa of Avila, *The Book of Her Life*, Chapter 40, §22, 284.

[10] St. Teresa of Avila, *The Interior Castle*, "The Seventh Dwelling Place," Chapter I, §8, 440.

spiritual indifference. The soul is relieved of the wish to be loved and to be praised. She is beyond hope and despair.

4. Becoming One with God's Agape

The soul's position with respect to God is thus radically turned around by means of the mystic night. Initially, it was directed towards God by means of an identification with Christ. God functioned as a *vis a fronte* for the soul's desire, that is, as the object of the soul's longing. In the night of mystic suffering, however, this desire is sublimated, such that God no longer appears as the aim of the soul's desire, but as a *vis a tergo* sustaining it and driving it on. In other words, he is no longer experienced as a hidden and sublime presence that attracts the soul, nor is he a reality to be reached, or sought out. Instead, he becomes in and for the soul what he really is, viz., love spontaneously expressing itself in everything, love generously flowing through the soul and permeating everything that the soul does and experiences. Even praying is no longer an isolated act carried out by the individual soul. Instead, like the slow and steady turning of a mill, the soul's prayer is put into motion by a gentle current of living water. The soul is thus no longer transcendent to its activities, but immersed in them in such a way that every action of the soul becomes the expression of something acting in it. In this way, a radical change in the soul's relation to God is brought about. As its desire to be loved by God and united with him fades into the background, so the soul becomes nothing more than a living expression of God's love. God's love flows through the soul, expressing itself and its mercy for everything that is.

This love reunites the soul with the world, transforming the relationship between world and soul into a *marriage.* The new relationship with God that this brings about is also understood in terms of a marriage relationship. What the use of this term suggests is that a love that was once consumed with desire is here transformed into the love of *amor amicitiae*. But, insisting too strongly on the marital aspect of this union between soul and God, or soul and world, can be some what misleading, for it risks drawing our attention away both from a deeper change going on in the soul, and from the rather uncommon way in which the soul is brought into communion with something beyond it. St. Teresa, for example, describes high prayer as an unshakeable joy, a joy brought about by being and living in God. This specific kind of joy bears a close relationship with the disappearance of the major causes of human sorrow, viz., the need to be loved, praised, protected, embraced and so on. The desire to be loved and cherished, whether by other people of by God, fills life, as I already argued, with uncertainty and anxious cares. What mystical love brings about, however, is a transformation by means of which the holds of self-oriented hope and despair are dissolved and place is made for a love that enjoys things just as they are, without any hope of reward. To be freed from the desire to be loved and to be capable of loving all creation without discrimination is the deepest expression of happiness. To reach such a state, however, one must be very lucky – without God's grace, such a transformation is impossible for the mystic soul. It is not that the uncertainties and doubts of knowing whether one's life is pleasing to God are simply replaced by an unshakeable and steadfast assurance. On the contrary, the desire for God's love is sublimated in such a way that there is no longer any cause for despair, hope, or certainty. There is no longer any fear of hell nor any hope in heaven; instead there is simply a deep happiness welling up spontaneously in the soul, a happiness giving expression to the soul's freedom from hope and despair.

What the term 'marriage' refers to in this case is to a union of God with the world, or more to the point, to the immanent presence of God in the world. Most often, we understand the term 'marriage' as referring to a unity in which the self and the other remain distinct. For Teresa, however, marriage refers to a state in which the soul becomes the pure expression of the other, i.e., God. The soul does not give expression to *itsown* personal love for God, the other, the world and so on, for the active self, along with desire, was already lost in the mystic night. Instead, the soul has been transformed into a love of God that expresses itself in and through the soul, such that, taking the expression '*amor Dei'*, we pass from the objective genitive to the subjective genitive. The soul is immersed in God's infinite and spontaneous love and, being in this love, it is purified of its desire to be loved. It dies to itself. The love of the world finding expression in the mystic's love is thus not the personal love of one individual soul, but rather the expression of God's love. The soul is nothing more than the medium of this love. If, then, we find Teresa continuing to use the term 'marriage' to describe her love, it should be clear that what she is referring to is a loving unity in which one term, in this case, the soul, becomes the pure expression of the other, viz., God's love. This new kind of love, which is brought about by becoming one with God's love, expresses itself as divine mercy. With this, however, we stumble upon yet another form of love, the analysis of which would take up beyond the aims of this paper.

6

Between Mysticism and Medical Materialism

The Relevance of William James and John Dewey for the Question of Neurotheology

Dr. Jonathan Weidenbaum
Berkeley College, New York, USA

1. Introduction: The Brain and the Void

At the end of *Island*, Aldous Huxley's answer to his earlier dystopian masterpiece *Brave New World*, a man swallows a pill and experiences enlightenment. Stumbling upon the tiny civilization by way of shipwreck, our hero, a cynical and dissatisfied journalist from the West, is introduced to a unique fusion of mysticism and communal experiment. This is *Pala*: a culture as devoted to self-knowledge and spiritual awakening as the bleak of world of *Brave New World* is to behavioral conditioning and chemically-induced complacency. While both societies employ drugs as part of a more general quest to re-shape human nature, the pill ingested by the protagonist of *Island* is the "*moksha*-medicine" - a pharmaceutical designed to stimulate the kind of ecstatic perceptions testified by contemplatives East and West. The pill is a concoction of the art called *neurotheology*, a discipline which, as we learn mid-way through the novel,"thinks about people in terms, simultaneously, of the Clear Light of the Void and the vegetative nervous system."[1] Here, is the marriage of Buddhism with brain-science.

[1] Aldous Huxley, *Island,* 112.

Huxley is repeatedly lauded for his prescience, and most often for the developments he disliked. It is for this reason that he probably would have found relief the growth of at least one thing he advocated—namely the use of empirical means to probe the origins of religious experience. Like the fictional country of Pala from where it was born, the field of neurotheology appears as a most curious juxtaposition of old and new: Red-robed *Vajrayana* monks meditate with wires glued to their scalp; Carmelite nuns sit peacefully in soundproof rooms; aspiring prophets wear a "God-helmet" and receive electrical stimulation through their temporal lobe.

Neurotheology, broadly conceived,is the art of exploring the correlations between religious/mystical experiences and the nervous system. The discipline contains two approaches which, though distinct in principle, are found side-by-side in almost every major work of neurotheology. First, there is the innocuous task of simply investigating what *happens* in our brain when we undergo meditative and rapturous states of consciousness. And second, there is theattempt to actually *identify* some part of the brain as the defining core and origin of mystical and religious experience.[2]

But, can religious and mystical experiences be understood as products of the nervous system? None of the major world religions consider the most exalted states of consciousness to be mere events within our brain chemistry. Zen Buddhists envision *satori* as the direct grasp of the *Sunyata*, the inherently empty and interconnected character of all things. Sufi dervishes and Hasidic Jews seek to become one with God. Even Huxley was occasionally reticent to identify spirituality with the brain. It should be remembered that the author of *Island* also wrote *The Perennial Philosophy*, one of the loveliest anthologies of the contemplative life.

Huxley was certainly not the first to stimulate the nervous system in order to explore the nature of religious experience. More than seventy years before the publication of *The Doors of Perception*, William James used nitrous oxide to replicate the experiences of the mystic (as well as to understand the philosophy of Hegel!). As a pioneer of both the biological understanding of the mind as well as the scientific study of spiritual

[2] Or, in the case of Newberg and Waldman, more than one God-part of the brain.

states of consciousness, it could be claimed that James paved the way for neurotheology long before Huxley coined the name of the discipline.Of course, it should be noted that James argued for the possibility of human immortality, the complete irreducibility of our spiritual life to bodily states, the importance of studying the psychical and the paranormal, and a finite and supernatural god who enters directly into the life of the individual. If James is to be included among the neurotheologians, he is a most unorthodox one, and stands in sharp contrast to those who would identify religious experience with the brain in *any* way.

In his little book on religion, John Dewey, William James's countryman and fellow pragmatist, states: "He is bold to the point of rashness who asserts that intimate personal experience will never come within the ken of natural knowledge."[3] Espousing a thorough, if non-reductionist, naturalism, Dewey may seem aligned with the more hard-headed tendencies in neurotheism. But, "natural knowledge" for Dewey means doing justice to the full-blooded texture of our experiential life; and here is where much neurotheology falls short for a Dewean perspective, as we will discover below.

The pages which follow examine the relevance of William James and John Deweyfor the current vogue of neurotheology. The importance of the two classical American philosophers is found primarily in their overturning of conventional assumptions about the relationship of the brain, mind, and external world—assumptions still prevalent among many neurotheologians. The upshot is that a human being is not a vegetative nervous system on the one hand and the Clear Light of the Void on the other. There are other elements involved in the constitution of spiritual meaning—the overlooking of whichserves as the greatest hindrance to a proper account of the origin and structure of a religious experience.

It should be noted that it is not my goal to exhaust the contributions of James and Dewey for an understanding of either religion or the religious experience (for which whole books have been written), but only to discuss their immediate relevance for the field of neurotheology. Nor do I seek to offer a sweeping criticism of neuroscience, since many

[3] John Dewey, *A Common Faith*, 35.

contemporary neuroscientists—particularly the non-reductionist sort—would likely endorse this critique.

In *Art as Experience*, Dewey asserts that "there is no test that so surely reveals the one-sidedness of a philosophy as its treatment of art and esthetic experience." If *art* and *esthetic* are here replaced with *religion* and *religiousness,* therein, in the resulting statement, would be found the larger purpose of this study. Mining and unpacking the still-overlooked contributions of William James and John Dewey on this topic is a first step in the right direction.

2. Meaning and Experience

Perusing through some of the key works in neurotheology, one finds a remarkably similar account of the manner in which experience constructed. In *The "God" Part of the Brain*, Matthew Alper provides a description of what occurs when we perceive an apple:

> First, photons of light which are reflected off an apple are picked up by our retinas, which convert that information into electrical signals that are then processed by our brain. Consequently, all that we perceive as "real" is nothing more than electrical signals as they are interpreted by our organ, the brain. When we eat an apple, we "feel" its texture; we "smell" its aroma; we "taste" its flavor. Not until we integrate all of these various sense-impressions is our experience transformed into a coherent perception of the apple as a whole. Without such an internal processor through which to coordinate this medley of sense-impressions we constantly receive, it would be impossible for us to make sense of our experiences.[4]

This model of experience leads to questions which have dogged philosophy since the Ancient Greeks. They include the following: How can we *know* that the world fabricated by our brain matches up to that of the "real" or external world? What, for instance, is the status of *causality*, the operations of cause-and-effect we perceive in nature and which serve as the basis of the sciences? Are they simply based upon

[4] Mathew Alper, *The "God" Part of the Brain*, 17.

our previous experiences, mere habits of association (the theory of the classical empiricists)? If so, how can we be assured these same laws will continue in the future? Perhaps they are the built-in structures of our mind (the position of the rationalists).

It is relevant to note that traditional rationalists and empiricists (usually understood as antagonists) share a similar premise both with themselves and with our neurotheologians. It is this: Meaning is not found directly within experience at all. Rather some external source—habits formed by our prior experience, transcendental structures of the mind, or (and more currently) neural processes found within the brain—slaps meaning onto our experiences, and thereby structures them into coherent and consistent wholes. Neurotheologians offer a similar account of spiritual and religious experience. If the brain and nervous system constitutes reality, then to alter the nervous system is to alter reality, plain and simple."The medieval German mystic Meister Eckhart lived hundreds of years before the science of neurology was born," explains Newberg, D'Aquili, and Rause, "yet it seems he had intuitively grasped one of the fundamental principles of the discipline: What we think of as reality is only a rendition of reality that is created by the brain."[5] A fourteenth century monk is hereby converted into the forerunner of a subject-centered idealism combined with modern biology.

It is anachronistic and dishonest, however, to graft a post-Cartesian worldviewonto the claims of individuals and movements from another era, whether Asian or Occidental. It also results in a terribly shallow depiction of the kinds of experiencesthat the great mystics of the worldwere trying to promote. Consider the Japanese tea ceremony. The whisking of the bowl, the smoke rising gently out of the earthenware pottery, the positions in which the participants are seated, the near-choreographed motions through which the host slowly passes the tea to his or her guests: All of these elements, taken together, are understood and felt as *immediate* expressions of the Buddha-nature. To suggest that they are ancient techniques designed to tweak specific portions of the nervous system, and thereby induce a spiritual consciousness, is to split the meaning from the medium. The result is a ceremony that becomes impossible to understand. Why, for instance, *this* particular

[5] A. Newberg, E. D'Aquili, and V. Rause, *Why God Won't Go Away*, 35.

movement, *this* style of cup, *this* décor for the tea-house, *this* batch of flowers on the wall? Try answering these questions strictly through the language of neural and physiological processes—which taken alone, and without regard to any larger context,can only be blind and indifferent to these details. Anyone with a capacity for true religious and aesthetic perception sees that in regards to the tea ceremony, the experience in questionalready arrives replete with meaning; the latter is not added from the outside.

Both the age-old problems of epistemology and the artificial accounts of experience are products of the Cartesian legacy in our understanding of perception. Here, a first-person and *phenomenological* report ("I see a red chair") is combined with a purely *physical* description of the experienced environment ("waves of light make their way onto the retina of the eyes"). Now, while physical processes underpin and serve as conditions for our perceptions of the world, they are not the stuff of our experience. Certainly, patterns of light can be found on the retina of my eye. However, I neither see, nor ordinarily care about, the retina of my eye. I do not first receive visual representations which I *then* have to construct into objects. Rather I see a plush chair, a lovely and comfortable looking piece of furniture that I would like to sit on. The chair in fact, seems to call for my tired body, since I've been on my feet all day long. According to a discipline known as "ecological psychology," the chair *affords* me rest, and this is a quality I see directly in the chair.For ecological psychologists, our behavior is *entirely* indecipherable if our surroundings are understood solely in the language of physics, chemistry, and neuroscience. My true environment is the one I take notice of and interact with, and it is composed of things relevant to my purposes and interests. To mix layers of explanation, the felt experience on the one hand and the underlying material substratum on the other, is to invite confusion, something all-to-common in modern accounts of experience and cognition.

The act of reading the physiological conditions for perception into our actual experience of the world is a chief example of what James dubs as "the psychologist's fallacy." "The *great* snare of the psychologist," he explains in *The Principles of Psychology*, is the *confusion of his ownstandpoint with that of the mental fact* about which he is making his report."[6] It is therefore no surprise that in *Ecological Psychology in Context*, Harry Heft deftly traces the work of James J. Gibson, the founder of ecological psychology, to the later work of William James.

James's "radical empiricism," ancestor of both phenomenology and ecological psychology, is first and foremost a kind of program. Throwing aside all of our prejudices and assumptions concerning experience, we are attend to it rather closely, rejecting nothing we see in it and placing nothing inside it we don't. The result is James's novel concept of "pure experience," the idea that experience is the sole (if complex and heterogeneous) reality from which subject and object, mind and world are but expressions. Consciousness is not something or substance which exists in its own right, but is a mere function within experience. The sensory atomism of the British Empiricists, the splicing of our perception into discrete bits requiring some kind of glue to connect them, is entirely rejected. In fact, the connections and relations between things are found directly within the texture of experience. Finally, in experience as we actually live it—or more accurately, as we and the "external" world are lived out of *it*—there is no division between value and fact, "ought" and "is."

In his surmounting of all dualisms and his depiction of experience as a meaningful totality, James was a tremendous influence on John Dewey. From his early essay "The Reflex Arc Concept in Psychology" to his later books, Dewey would detail a notion of experience as the mutually constitutive relationship between sentient beings and the surroundings through which they exist. "Life denotes a function, a comprehensive activity," he explains in *Experience and Nature*, "in which organism and environment are included. Only upon reflective analysis does it break up into external conditions—air breathed, food taken, ground walked upon—and internal structures—lung respiring, stomach ingesting, legswalking."[7]As with Gibson and the ecological psychologists, Dewey does not so much ignore the physiological processes involved in our acts of cognition and perception as make them subservient to the continual adjustment between a living agent and an external world.

[6] William James, *The Principles of Psychology*, Vol.I, 196. Italics are in the original.

[7] William James, *The Principles of Psychology*, Vol I, 9.

Dewey holds that the *felt* character of experience needs to be apprehended on its own terms. Throughout many of his writings, the consequence is nothing less than what James called "a thick universe;" one in which time and space are innately significant and not empty Cartesian coordinates, qualities belong as much to things as to the "inner" life of human beings, and experience is of actual objects and not mental *representations* of objects. For both James and Dewey, meaning is not an addition to experience from elsewhere. Situated against the context of their ideas, the calm gestures of the participants in a tea ceremony can be understood as *inherently* meaningful.

3. James, Mysticism and Medical Materialism

While a number of James's writings have pertinence for the relationship between mystical experiences and the brain, it is the chapter on "Religion and Neurology" from *The Varieties of Religious Experience* in which he comes closest to tackling a doctrine resembling the more reductionistic of today's neurotheology. Labeled by James as *medical materialism,* this is the view that religious experiences are dismissible as mere products of our body and nervous system. James's rebuttal goes as follows: Unless it can be demonstrated beforehand that *only* religious experiences are so reducible, and not scientific and skeptical modes of perception as well, then the position of medical materialism is arbitrary—the result of prejudice rather than impartial observation. On the other hand, if *all* kinds of consciousness are deemed as the consequence of bodily states, and therefore without *some* connection to extra-psychical facts, then the conclusions of the medical materialists must be equally suspect. James concludes that we have little choice but to evaluate religious and mystical intuitions with the same criteria as with any other experience: "immediate luminousness," "philosophical reasonableness," and "moral helpfulness."[8]

Of course, it is always possible that an experience is a product of the nervous system and yet also related to facts beyond the confines of the skull. In holding this position, many neurotheologians would not only fail to recognize themselves in medical materialism, but would even be relieved to see that I am employing the arguments of James to

[8] See, William James, *The Varieties of Religious Experience*, 29-32.

fight a straw man. Newberg, D'Auili, and Rause argue for the possible veridicality of mystical experience, and even provide an argument against dismissing religious states of mind roughly similar to James.[9] Nevertheless, the same authors go on to claim that the only place God "can manifest his existence would be in the tangled neural pathways and physiological structures of the brain."[10] And here, even the most open-minded of neurotheologians impale themselves on yet another dilemma. It is this: The extent to which our cognitive states involve a reality beyond the confines of the nervous system, the less defining brain activities are for such experiences; and the larger the role of the nervous system is in creating the meaning and "flavor" of our experiences, the more we collapse into all of the epistemological problems pointed out in the previous section. In arguing that our perceptions of the world provide us "second hand neurological perceptions" only, images to be assembled by the brain, Newberg, D'Aquili and Rause affirm that even *science* is a kind of mythology.[11] If so, why trust the careful findings of the neurotheologian over the ranting of the fundamentalist? The latter would spare us the cost of EEG machines.

In basing religious experiences within the brain, neurotheologians fall into the same subject/object dualism which has befuddled philosophers for centuries. This is a particular irony for those who equate genuine religious experience with the dissolving of all such dualisms, including that between the inner self and the Absolute as championed by the authors of *Why God Won't Go Away*.[12] Once again, neurotheology violates the very experiences they seek to explain.The *Upanishads* speaks of the identification of the soul with the Ultimate Reality—atman with *Brahman*—and not the mere *feeling* or replica of such a relationship.

---

[9] In chapter eight of *Why God Won't Go Away*, the authors state: "If you were to dismiss spiritual experiences as "mere" neurological activities, you would also have to distrust all of your brain's perceptions of the material world. On the other hand, if we do trust our perceptions of the physical world, we have no rational reason to declare that spiritual experience is a fiction that is 'only' in the mind."

[10] A. Newberg, E. D'Aquili, and V. Rause, *Why God Won't Go Away*, 53.

[11] See chapter nine of *Why God Won't Go Away*.

[12] A. Newberg, E. D'Aquili, and V. Rause *Why God Won't Go Away*, 101.

In his essay on human immortality, James agrees that thought is a function of the brain. But, James here opposes a *transmissive* to a *productive* function, and offers the possibility that the cerebral cortex serves as a conduit through which a wider consciousness is narrowed into our practical, day-to-day awareness.[13] This is similar to Huxley's perspective in both *The Doors of Perception* and *Island.* Dr. Robert MacPhail, grandson of Pala's founder (and one of Huxley's many philosophical voices in the novel), explains that "the *moksha*-medicine does something to the silent areas of the brain which opens some kind of neurological sluice and so allows a larger volume of Mind with a large 'M' to flow into your mind with a small 'm.'"[14] Like a light shining through stained glass (James's analogy), there is no difference in principle between the divine ground of consciousness and ourselves, one is in fact a segment of the other. For neurotheologians, the brain remains the seat of mystical experience, even if the sacred exists. For James (and Huxley), religious ecstasy is quite literally the return of our essential being to its source like a spark into a bonfire; the flight, as described by Plotinus, of the "solitary to the solitary."[15]

4. Dewey, Religion and Reification

In recounting a true story of James and Dewey sitting at a Ouija board in 1905, Richard Gale imagines "a big smirk" on Dewey's face, while "the sweat of earnest conviction was pouring off James's."[16] Dewey is a thorough naturalist for whom the objects of religious and aesthetic veneration do not descend from the heavens, but are woven out of the fabric of our concrete experience. *A Common Faith* and *Art as Experience*, both published in the same year, discuss the manner in which our heightened perceptions of the world are projected outward into separately existing things, the material of the fine arts and the supernatural respectively.

"There is no reason for denying the existence of experiences that are called mystical," affirms Dewey in *A Common Faith*, for "there is

[13] William James, *Human Immortality: Two Supposed Objections to the Doctrine.*

[14] Aldous Huxley, *Island*, 168. Also see *The Doors of Perception*, 21.

[15] This is the last line of the *Enneads.*

[16] From his appendix to *The Divided Self of William James.*

every reason to suppose that, in some degree of intensity, they occur so frequently that they may be regarded as normal manifestations that take place at certain rhythmic points in the movement of experience."[17] The idea of experience possessing rhythmic points is central to Dewey's phenomenology, since mind is the result of an embodied and environmentally embedded organism; a "live creature" alternatively falling out of, and then back into, harmony with its external surroundings.[18] It is precisely this dynamic character of experience which informs the nature of meaning: "We envisage with pleasure Nirvana and a uniform heavenly bliss only because they are projected upon the background of our present world of stress and conflict."[19]

Mystical states of consciousness, as with aesthetic ones, are ecstatic partly because they are an intensification of the rich contrasts already found within any truly fulfilling experience—what Dewey calls "having *an* experience."[20] Consider the very language of religious and spiritual intuition: There is a movement from *darkness* to *light*, from being *lost* to being *found*, from *confinement* to *liberation*. Now, neurons, taken in isolation, can know nothing of these contrasts. Self-transcendence is not significant by itself, but only as a release from the labors and exigencies of our day-to-day existence.[21] What *possible* relevance can confinement followed by a sudden freedom have for a nervous system floating in a vacuum? It is the entire, purposeful organism which feels suffocated and pines for liberty. Aesthetic and religious meaning is possible only for a nervous system *in* a body, and "not as marbles in a box but as events are in history, in a moving, growing never finished process."[22] Thus, neurotheology can never, in principle, elucidate the character of religious experience. At best, it can examine one of its underlying conditions.

It is worthwhile to examine this argument against neurotheology from another angle. According to the great bulk of neurotheologians,

---

[17] John Dewey, *A Common Faith*, 37.

[18] The notion of a "live creature" is borrowed from *Art as Experience.*

[19] John Dewey, *Art as Experience,* 15.

[20] See his famous third chapter from *Art as Experience.*

[21] John Dewey, *Art as Experience*, 21.

[22] John Dewey, *Experience and Nature*, 295.

spiritual experience is a product of the brain. Now, either the brain is the seat of meaning or it is not. If the brain is the origin of all significance, and operates upon purely neutral and meaningless sense experiences, then we are left with the question of how the movement from, say, defilement to purity is felt as meaningful. How can the brain, by itself, know the significance of such a contrast? If the answer is "from the senses," then the nervous system is not the seat of all meaning after all, since what the senses present us is already loaded with significance. In that case, neurotheologians are preoccupying themselves with only a small (if necessary) part of the story.

Some neurotheologians contend that evolution has implanted such meanings already within the brain.[23] In this case, the various artistic expressions and rituals found among the world's religions, from the whirling of a Sufi dervish to the Stations of the Cross adorning the wall of a cathedral, are constructed to "turn on" these inner capacities of our nervous system like an operator on a switchboard. But, this permits, as I have pointed out earlier, a most artificial understanding of the means by which these forms of art influence the experiences of a believer. The landscape painters of Asia do not intend to alter something inside of our brain. Rather, the *tathata* or "suchness" of things is already present in the lines and contours of the painting, and the artist simply wants us to open our eyes and *see*.

One of Dewey's core arguments in *A Common Faith* is that the heightened aspects of our experience are regularly interpreted as independent realities; they are hypostatized "into a supernatural realm for safe-keeping and sanction."[24] There are many consequences of this act of reification. Experiences available for all human beings are not only placed in the possession of aclerical and societal elite, they are used to divert energy away from solving social and political problems and toward the worship of imaginary entities and beings. "Men have never fully used the powers they possess to advance the good in life," Dewey explains, "because they have waited upon some power external to themselves and to nature to do the work they are responsible for

[23] Matthew Alper and Michael Persinger offer this kind of explanation. See *The God Gene* and the *Neuropsychological Bases of God Beliefs* respectively.

[24] John Dewey, *A Common Faith*, 73.

doing."[25] Although Dewey does find a place for the word "God" in *A Common Faith,* it is used by him to labelthe continualuniting of our imaginedideals withconcrete actuality, possibility withfact. We are thus reminded that human agency does not occur in a vacuum, and that even our loftiest efforts for the good involve a taking up of what our situation provides.[26]

Many neurotheologians share a similar goal with Dewey. In *The Mystical Brain*, Michael Persinger asks us to envision the possibility of making mystical perceptions available without the dogmas of organized religion. Some argue that neurotheology will finally democratize spirituality by taking the religious experience out of the jurisdiction of theologians and church doctors, secret rites and esoteric texts. The problem is that neurotheologians are an elite themselves, with not only an intimate knowledge of the neural pathways of the cerebral cortex which most of us don't have, but with expensive and state-of-the-art machinery that no average person can afford. Of course, *Moksha*-medicines and God-helmets can become widely available in the same way as cars and dishwashers. But, once again a new clerical elite comes into being, for manufacturers will not only be needed to continually create such technologies, but to either sell them for profit or disseminate them in thc manner of a priest handing out wine and wafers at a Catholic mass. One need not strain to imagine an unscrupulous demagogue or future technocracy exploiting such *Moksha*-medicines, for Huxley has conveniently done it for us in *Brave New World.*

5. Conclusion: Neurotheology as Theology

Perhaps the process of reification, as pointed out by Dewey, can actually illuminate a few things about the unstated goals of neurotheology. It is conceivable that neurotheologians engage in their own form of hypostatization, and seek a "god-gene" or god part of the brain for a variety of personal reasons. Those neurotheologians sympathetic to religious belief and practice are thus able to fix a distinguishable form for their spiritual needs and even locate verifiable evidence for their faith; while those against religion can identify the great devil sitting behind

[25] John Dewey, *A Common Faith*, 46.

[26] John Dewey, *A Common Faith*, 51-4.

the collective misery of humankind. In both cases, there is a kind of transcendentalism at work in the project of neurotheology, a condensing and shelving of the most intense elements of our experiences into a place beyond the reach of our everyday life. In this way, neurotheology is theology (or demonology) after all.

References

1. Alper, Matthew, The *"God" Part of the Brain: A Scientific Interpretation of Human Spirituality and God,* Naperville: Sourcebooks, Inc, 2006.
2. Dewey, John, *Art as Experience*, New York: Penguin Books, 1934.
3. Dewey, John, *A Common Faith*, New Haven: Yale University Press, 1934.
4. Dewey, John, *Experience and Nature,* New York City: Dover Publications, Inc, 1958.
5. Dewey, John, "The Reflex Arc Concept in Psychology," in *Pragmatism; The Classic Writings*, ed. H. Standish Thayer, New York: Mentor Books, 1970.
6. Gale, Richard M., *The Divided Self of William James,* Cambridge: Cambridge University Press, 1999.
7. Heft, Harry, Ecological *Psychology in Context: James Gibson, Roger Barker, and the Legacy of William James's Radical Empiricism,* Mahwah: Lawrence Erlbaum Associates, Inc, 2001.
8. Huxley, Aldous, The *Doors of Perception*, in *The Doors of Perception and Heaven and Hell.* New York: Penguin Books, 1968.
9. Huxley, Aldous, Island, New York: Harper Perennial Modern Classics, 2009.
10. James, William, Essays *in Radical Empiricism*, Lincoln: University of Nebraska Press, 1996.
11. James, William, *Human Immortality: Two Supposed Objections to the Doctrine*, New York: Dover Publications, Inc, 1956.
12. James, William,The *Principles of Psychology, Volume One*, New York: Dover Publications, Inc, 1950.
13. James, William, *The Varieties of Religious Experience*, New York: Mentor Books, 1958.
14. Newberg, Andrew and Waldman, Mark Robert, How *God Changes Your Brain: Breakthrough Findings from a Leading Neuroscientist*, New York: Ballantine Books, 2009.
15. Newberg, Andrew, D'Auili, Eugene, Rause, Vince, *Why God Won't Go Away; Brain Science and the Biology of* Belief, New York: Ballantine Books, 2001.
16. Persinger, Michael A., *Neuropsychological Bases of God Beliefs*, New York: Praeger, 1987.
17. Plotinus, The Enneads, trans. Stephen Mackenna,New York: Penguin Books, 1991.
18. Raynauld, Isabelle (dir.), Mystical *Brain*; Scientists meet spirituality head-on (DVD). Alive Mind, 2010.

7

Sobering Up To the Other

Levinas' Paradoxical View on Mystical Enthusiasm

Dr. Roger Burggraeve
Faculty of Theology
Katholieke Universiteit Leuven, Leuven, Belgium

Introduction

The philosophical thought of Levinas can be described as a thinking 'unto-God', for which the face of the other, with its ethical appeal to responsibility, is held as the 'trace'. In this thought we discover a double, apparently contradictory approach to mystical enthusiasm. What is most known is his very critical stance towards mysticism, as it is found especially in the period of his first major work, *Totality and Infinity* (1961). In a first movement we will describe the source and dynamics of this critique. What is less known is his positive attitude towards mysticism, which we encounter especially in the period of his second major work *Otherwise than Being* (1974). In a second movement we will then make more explicit the very unique modality of this positive approach so that it can be made clear how both approaches do not annul but on the contrary need each other. In a third movement we shall explore particularly the possibilities implied by Levinas' positive approach to mysticism for a Christian view, without neglecting his critical evaluation of a fusional mystical enthusiasm.[1]

---

[1] The cited studies of Levinas are listed below in alphabetical order. Citations in our text are indicated with an abbreviation of the original French edition, along with the cited page(s). The cited page(s) from the available English translation is indicated

1. Radical critique on mystical enthusiasm

In the period of his first major work, *Totality and Infinity* (1961) and of the compilation of his essays on Judaism of 1963, "Difficult Freedom", Levinas is quite disapproving of 'mystical enthusiasm'. Alongside an outspoken mistrust towards a cosmic religiosity, which starts from nature towards the divine (as if nature were only the transparency of the 'amazing' or 'wonderful' and were not, at the same time, marked

---

after the forward slash (/). Abbreviations used: **AE**: *Autrement qu'être ou au-delà de l'essence*, La Haye : Nijhoff, 1974. [English translation (ET): *Otherwise than Being or Beyond Essence*, translated by A. Lingis, The Hague/Boston/London: Nijhoff (Kluwer), 1981.]; **AV**: *L'au-delà du verset. Lectures et discours talmudiques*, Paris : Minuit, 1982. [ET: *Beyond the Verse. Talmudic Readings and Lectures*, trans. G.D. Mole, Bloomington & Indianapolis: Indiana University Press, 1994.]; **CPP**: *Collected Philosophical Papers*, trans.A. Lingis, Dordrecht/Boston/Lancaster: Kluwer/Nijhoff, 1987; **DL**: *Difficile Liberté. Essais sur le Judaïsme*, Paris : Albin Michel, 1963 (1st ed.), 1976 (2nd ed.). [ET: *Difficult Freedom. Essays on Judaism*, trans. S. Hand. Baltimore : The John Hopkins University Press, 1990.]; **DVI**: *De Dieu qui vient à l'idée*, Paris : Vrin, 1982. [ET: *Of God Who Comes to* Mind, trans. B. Bergo, Stanford: University Press, 1998.]; **EE**: *De l'existence à l'existant*, Paris:Vrin, 1978 (2nd ed.). [ET: *Existence and Existents*, trans. A. Lingis, The Hague: Nijhoff, 1978.]; **EFP**: "Entretiens", in F. Poirié, *Emmanuel Lévinas. Qui êtes-vous?*, Lyon: La Manufacture, 1987, 62-136. [ET: "Interview with François Poirié," in **IRB**, 23-83.]; **EN**: *Entre nous. Essais sur le penser-à-l'autre*, Paris : Grasset 1991. [ET: *Entre nous. Thinking-of-the-Other*, trans. M.B. Smith and B. Harshav, London/New York: Continuum, 2006]; **HAH**: *Humanisme de l'autre homme*, Montpellier: Fata Morgana, 1972. [ET: *Humanism of the Other*, trans. N. Poller,Urbana & Chicago: University of Illinois Press, 2003.]; **HN**: *A l'heuire des nations*, Paris: Minuit, 1988. [ET: *In the Time of the Nations*, trans. M.B. Smith, Bloomington & Indianapolis: Indiana University Press, 1994]; **IRB**: *Is It Righteous to Be. Interviews with Emmanuel Levinas*, ed. J. Robbins and trans.J. Robbins, M. Coelen, with T. Loebel, Stanford (CA): Stanford University Press, 2001; **NP**: *Noms Propres*, Montpellier: Fata Morgana, 1976. [ET: *Proper Names*, trans. M.B. Smith, Stanford: University Press, 1996.]; **PI**: "La philosophie et l'idée de l'Infini," in *En découvrant l'existence avec Husserl et Heidegger*, Paris: Vrin, 1967, 165-178. [ET: "Philosophy and the Idea of Infinity» in **CPP**, 47-59]; **SaS**: *Dusacré au saint. Cinq nouvelles lectures talmudiques*, Paris: Minuit, 1977. [ET: in **NTR**, 89-197, entitled "From the Sacred to the Holy. Five New Talmudic Readings".]; **TI**: *Totalité et Infini. Essai sur l'extériorité*, La Haye: Nijhoff, 1961. [ET: *Totality and Infinity An Essay on Exteriority*, trans. A. Lingis, The Hague/Boston/London : Nijhoff, 1979.]; **TrID**: *Transcendance et intelligibilité* (suivi d'un entretien), Genève: Labor et Fides, 1984, 33-68 (Entretien avec Emmanuel Levinas: 2 juin 1983, à Genève). [ET: "Discussion Following 'Transcendence and Intelligibility' (1984)," in **IRB** 268-286.

by ruthlessness), he also criticises sharply the so-called 'religious enthusiasm' and a certain mysticism of emotional interiority that is coupled with it.

1.1. Mithnagdic background

This unambiguous critical approach – leading up from his Jewish background to a 'strict and demanding' form of an ethically oriented religiosity in and through the 'doing' (of the Torah) – can be better understood if it is linked with his particular Jewish Lithuanian background, namely the 'Mithnagdic' spirituality of the strict application to the Scripture and Talmud and to the writings of the great masters of the tradition. This spirituality stands in stark contrast to the 'Hassidic' spirituality, of which the *Tales of the Hasidim* (*Chassidische Erzählungen*, 1965) of Martin Buber are an eminent expression. Hasidism came into existence midway through the eighteenth century as a sort of devotional Judaism among the frequently illiterate rural Jews of the Ukrainian provinces of what were then Poland-Volhynia, Podolia, and Galicia. The main proponent was Israel Ben Eliëzer (1700-1760), also known as Baal Shem Tov, meaning 'friendly Master of the Name (of God),' and 'possessor of the good name,' or 'entrusted with the people.' He taught that true religion consisted in a sincere and joyous love of God. The core of this living religiosity is 'enthusiasm' ('*hitlahavut*') that expresses itself concretely in a heartfelt experience of and participation in God's omnipresence, both in fervent prayer and in daily life, with all its tasks and duties.

Hasidism met with heavy resistance, especially among the Jews of Lithuania, the homeland of Levinas. In some cities of Lithuania and in Vilnius in particular, the Jewish communities developed not only their religious and social life, but also their multi-faceted intellectual life. Lithuania was the land where Judaism reached its spiritual peak (EFP 64/24). This intellectual Judaism was rooted in the hard discipline of studying the Talmud in the 'Yeshiva' or 'academy of higher study of the Talmud', where the Talmud was no longer studied privately but in a group and under the direction of a learned teacher or 'master' (*Rabbi*). Resistance against Hasidism was initiated by Elijah Ben Solomon

(1720-1797), also called the Gaon of Vilna,[2] and carried on further by his disciple Rabbi Hayyim Volozhiner (1749-1821)[3] and the so-called *Mithnagdim*, literally 'opponents'.[4] They played a key role in the resistance against the popular movement of Hasidism, "demanding more fervour than knowledge", denying Talmudic study its primary place in Jewish religious life (AV182-183/151). With a certain fierceness, the Lithuanian Mithnagdim precisely went against the excessive preference for enthusiasm, because they were convinced that "by grouping the communities around spiritual personalities with charismatic power the *Tsadikim* or the 'miraculous Rabbis', who did not refuse the adoration of the faithful, changed the true relations between disciple and master, and undermined the fundamental principles of Jewish monotheism" (AV 182-183/150-151). Fighting the excesses of the Hasidic movement, they attempted to safeguard and develop the essential importance of a persistent and thorough study of the holy Texts and commentaries as the primary Jewish form of religiosity.[5]

1.2. Religious enthusiasm called into question

Levinas was clearly influenced by Mithnagdic Judaism and its suspicion against religious enthusiasm.[6] Levinas understands enthusiasm as the

---

[2] Cfr. J.-F. Malthète, "Gaon de Vilna, 1720-1798," *in*: Y. Plasseraud, H. Minczeles (eds.), *Lithuanie juive 1918-1940. Message d'un monde englouti*, Paris: Éditions Autrement (Collection Mémoires n° 44), 1996, 193-206.

[3] In his Jewish writings, Levinas points several times to Rabbi Hayyim Volozhiner, the favorite student of the Gaon of Vilna. He even dedicates a detailed and penetrating study to him, which at the same time also throws considerable light on his own thinking: "'In the Image of God', according to Rabbi Hayyim Volozhiner" (1977) (**AV** 182-200/151-167). In a much later study, "Judaism and Kenosis" (1985), he explicitly retraces his thinking (**HN** 138-151/114-132).

[4] Cf. A. Nadler, *The Faith of the Mithnagdim. Rabbinic Responses to Hasidic Rapture*, Baltimore & London: The Johns Hopkins University Press, 1997.

[5] The numerous Talmudic readings and lectures of Levinas appear as a very unique incarnation of all that phenomena, and they have appealed to many generations of 'enlightened' young Jews and has maintained its ties with Judaism: "Four Talmudic Readings", 1968; "From the Sacred to the Holy", 1977; "Beyond the Verse", 1982; "In the Time of the Nations", 1988; "New Talmudic Readings", 1996.

[6] His first collection of essays on Judaism, *Difficult Freedom*, appearing first in 1963 and then again, reworked and expanded, in 1976, is a pregnant illustration of the basic Mithnagdic rationality from which Levinas interprets Judaism and calls for

possibility of achieving a lived-through interwovenness with God or the divine. The Greek word 'entheos', the root of 'enthusiasm', literally means: 'having a god in oneself, to be possessed and taken up by a god'. This easily leads to a 'pan-en-theistic' religiosity wherein the divine and the human thus become one that they are fused: all in God and God in all. Whatever the many forms of appearances may be, Levinas interprets 'enthusiasm' as an implanting and immersion into the godhead, just as a butterfly is sucked up in the fire: the fusion of the human with the divine. Out of a kind of 'spiritual' hunger for religious depth-experience, one strives for the self-surpassing of one's own 'I' up to the divine other, for a direct and pure union with the divine, for an intimate, comforting, sweet and encompassing nearness to, or rather *in* the divine presence. This 'sublimation' *in*to the godhead takes place in and through ecstasy, rapture, 'top experience', where the boundaries and separations become 'annulled' as a consequence (DL 29/14).

The path *par excellence* in order to reach this religious participation can be found in the *feeling*, as the common meaning of the term enthusiasm immediately suggests indeed. Levinas describes religious enthusiasm then as an "invasion of God across an inward emotion" (TI 186/211). Via the emotion of enthusiasm one searches for a lived-through experience of intense interiority and 'spirit', with the intention to take part directly in the 'intimate' divine presence in itself, or rather in the feeling that experiences and within which one feels oneself alive. One does not choose for the external detour of care for the world or for the other; or for the detour of the study of the 'exterior' text (Bible and Talmud), one opts resolutely for the 'short' and direct path to the inside, for the descent into one's own interiority, in order then to let go of oneself in the intensely felt interiority. One searches for an intense subjective

an intellectual and philosophical approach to the 'Jewish texts,' which according to him 'give to think' - which is to say, represent a specific form of thinking by which they resist the tests of an insistent and 'strict,' critical reflection. And this Mithnagdic rationality not only influenced Levinas' interaction with Jewish texts and traditions, but also equally his philosophical thinking. His intellectual Judaism meets with the Western preference for thinking manifest in Greek thought and renewed in the Enlightment. Both Jewish and Western 'modern' intellectualism reinforces each other in his thinking, arriving at what he himself refers to as his "allegiance to the intellectualism of reason" (TI XVII/29).

experience of being grafted onto, or rather into the divine reality that is discovered and experienced not outside but inside the deepest self as the core of one's own true self. In religious enthusiasm there is no separation anymore, but an inextricable and direct 'in-presence' of the divine within the subjective, and vice-versa.

Insofar as religious enthusiasm leads to an absorption of the 'I' in a captive and alienating Ground, Levinas unrelentingly places this divine under criticism, however deeply moving the experienced 'One-All' may be. He moreover suspects religious enthusiasm of promoting – precisely on the basis of its inherent cult of feeling – a subjective, uncontrolled simmering of forces and passions. It can be the expression of an infantile yearning to return to the mother's womb, wherein one is redeemed by means of a fusing union from the calamity of separation. Then religious enthusiasm runs the risk of not being much more than a narcissistic projection of one's own unfulfilled dreams and wishes. Religious experience left to itself easily becomes shameless and immodest. Certain ambiguities and images simmer upwards unconsciously with the feeling out of our 'depths' and these make us so drunk that we lose our lucidness and thus our independence. And this then leads us to an 'apostasy' with regard to ourselves. Hence, Levinas remains faithful to the Western intellectualism that sees reason as an important source of freedom and independence (DL 68/44). In order to safeguard the 'soul' against all possible tyrannies that lie lurking on its ground, it must be assisted by reason. It must see to it that the 'I' remains separated and independent: 'ab-solute' in the literal sense of the word, namely 'set free'. In this regard, just as Plato puts it, 'the dialogue of the soul with itself' is the very breath of freedom (TI 16/45).

It is then not surprising that Levinas nurtures a huge distrust towards every religious revival, namely the loudly resounding cry time and again to return to interiority and spirituality, to religious experience and enthusiastic religiosity, in short to the 'true' religiosity of the 'soul' (DL 19/6). He discovers therein the ever returning threat of "the violence of the sacred" (TI 49/77). The divine transports and stupefies humans and extracts them from their own capabilities and intentions. This exaltation leads to the loss of self or the fusion and the convergence with the great and comforting, divine Mystery, without there still being any sufficient distance and separation: "In the mystical participation the identity of the terms can be lost. They are then divested of what constituted their very substantiality. The participation of the one term in another does not consist in sharing an attribute; one term *is the other*. The *private* existence of each term, mastered by a subject that is, loses the private character and returns to an undifferentiated background; the resistance of one submerges the other, and is thus no longer an existence of the one. We recognize here the *there is*" (EE 99/61), the impersonal, a field of anonymous forces, absence of beings, begin in general, 'no-thing-ness', 'no-one-ness': the indeterminateness constitutes its acuteness. Rather than to a – human or divine – subject, the notion of the *there is* leads us to the absence of humans and God, the absence of any being, "before all Revelation, before the light comes" (EE 99/61): the situation of chaos, absolute darkness and indifferencc – without any kind of separation and differentiation.

In the enthusiastic participation in the divine, the 'I' disappears; it literally becomes 'consumed' and annulled. The 'I' is paralysed in its experience of identity. It is transported outside of its knowing and willing. True freedom, however, would feel insulted at such uncontrollable overwhelming. The immersed participation in the divine "annuls the link between persons by making beings participate, albeit ecstatically, in a drama not brought about willingly by them, an order in which they founder. This power of the Divine seems to offend human freedom and to be contrary to the education of man, which remains *action on a free* being. Not that liberty is an end in itself, but it does remain the condition for any value man may attain. The Sacred that envelops and transports me is a form of violence" (DL 29/14).

1.3. Religious atheism as condition for mature religiosity

Out of this consideration on the violence inflicted on the 'I', which is inherent in different forms of religious enthusiasm, Levinas stubbornly arrives at stating time and again that religious atheism is an essential condition for the unfolding of human independence. Whoever takes seriously the independence of the human shall reject that which endangers this independence. The independent will establishes itself precisely as will in and through this religious atheism or through this refusal of a god who, from the inside out, would inhabit or direct it (TI 61/88-89, 202/226). For those who see God as a "fairly primary sort of God, who dishes out prizes, inflicts punishment or pardons sins" (DL 190/143) this atheism is most normal and healthy, and actually a necessary reaction. Levinas speaks in this regard about "the legitimate demandsof atheism" (DL 190/143) or stronger still about the unassailable position of atheism. This implies that religious atheism should not be conceived of as "equivalent to a diabolical pride" (TI 52/79) or as disobedience, but only as a happy affirmation of one's own independence.

There is more, however, for this religious atheism is not only the condition for the growth towards independence of the 'I', but also for a mature religiosity, or better still for a 'religion of adults', i.e., of free and responsible beings (DL 25/11). The relationship with God must be such that the independence of humans is not annulled but, on the contrary, is promoted. As long as humans are not seen as autonomous beings in religion but are, on the contrary, absorbed into the divine, there can be no talk of a mature religion. Hence, monotheism according to Levinas obliges itself to run the *risk* of religious atheism: "The path that leads to the one God must be walked in part without God" (DL 190/143). It must accept that the 'I' that becomes aware of its autonomy and thereby arrives at a rejection of all reducing religious participation, can get stuck in this atheism. Only through this religious atheism can the mature 'I' climb up to a full understanding of the Transcendent. Only a radically separated and independent being can stand open to a possible revelation from God, without it being brought out of itself through the contact with God and lose its separation. Only an independent 'atheistic' being can be a full fledged conversation partner (DL 31/15). The mature religious person, namely the one who acknowledges and affirms God, wants to know what he does and why; such a person wants to judge and take part in full lucidity as a true partner in the relationship. That is why it is for Levinas "a great glory for the Creator to have set up a being who affirms Him after having contested and denied Him in the glamorous areas of myth and enthusiasm; it is a great glory for God to have created a being capable of seeking Him of hearing Him from afar, having experienced separation and atheism" (DL 31/15-16).

Finally, we would like to point out how religious atheism is not of a temporary or passing nature. It is not so that humans must become atheist in a first phase in order to give up atheism in a second phase. They must, on the contrary, remain atheist *in order* to be able to enter into a relationship with God in an authentic way. If religion, to be understood as the relationship with the Transcendent, is not to be degraded into a reducing participation then humans must time and again integrate their independence and thus their 'religious atheism' in that relationship itself. Monotheism conquers, in other words, religious atheism by taking it up in itself and retaining it as the condition for religion itself: an authentic human relationship with the Transcendent (TI 50/78). With this, Levinas confirms *and* surpasses at the same time the thesis of the 'enlightened' or modern, *axiological humanism*, that often brings along in its tracks an *axiological atheism.* In order to safeguard human dignity and freedom, this atheism radically rejects all theological and religious views that stand in the way of human emancipation and unfolding. Levinas sees in this, however, only a first and not a definitive step. While axiological atheism denies God *in order* to promote the human, the affirmation of the irreducible value and dignity of the human does not lead for Levinas to a total negation of God but, on the contrary, to a purification of the concept of God.

1.4. Religious atheism affirms God's transcendence

This purification implies a qualified confirmation of God's radical and irreducible transcendence or 'holiness'. Levinas makes a sharp distinction between "the sacred" ("le sacré") and "the Holy" ("le Saint") (SaS 88/140). He describes the Holy in its literal sense as the pure, the separateness, the beingness without mixture, that is fundamentally applicable to God as the Transcendent One (think of the Latin 'sanctus', that refers back to 'sancire', to separate). Over and against that he describes the sacred as the "anonymous divinity": "faceless gods", "impersonal gods to whom one does not speak" (TI 115/142). "The sacred is neither an object nor a person who speaks" (EN 60/39), "being-without-beings", the "neuter" or the 'there is' (EE 93-94/57-58): the impersonal process of being that depersonalises beings – and humans in particular - through 'immersed participation' or 'reductive fusion' (TI 202/226).

It is precisely against this anonymous and depersonalising divinity that Levinas stubbornly lodges protest by affirming the radical transcendence of the Infinite, literally 'non-finite', non-identical and irreducible to the separated human subject. Levinas also refers back to an idea from the Jewish Kabala, retaken by the already mentioned and by him admired Haïm Volozhiner, namely the 'Tsimtsum' or 'originary contraction of the Divine', God's withdrawal or 'anachoresis' (AV 200/166). This idea was developed for the first time by Luria (1534-1572), the founder of the 16th century renewal movement in the Jewish Kabala mysticism. The core of the 'tsimtsum' is the concept of divine self-limitation. We can best translate 'tsimtsum' with 'self-contraction' or concentration of the divine. By means of contracting into Himself, God wants to liberate space outside of Himself for something other than Himself. By means of withdrawing into His fathomless depth and, as it were, disappearing, He makes place for humans as independent and free creatures. In this manner, Kabala mysticism attempts to resolve the antinomy between God's omnipresence and the existence of free creatures outside of God. Or rather it transforms the contradiction into a paradox: the perfection of God consists precisely in that He rids Himself of the perfection of His omnipresence until He becomes, as it were, 'Nothing' (Rosenzweig), and thus makes place for humans as radically separated and independent beings (TI 76/103). This implies that the self-emptying or 'anachoresis' (contraction) of the Infinite is essential for God's transcendence. Levinas expresses this in a philosophical manner as follows: "The Infinite realises itself by withstanding the invasion of a totality, in a contraction that leaves place for the separated being. Thus relationships that open up the way outside of being take form. An infinity that does not close in upon itself in a circle but withdraws from the ontological extension so as to leave a place for the separated being exists divinely. Over and beyond the totality it inaugurates a society. The relations that are established between the separated being and Infinity redeem what diminution there was in the contraction creative of Infinity. Man redeems creation. Society with God is not an addition to God nor a disappearance of the interval that separates God from the creature.

By contrast with totalisation we call it religion. Multiplicity and the limitation of the Infinite, creator, are compatible with the perfection of the Infinite; they articulate the meaning of this perfection" (TI 77/104).

We can conclude our first movement by stating that for Levinas religious atheism is indispensable to safeguard the independence and autonomy of the human as well as the radical transcendence of God. Both indeed create the conditions for a non-fusing bond between God and humans, and thus for a religious experience that does justice to both God's alterity as well as our own human freedom, without the one coming at the expense of the other.

2. Ethical and 'religious' re-assessment of mystical enthusiasm

In the period of Levinas' second major work *Otherwise than Being or Beyond Essence* (1974), preceded by a few essays compiled in *Humanism of the Other* (1972), and further developed in *Of God Who Comes to Mind* (1982) and *Entre Nous. Thinking-of-the-other* (1991), the idea of enthusiasm appears once again but the one-sided negative connotation has rather disappeared. In 1975, I posed a question to him in a letter concerning the bond between his Mithnagdic background and his critical approach to enthusiasm and his answer was short but clear: "Distrust towards mysticism? Without doubt, certainly! *For enthusiasm* (emphasis by Levinas) = possession by God – as it doesn't mean ecstasy and drunkenness, but awakening and sobering up".[7] This reflection has led me to nuance and reconsider Levinas' view on mysticism, namely in his second major work and the writings preparing and elaborating it, and to discover a quite unique mystical dimension. The validity of this interpretation is confirmed by two articles: (1) "From Consciousness to Wakefulness" (1974), taken up in "Of God Who Comes to Mind" (DVI 34-61/15-42); (2) "Philosophy and Awakening" (1976), taken up in "Entre Nous" (EN 93-106/66-77).

[7] "Correspondance Roger Burggraeve – Emmanuel Levinas (le 10 juillet – le 4 août 1975), in : R. Burggraeve, *Emmanuel Levinas et la socialité de l'argent*, Leuven: Peeters, 1997, 87-98, i.c. 97 : "Méfiance à l'égard de la mystique? Sans doute, certes! *Pour l'enthousiasme* = possession par Dieu – dans la mesure où il signifie non pas extase et ivresse, mais éveil et dégrisement".

2.1. Outward movement toward the wholly Other

Levinas directly links his later revaluation of mysticism with the ethical relationship to the other. We can call it a form of 'ethical mysticism'. In the period of his first major work *Totality and Infinity: An Essay on Exteriority*, he starts from the self as the same *par excellence*, to explicate – as aforesaid - the radical separation and structural autonomy of the human subject, being also the basis for his suspicion against mystical enthusiasm. We can discover in this affirmation of the self as 'the same' a continuation of the 'enlightened thought', which he of course develops in his own unique way by his phenomenology of enjoyment, labour, possession, habitation and knowledge as representation (TI 107-183). What is really new to his thought 'beyond enlightenment' is that he searches for the wholly other rather than the same. Concretely, he discovers and makes explicit that 'metaphysical alterity' on the basis of a phenomenology of the face of the other that by means of its essential exteriority transcends the same (the self) irreducibly. Inspired by his teacher and the promoter of his *Doctorat d'état* or habilitation, Jean Wahl (1888-1974), he qualifies this as the movement of transAScendence (outward and upward) (TI 5/35, 12/41).[8] Metaphysics directs itself towards the absolute as a term, on the basis of a desire that is and remains not only factual but also in principle inadequate and disproportional: "The term of this movement, the elsewhere or the other, is called *other* in an eminent sense. (…) The metaphysical desire tends toward *something else entirely*, toward the *absolutely other*" (TI 3/33). In concretising the metaphysical desire for the wholly other, Levinas discovers the deformalisation of this alterity in the face of the other as the immediate expression of its otherness through its gaze and word (TI 37/66) and as ethical appeal to responsibility for the other as other (TI 172-175/197-201). Levinas likewise calls this "the 'curvature 'of the intersubjective space" (TI 267/291).

By means of its metaphysical and ethical expression the face brings about a de-levelling in being, literally a 'trans-ascendence' of the other. This leads Levinas to speak about the 'height' and 'holiness' (TI 169/195), or even about the 'divinity' of the face (TI 273/297): "The dimension of the divine opens forth from the human face" (TI 50/78).

[8] Cf. "Jean Wahl: Neither Having nor Being," in: HS 110/74, 119/81.

The metaphysical and ethical otherness of the face introduces in me the idea of the Infinite – it is literally an 'infused idea', coming from elsewhere, as also Descartes suggests (PI 171-172/53-54): "The face of the other at each moment destroys and overflows the plastic image it leaves me, the idea to my own measure – the adequate idea" (TI 21/51). I discover God as the wholly other in and through the face that awakens within me an idea that is never adequate with the alterity of the face: the idea of the Infinite that 'infinitises' itself. And the appeal that proceeds from the face of the other summons me to a responsibility that is never ever sufficient, meaning to say to a responsibility that likewise 'infinitises' itself (TI 50-51/78-79). In that way "the other is closer to God than I" (PI 174/56) and God remains the radically transcendent, the wholly Other, notwithstanding God's proximity through His trace in the face that touches me ethically. In this way "any sort of evasion of God across an inward emotion" becomes impossible (TI 186211). By means linking the idea of God as the idea of the Infinite with the alterity of the face, Levinas affirms his critique on mystical enthusiasm to the extent that – as aforesaid - it not only swallows up the autonomous subject but also assails the transcendence and holiness of God.

2.2. Inward movement toward the 'other in me'

The movement of transascendence towards the o/Other prepares the later positive appreciation of mysticism. It will be made clear how this re-appreciation is only possible thanks to a re-interpretation of mysticism no longer as enthusiasm but as a sobering up, or rather as enthusiasm in and through sobering up.

Before we sketch this reassessment of mysticism, we must first reflect on the re-orientation or 'turn' that takes place in the thought of Levinas in the period of his second major work. After sketching phenomenologically the surpassing of the 'I' by the epiphany of the face in the period that culminates in *Totality and Infinity*, Levinas poses a new question. We can call this a Kantian question in the sense that he goes in search of the condition of possibility of the ethical relationship between the other and me. What makes it possible for that which happens to indeed happen? By posing this question Levinas expresses inadvertently a doubt about his first description of the 'I' as 'the same par excellence' or as a 'being' that is interested in the persistence and unfolding of its own being. He describes this being 'at first sight' as follows: "The natural tension of being on itself that I have alluded as egoism. Egoism is not an ugly vice of the subject's, but its ontology, as we find in the sixth proposition of Part III of Spinoza's *Ethics*: 'Every being makes every effort insofar as it is in to persevere in its being'; and in Heidegger's expression about existence existing in such a way that its being has this very being as an issue" (NP 104/70-71). The question is whether there was not something essential that escaped his attention or rather was unconsciously overlooked. Is the first, spontaneous description of the 'I' as sameness and energy, realisation and expression of its own being correct? Is that which at first sight is given indeed the true nature of that which presents itself? May we trust our first impression? Should we not retrace our steps in order to discover, under the surface of that which so eagerly unveils itself as sameness and (interested) being, a more original but hidden – or even repressed – dynamism? Concretely: has everything truly been said about the 'I' when its is labelled as the same and as being interested in its own attempt at being? Is 'being by and for itself' the alpha and omega of the human 'I'? To answer this question Levinas, as a true blooded phenomenologist, in line with Edmund Husserl, is convinced that he has to return 'to the real thing' ('zur Sache selbst'), that means to the forgotten and overlooked dimension of the 'I', namely the true 'soul' of the 'I'.

For the deformalisation or the concretization of this return – this way backward – he appeals on his promoter and philosophical mentor, Jean Wahl, who in metaphysics introduced not only the transascendence but also the transdescendence movement. This downward *and* inward movement consists in descending into the subject, into the 'underground' of the subject, beneath its consciousness and self-determination, in order to discover there that by which the subject is already marked even before it comes to consciousness and activity.

The ethical encounter with the other is the event – a form of radical empiricism – of being touched by the vulnerable face of the other. We are literally 'moved' and affected by the epiphany or appearance of the other. Inspite of ourselves we are appealed to by the nakedness-destitution of the other, that menas we are called to responsibility. The question now is what has to be presupposed in the 'I' so that the 'I' can be appealed: what is the condition of possibility of this being appealed? The answer is that in order to be touched by the other, we must be touchable! The 'hetero-affection' by the face is only possible if the subject, the 'I', is 'affectable'. Even before I take up my responsibility for the other, I must in my being already *be* responsible. I don't make myself responsible but I discover myself as put in the 'situation' – being 'created' – to be responsible: that's my 'human condition' which precedes every form of option, decision making and activity. This is my 'original state', or better my 'pre-original' state, in the sense that I'm not by myself – by my choice – the origin of my 'being-responsible-for-the-other': my condition of being responsible precedes my being the 'origin' or the active and dynamic source of my acting responsibly. Therefore, we have to redefine the subject as 'otherwise than being': the being of the 'I' is not simply 'to be', but in its 'being' the I is already 'beyond being': "being's *other*; not *to be otherwise*, but *otherwise than being* (AE 3/3). As a being that is concerned with its own being and its own identity (*sameness*), the 'I' in its being is already marked by 'the other than its own being'. Even before I attune myself actively to the well-being of the other, I am already – in spite of myself, thus in my very being – attuned to the other. I am engaged to the other, before my initiative to engage for the other. I discover myself as already marked by an event that radically precedes me as a conscious 'origin' of meaning, choice and activity. Levinas qualifies this heteronomous being-made-responsible-for-the other as the human condition of 'fraternity prior to freedom': "I am bound to the other before any liaison contracted. Here there is a relation of kinship outside of all biology. The community with him begins in my obligation to him. The neighbour is a brother. A fraternity that cannot be abrogated, an unimpeachable assignation, proximity" (AE 109-110/87).

To indicate this further Levinas uses the terms that evoke directly the idea of an ethical mysticism, namely animation and inspiration. My passive being affected by the fate of the other is the very intrigue of my subjectivity, namely being 'animated' and 'inspired' in the sense of 'being enraptured and enthused' by the other than myself (AE 84/67): "The proximity of the neighbour in its trauma does not only strike up against me, but exalts and elevates me, and, in the literal sense of the term, inspires me. Inspiration, heteronomy, is the very pneuma of the psyche" (AE 160/124). This leads Levinas to the idea of 'soul', in the sense that the other is the soul – the heteronomous principle of life and meaning – of the self. And note well, soul should not be equated here with consciousness, since it precisely concerns the opposite of consciousness, knowledge and act. The one who is irreducibly different – the other – has made itself in such a way master of the same – the self – and this in an immemorial past, that it becomes the driving force that propels the self forward. Levinas rightly labels the soul conceived of thus as 'the depth of the psychical' or as the '*de profundis*' of the spirit. This concerns a radical and irreducible passivity, which is laid under one's own 'inner depth'. Hence, Levinas, in his iterative and emphatic language, speaks about the infinitely withdrawing transdescendence into "the soul within the soul" (DVI 47/24). Hence, Levinas also speaks, not coincidentally, about "the other in the same" (AE 147/116), "transcendence in the immanence" (DVI 47-48/24-25). We can also rightly qualify this as 'transdescendence': the 'extra-ordinary' that has nestled itself in the 'ordinary'; the higher that has withdrawn into the lower, in an inaccessible and immemorial depth.

In a paradoxical manner Levinas qualifies the 'animation' or 'ensoulment' by the other as the 'incarnation' of the subject. Another word for this ethical incarnation is 'sensibility', literally 'being sensible' through the bodylines of the subject: "Animation can be understood as an exposure to the other, the for-the-other, which refers to maternity, which sensibility signifies" (AE 89/71). "Here the psyche is the maternal body" (AE 85/67). In my sensibility, both emotion as 'shock and shivering due to the other' as well as bodily tangibleness and vulnerability, are contained. My body is, on the basis of its sensoriness, my ethical directedness: eyes, ears, nose, hands are of the nature that they present themselves as the 'antennae' of my 'soul', or better of my being ensouled for the other. In this sense my body is my soul. I already bear the other in my body: through my 'lived body' (*body subject*) I am sensible for the other's vulnerability, manifesting itself to us through the other's body. My 'own body' (*corps propre*) is ethically ensouled in the sense that it bears an ethical signature or 'tattoo' in itself: the other has been etched indelibly in my body, in the sense that my bodily being subject in its 'being' stays directed and 'exposed' to the other. That again reveals my human condition, my 'creaturality' or 'creature status', as Levinas also calls it (AE 117/92). I am, in and through my exposed and vulnerable – sensible – body, already connected with the other, even before I can actively link and identify myself with my body as 'my body' (AE 96/76-77). This bodily sensibility is the condition of possibility of the above-mentioned brotherhood. Being an ensouled body here means "being-in-one's-skin, having-the-other-in-one's-skin" (AE 146/115): I am able to be 'occupied' with the other because the other already 'occupies' me, in the sense that the directedness towards the other marks and ensouls my bodylines and precisely in so doing makes it 'sensible' for the other. Through my body, I can suffer of the other's suffering and therefore I am for-the-other (AE 114/90). And this creatural sensibility is not only corporeal but also 'passive' in the literal sense of the word: the bearing of the other is 'passion', that means bearing the passion and suffering of the other. That's why Levinas describes this bodily sensibility as 'compassion' (AE 150/117): "suffering of the other, my pity for his suffering, his pain over my pity, my pain over his pain, etc" (AE 150/196). Compassion, what etymologically means 'suffer with the other', has an ethical meaning, because it is anchored in our bodily ensoulment by the other, in our 'being-for-the-other'. My sensibility by-and-for-the-other implies the 'birth pangs' that it entails, precisely because it is a bodily bearing: "groaning of the entrails" (HAH 94/114).

This bodily sensibility as ethical animation reveals finally the 'extra-versive' meaning of the 'the other in the same'. The 'I' is awakened out of itself and is driven outwards – out of itself: "the awaking of the same by the other, sobering up from its identity and its being" (DVI 57/30). The 'through the other, despite oneself' is radically and irreversibly 'for the other': "explosion of the other in the same" (DVI 55/29). The 'I' is awakened as such by the other, that it is moved to vigilance. It is turned inside-out: despite itself it is turned away from itself towards the other than itself, the vulnerable other. The ethical animation does not revert back to its own self, but to the other than itself. In this regard the animation remains heteronomous. As inspiration it is enthusiasm, meaning to say a driving force and a 'being-inspired' (in the passive sense of the word). This enthusiasm, however, is never ecstasy and intoxication but on the contrary a sobering up. By means of 'the other in the self', the self is brought 'outside itself' towards the other, for the sake of the other. The animation results in 'ex-ternality', to be understood dynamically as an 'externalisation' or rather as an externalisation that never stops, an externalisation that infinitises itself: "trauma, not thauma" (EN 103/75). No mystical ecstasy therefore, but a sober and lucid dedication to the being and the well-being of the other, an incessant bursting and restlesness, ethical insomnia, 'ex-cess' in the literal sense of the term: "The Same, disturbed by the Other who exalts him. To live is not an ecstasy, it is an enthusiasm. Enthusiasm is not drunkenness, it is a sobering up. A sobering up always yet to be further sobered,a wakefulness watchful for a new awakening" (DVI 57/30).

2.3. Inward movement toward the Infinite in me

Levinas, however, still takes a step further, through which we arrive at a religious transdescendence, leading us to a religious understanding of ethical mysticism. He discovers in the ethical movedness by and solidarity with the fate of the other – pre-original, trans-biological, ethical fraternity – a 'divine affection', namely the human subject's being affected and marked in spite of itself by the Infinite. The term 'Infinite' has to be understood literally as 'In-finite', namely as the Infinite 'in' the finite *and* as the 'non-finite' that is radically separate and distinct from the finite. The subject thinks more than it thinks when it thinks the idea of the Infinite. Thereby the more is situated in the less, without this more is absorbed in and by the less – and without the less is absorbed by the more! Insofar as the 'I' is in its being – in its createdness - attuned to the other, and thus bears the other in itself despite itself, it actually bears something that it neither can conceive of nor contain, which is precisely the radically other and thus the Infinite. In this regard the Infinite is the denial of the finite: radical and irreducible difference, making impossible mystical fusion and participative identification. But, this denial does not place the Infinite outside of the finite, for the Infinite is located in the finite. With the already mentioned word-play, Levinas states that "the *in* of the Infinite signifies at once the *non-* and the *within*" (DVI 107/63). At this we come across the divine transcendence in the human immanence, or the immanence of God's infinite transcendence.

The idea of the Infinite in me, that in no way whatsoever coincides with me as finite, can only be understood as the radical passivity of the consciousness, in the sense that my consciousness is 'touched' or 'affected' by something that is radically different from itself. And this non-assimilable alterity, that is situated in, or rather under the consciousness, awakens the consciousness to the other, in an unending, sobering up and extra-versive movement as well: pure goodness. In this regard, the consciousness is that which in its underground bears the Infinite, a consciousness aroused by the other: in spite of itself, driven from its underground out of and above itself towards the other. In this regard, the radical difference between the Infinite and the finite 'I' is at the same time a radical non-indifference for the one different from itself, meaning to say for the other. The intimate *and* transcendent infinity of God should thus not to be understood in a neutral but, on the contrary, in an ethically qualified manner.

This means that the idea of the Infinite for Levinas is at the same time the idea of the Good – the Good beyond the self-interested being – or better the idea of 'the Good in me', the idea of the in-dwelling God. Even before I come to myself via the acts of my own self-consciousness I am already awakened by God to myself. God is the intrigue of my soul, or better still the soul of my soul. This likewise leads Levinas to describe the subject as a theological being, whereby 'theological' has no confessional but only a strictly philosophical meaning. In an almost shocking manner he states: "the psychical is originally theological" (TrID 39/271), whereby he not only puts behind him the current Western definition of the human as *animal rationale* but also brings it into a radical crisis (TrID 40/271). He also speaks about the essential "religiosity of the self" (AE 150/117), in the sense that the subject, insofar as it is driven by that which is different than itself – the other – *and* thus stands directed towards the other, is likewise affected and moved by God as the Good. The human is of a divine signature, or to put it with a biblical metaphor: the human is the image of God, even before the human is a reasonable, conscious and free being (AV 120-121/96-97).

This religiously founded awakening by the Infinite is manifested in the trace of the ethical awakening as an extraversive movement that always sobers up the subject: "A sobering up always yet to be further sobered, a wakefulness watchful for a new awakening" (DVI 57/30), "the awakening from which the vigil lives" (DVI 56/29), "permanent revolution of sobering up as concrete life; the vivacity of life as excession; ecession of life: a sobering up always in need of sobering up, a wakefulness on the eve of a new awakening" (EN 105/76). To synthesise: "Transcendence or awakening that is the very life of the human, already troubled by the Infinite" (EN 106/77): God as thorn in the flesh. This uneasy, extraversive movement of 'the awakening of the awakening' means that the human subject cannot resign itself to itself nor close itself up in itself, to rest in itself and to be able to fall asleep. It is driven out of its own being by the Good as the Infinite in its soul towards the other than itself. The paradox of this movement of sobering up is that it is at the same time a dynamics of longing: overflowing desire, not based on need and search for satifisction but feeding itself with an ever-new hunger: the fullness of a desire, never full enough, "unquenchable desire" (HAH 46/94), leading to a "proximity to the other, never close enough" (*un proximité jamais assez proche*), thus without any form of reductive or seductive and violent fusion (AE 140/90). The Infinite in the finite, the Good in me, is a fire that burns in the depths of the soul: the flame of the desire by and for the other. A flame whereby the 'I' reaches from underneath, from its underground that lies deeper than all capability and all activity of the consciousness, for the other – above the grasping and comprehending consciousness: desire leading towards the good, out of the Good, whereby the consciousness is already 'brandmarked' pre-originally. And precisely because God as the Infinite is also the Good, this desire is inspired, literally blown and propelled by the Good – God – in me. And this drivenness by God brings me as well to ecstasy, literally to a coming to stand outside, in a movement towards God as the Good, thanks to a highest and infinite non-indifference for the other (DVI 110-111/66-67). An ecstasy is thus not of drunkenness but as ethical and divine sobering up to the other. Levinas qualifies this "entering into the Beyond by ecstasy that remains relationship." And to corroborate this idea he refers to Plato who "affirms the value of the delirium that comes from God, 'winged thought.' Delirium here does not have an irrationalist significance. The fourth type of delirium is reason itself, rising to the ideas, thought in the highest sense. Possession by a god, enthusiasm, is not the irrational, but the end of the solitary or inward thought, the beginning of a true experience of the *new* [the other] – already desire" (TI 18/48, 20/49-50).

We can conclude our reflections on the second movement, namely the movement of transdescendence, by stating that the mystical view of God as the Infinite and the Good in me – 'entheos' or enthusiasm, where the difference between possessing and possessed doesn't disappear (HAH 80/55) – finally brings Levinas to the strong conclusion that this 'religious enthusiasm' – this being ensouled by the Infinite as the Good beyond being – is likewise the *conditio sine qua non* of our ethical movedness by-and-for-the-other, of our ethical destiny that precedes every consciousness and every free choice. I can only be ethical, that is to say, called in spite of myself to responsibility for the other, if I am inspired by God as the Good beyond being, that means as the Infinite who is more intimate than I am intimate with myself. Hence, my religiosity, my being animated by the Infinite as the Good, my 'divine signature', counts as the condition of possibility of my ethical 'otherwise than being', i.e. my non-indifferent directedness towards the other because of the other: "the Infinite awakens me to vigilance, to watchfulness over the neighbour" (DVI 57/30). It is the divine goodness in me that makes possible my ethical goodness that inspires me and appeals to me towards it, without forcing me or without any form of necessity.God as the Infinite in me, who rouses me to the good, neither denies nor alienates my freedom but invests it with an 'extra-ordinary' election and thus unicity. In that way, the 'inspired I' becomes by means of its ethical being and acting a prophet of the Infinite: "Here I am", or more correct in French: "me voici", an accusative form without nominative (AE 14/11, 159/124), like the biblical, Hebrew 'Hineni' (104/97).

With this, Levinas returns to a thought that he has encountered in his own Jewish Mithnagdic tradition, namely the thought of Rabbi Hayyim of Volozhin in his book *Nefesh ha'Hayyim* (*The Soul of Life*) (AV/151/167). Notwithstanding his rejection of mysticism, or at least in its Hassidic excesses, he himself develops a mystical view: God is the soul of the universe and of all the worlds. And the human being, not understood in the light of the rational animality of the Greeks but in the light of the biblical notion of being created in the image of God, is the soul of the world(s) because God is not only the soul of the world but also of the human. Man is responsible for the world because he is ensouled by God. This shows a mystical vision on the inspiration of the lower by the higher and of the higher by the lower, the lower being for the higher. "It is not through substantiality – through an in-itself and a for-itself – that man and his interiority are defined, but through the 'for-the-other': for that which is above self, for the worlds (but also, by interpreting 'world' broadly, for spiritual collectivities, people and structures)" (AV 194/161).

3. Christian perspective on 'sobering enthusiasm'

Finally, we would like to pose the question what Levinas' paradoxical view on mysticism can mean for a Christian view on God and humans and their relationship?

3.1. Created in God's image, not in God's likeness

Firstly, his critical suspicion against mystical enthusiasm offers the possibility of getting rid of a certain concept of Divine Providence. And this in favour of a view of the human as the image of God, whereby God's transcendence as well as human freedom and responsibility are done justice. Divine Providence can beunderstood as an all-disposing and arbitrarily ruling by an omnipotent and omniscient God, in whose abiding mystery and impenetrable dispensations one can only share by unconditionally subjecting oneself to 'God's will'. But, then one literally gets ensnared "in the invisible meshes" of God (TI 49/77). In such a conception, human life is reduced to nothing else than the enactment of a drama that has begun without our knowing and willing, and the unravelling of which an invisible and ungraspable other – God alone – knows before we do. A drama, therefore, that proceeds towards its goal without our being able to hinder this process or to determine or change ultimately its direction and outcome. Our existence has no meaning of itself, but only insofar as it is an exponent of this "drama of salvation or of damnation that would be enacted in spite of me and that would make game of me" (TI 52/79). The shadow of a certain fate is being outlined, as it were, which does not come from ourselves but which infiltrates unnoticed in our intentions in order to steer it and make it serve an encompassing 'masterplan' that is only accessible to God who surpasses all and oversees all things. In such an experience of Providence the human is ultimately enfolded by a totality wherein all takes place in the way that the 'Principle' of that totality has weighed and disposed of from the beginning.

In so doing, however, the separateness and structural independence of the 'I' is simply denied and destroyed. We can label this concept of the history of salvation as an interpretation of a theatre play, which intends to force through with all violence a certain thesis, and which – even though it is still so transcendent – brings no articulation of a real life through freedom. The human being as a person, as an agent of history, seems less real than the human being as a figure or statue. The freedom of conscious humans is enveloped by a kind of sublime and sacred *fatum* in which, instead of *being*, humans *figure*. God the Director effaces God the Creator. He commands actors rather than freedoms (DL 163/121-122).

A Christian view is faced time and again with the challenge to do justice both to God as Creator as well as to humans as free and responsible creatures. For that purpose, a dynamic interpretation of the human as 'image of God' offers a possibility. In the first creation story God says: "Let us make humankind in our image, according to our likeness" (Gen 1, 16). But, when we read further how God really creates the human, it only says: 'So God created humankind in his image; in the image of God he created them" (Gen 1, 27). God creates the human therefore only according to God's image, but not in God's likeness. Is it a memory lapse by the author? Should image and likeness actually be seen as synonyms? Or is there more to this than that? The finding that God creates the human according to God's image, not according to God's likeness, is quite important. By creating the human according to His image, God sets His signature in the human. God lays the divine in the human: the Infinite in the finite. In other words, the human is marked by divine Love. Like a musical instrument, the human is divinely disposed and thus attuned to love, to the other. But, it also stops there. God creates the human according to God's image as possibility and condition. In the human there lies only a divine sensitivity or 'seed'. It is then up to the human to substantiate fully for himself or herself one's likeness with

God, starting from the seed of love that God has poured into his or her heart. That divine seed should then germinate. That is the task of humans. On the one hand, there is the gift, the Infinite in the human: the divine that, as the good, is planted in the human like a seed. On the other hand, everything else should still take place. If the human does not nourish that seed and does not create the correct conditions so that it can germinate and grow, nothing will happen. It is thus entirely up to human freedom, creativity and responsibility to substantiate concretely that divine love that has been planted, in and through love for others and the world. It is a task that is entrusted to every human. Thanks to God, we as human beings are marked by the divine; thanks to ourselves we substantiate this divine signature. Orthodox theology calls this 'theosis', divinization. In this way, the irreducible uniqueness of both God as well as humans is safeguarded and at the same time a bond of cooperation is made possible: a human independence that is based on dependence on God, or stronger still a reciprocity, the reciprocity of a covenant, that is based on asymmetry.

3.2. Ensouled by the Holy Spirit

Also Levinas' movement of transdescendence offers possibilities for a Christian 'thorough reflection' starting from Spirit-theology, which has been all too often neglected, although it is an essential ground of Christian mysticism. We can link Levinas' idea of God as the 'Good in me' to the idea of the 'Spirit': God infused in us, the immanence of God's ethically qualified transcendence. According to the Biblical tradition God is not a supreme, neutral being or 'unmoved Mover' (Aristotle); God is moved by and for his creation, the world and humankind. The Infinite is always qualified in ethical terms, being the Righteous and the Merciful, the Loving One. Throughout the history of Israel, in a historico-dynamic way, God reveals Himself slowly but surely as a God who associates with people. Think of the God-revelation on Sinai where the Lord reveals Himself as 'I will be with you' and this promise suffices to let Moses liberate his oppressed people from the house of slavery. Likewise, in the Torah (Law), and even more strongly in the prophets, it is clear that God's association with people develops a well-defined preference: he associates himself especially with the misery of the poor, the widow, the orphan and the stranger who stays in the land. In Israel, they were symbolic of the one who suffers, or rather; they acted as the concrete forms in which the vulnerable nakedness of people appears. It is far from accidental that God associates Himself with the destitute. God conforms to them so that He becomes, as it were, a suffering God. This could be called *the passion of God.* He descends from upon high; He relinquishes His glorious majesty in order to empty Himself and to make Himself small, by conforming to, or stronger still, by identifying with, the misery of the ones who suffer. In other words, what we are faced with here is a very specific self-emptying of God. It reveals itself not as a masochistic self-destruction, but rather as an ethically qualified self-emptying, as a profound alliance with all who are forgotten, disenfranchised and oppressed in this world. God makes Himself small along with the small: he is an associating God. That is not only what Jesus announces through his message of the coming Kingdom, but what he also realises in flesh and blood. Through Jesus' words and life, to the extreme of his suffering and dying on the cross, we discover and receive the ethical being of the loving God as our grace: God's ethics of love is our 'given and received love'. In and through Christ, 'God-man', the 'persecuted truth' (Kierkegaard) of the One allied with the vanquished, thc poor, the persecuted is revealed and incarnated: a radical kenosis or self-emptying of God, the humility of the Infinite. This 'defeatism' of the Infinite, this divine timidity that does not dare to dare - the non-audacity of the Good beyond being in and through the humankind of Jesus, can be called 'the transubstantiation of the Creator into the creature': in Jesus, a fine historical being, the Infinite or "the Word became flesh and lived among us" (Jn 1:14a).

In contrast to, or better as fulfilment of this Christological approach to God, whereby Jesus as the Christ still remains 'outside the human', the pneumatological approach to God as'Holy Spirit' introduces the Infinite that is Love 'inside us'. Think of the affirmation of Paul in the letter to the Romans: "God's love has been poured into our hearts through the Holy Spirit that has been given to us" (Rom 5, 5). The ethically qualified God does not remain external but becomes internal, intimate. Through the Spirit 'dwelling' in us we are animated and ensouled by the divine love, not to coincide with God but to be inspired beyond ourselves by the Infinite. As revealed by Jesus, God's Christ, we are inspired and called to be the bearers and witnesses of the Infinite. This 'interiorisation of God' seems to make meaningful Jesus' remark in the gospel of John: "It is to your advantage that I go away, for if I do not go away, the Advocate will not come to you; but if I go, I will send him to you" (Jn 16, 7).

And there is still more, because the radical passivity of the grace of intimate divine love provokes – calls to - the radical activity of ethical engagement. In other words, the 'in-dwelling' of God as Spirit in us not only means a gift of grace but also a dynamics of ethical inspiration: 'a gift that gives to give'. The love of God in us through the Spirit makes us literally 'ec-static': exposed to the other, being for-the-other, dedicated to the other, despite ourselves but not without ourselves. Because through the infused Spirit God's love became our soul, or rather the soul of our soul, we are appealed and made able to love the other: "We love because he first loved us" (1Jn 4, 29). By means of the Spirit, who is nothing else than God's love, in our spirit – up to our very flesh – we are borne and moved, literally 'in-spired' or 'en-souled,' to an infinitising love just like the 'agapè' of God Himself. In this regard, my love for the other than myself, the other and the whole of creation, does not spring forth from myself. It is rather a kind of irradiation of God's love in and through me, despite myself. Not I, but the Spirit of God in me, loves the other – as Augustine would have put it. Thanks to the Infinite, I as a finite being am love for the other and the world. We can also call this a divine 'vitality' that awakens us as such and sobers us up that we are stirred towards the other or rather stirred time and again – up to infinity: the life of God in this world.

Conclusion

It is apparent from all this that mysticism does not stand at the margins in Christianity, but takes on or rather deserves a central place. It likewise means that an authentic mysticism cannot be separated from ethics: the divine gift of love in our soul, poured out by the Spirit, awakens us and sobers us up, drives us out of ourselves, at the service of the other: 'extra-ver-sive spirituality of responsibility'. Likewise, we should not forget the lesson of Levinas' initial critical stance towards mysticism.

Indeed the danger remains real – even on the level of transdescendence, and of the Christian spirituality of 'ensoulment by the Spirit of love' – that enthusiasm transports us as such that we end up in a fusing ecstasy and drunkenness – a drunkenness that sucks us down into the depersonaliseddarkness of the 'there is': at the cost of God, at the cost of ourselves *and* at the cost of the other. We accentuated therefore the recurrence of awakening, or the vigilance as the waking up in awakening, which one also can describe as the "shiver of incarnation", through which *giving* takes on meaning, as the original dative of the *for the other*, in which the subject becomes heart and sensitiveness and hands that give: incessant solicitude for solicitude, the *glory of a long desire*, not a proof but a prophetic witnessing of the Infinite (DVI 20/73).

8

"I Live, Not I; It is Christ Who Lives in Me" (Gal 2:20)

A Yogic Interpretation of Paul's Religious Experience

Dr. Joseph Pathrapankal CMI
Dharmaram Vidya Kshetram, Bengaluru, India

The basic and final goal of all religions is promotion of union between their devotees and the God these religions profess and proclaim. This union can have manifold articulations: either as the final union with God after the life in this world or as an experience of a divine union already during the earthly life. Here again, the issues and the catena of divine experience could be considerably different one from the other, and hence it is difficult to delineate the principles and nuances of such divine-human union and its various manifestations. Some writers would call it mysticism, while others would give some related expressions to articulate such a profound union. The main purpose of this study is to see how Paul, an energetic apostle in the early church, also had such an experience of aunion between himself andChrist, in whom he believed, an experience which lies at the very basis of his life and mission. The purpose of this analysis is to explain this Christ mysticism of Paul from a Yogic perspective in the hope that this attempt would contribute towards an Indian interpretation of a biblical text, an exercise in biblical exegesis which is currently undertaken by some Indian exegetes.

1. The Basis of Yogic Experience

Basically *yoga* means 'union', related to the English word 'yoke' and the Latin word 'jugum'. Hence, *yoga* comes to mean a method of spiritual union of the human with the divine. Consequently, yoga is a method by which an individual may become united with God, the Reality who underlies this apparent, ephemeral and unreal universe. To achieve such a union with God is the perfect yoga, which in Christian language is often called mystic union. Many Christian saints are said to have had this profound union and their writings are studied and analyzed at length all over the world.

The basic call of all humans is to reach the divine, whether it is in the Christian, Hindu or Islamic traditions. The nuances regarding the efforts that are to be made use of in order to reach the divine may vary from religion to religion. Although all humans have a divine element in them and hence are basically divine, there is a process which each human person has to undertake to unravel the divine in them and experience it. Whereas in Hindu religious tradition it is known as the *atman* becoming aware of the *brahman* and assimilating itself with the *brahman* beyond this world of the unreal and the transitory, the Christians speak of the human mind, will and spirit surrendering themselves to the divine Spirit in such a way that they find their ultimate joy and peace in the divine. The Hindu tradition proposes *jnana, bhakti,* and *karma* as three ways (*margas)* for the attainment of this goal and the Christian tradition has it as faith, love and hope as the three means of reaching the goal of human life.

The Christian tradition about salvation has two levels: one is the level of the Old Testament which the Christians share with their brothers and sisters of Judaism, and the other is the specifically Christian, namely, one in which the Christians find the realization of their religious aspirations in the person of Christ. At the same time, it is important that Christians living in the midst of other religions try to understand their religious categories within the framework of their own culture and religious climate and articulate them in a way that makes the Christian thought more tuned to their own culture and religious thinking. Hence, we are trying to analyze how Paul who was a Jew and a Christian at the same time tried to reach the goal of his religious call, and explain the whole process of it as a yogic experience.

2. Paul, the Blameless Pharisee

It was with a certain sense of pride and legitimate satisfaction that Paul in his letter to the Philippians recalled his Jewish identity and religiosity: "I was circumcised when I was a week old. I am an Israelite by birth, of the tribe of Benjamin, a pure-blooded Hebrew. As far as the keeping of the Jewish law is concerned, I was a Pharisee, and I was so zealous that I persecuted the Church. As far as a person can become acceptable to God by obeying the commandments of the Law, I was without fault" (Phil 3:3-6). The Pharisees were known for their strict and scrupulous observance of the Law of Moses, known as the Torah, and they were the most religious-minded people among the Jews. This naturally led them to consider themselves as the paragons of virtue and hence they were tending to despise others who were not so strict with regard to the observance of the Law, as is clear from the parable of the Pharisee and the Publican (Luke 18:9-14). The Law was supposed to be given to Israel through the mediation of Moses on the occasion of the making of the covenant on Mount Sinai. Hence, Covenant and Law were to be understood as closely related; the latter as the means and expression of the commitment to the former. But, in course of time, especially after the Babylonian captivity, the Law was dissociated from the Covenant as well as from its personal dimensions, and it was understood more as an area of self-effort to make one upright and acceptable to God. Psalm 119, written after the Babylonian captivity, gives this impression to a great extent.

As such, there was nothing wrong about one obeying the law, and hence Paul could call himself a blameless Pharisee. But, the major theological problem in it was that it was basically a denial of God's grace and thereby one's dependence on God. A person committed to such a philosophy of life could hardly depend on God, and such persons would consider themselves as ideals for others to follow. Moreover, they would be obstinate in their convictions and would not enter into any dialogue or compromise with others. In fact, Paul also was so sure of his religious excellence that he would not give in to any other teaching and practice besides his own religious convictions. Hence, he had concluded on the basis of Deuteronomy 21:23 that Jesus of Nazareth was a cursed one because he was hanged on a tree (Gal 3:13). That conviction gave him the impetus and the urge to destroy the religious movement Jesus of Nazareth had inaugurated, which only gained strength and enthusiasm among his followers after he had been crucified (Acts 9:1-2). Hence, Paul wanted to destroy this new religious movement by all means. He did his best to persecute the followers of Jesus in Jerusalem and then set out for Damascus with the authorization of the High Priest to persecute the followers of Jesus over there. It was nothing less than a militant approach to religion.

3. The Damascus Experience

The Acts of the Apostles narrates the event of Paul's encounter with Jesus of Nazareth near Damascus in a very dramatic manner. As Paul was proceeding to Damascus to arrest men and women who were following Jesus, for which he had the official and written authorization of the High Priest from Jerusalem, he was confrontedby a very strange question: "Saul, Saul, why do you persecute me?"(Acts 9:4) To the question of Paul as to who it was who asked him, the answer was simple enough: "I am Jesus whom you persecute" (Acts 9:5). Paul had heard about Jesus of Nazareth; he may have even met him somewhere during his stay in Jerusalem in the School of Gamaliel. But, he had never thought that this Jesus, who was already crucified, had an authority and a challenge about his person to confront such a respectable Rabbi like Paul. In fact, the details of what happened remain unknown. Paul was asked to get up and go into the city, where he would be told what he has to do (Acts 9:6). Paul obeyed.

In his letter to the Galatians Paul narrates this event as a "revelation of God's Son" (Gal 1:17) to him and he explains in no unclear terms the change which he underwent, a change about which he did not want to consult any human agency. Rather he went all the way to Arabia to think and reflect on the meaning of what had happened to him. Paul was always a committed person. As a Jew he was fully committed to the convictions and practices of Judaism, which gave him the urge and the persuasion to destroy a splinter group of Jews who claimed that Jesus of Nazareth was the Messiah and Lord. The life-style of these followers of Jesus was all the more repugnant to Paul because in all other matters these followers of Jesus lived a Jewish way of life and consequently it was an affront to his own religion to have to tolerate such a heretical group. But, then the revelation came to him on the way to Damascus that the whole issue was different from what he had so far thought. Jesus the crucified one was alive and he was one with his followers whom he was persecuting, so much so that persecuting his followers was tantamount to persecuting Jesus himself. At last, Paul had to change his convictions; he had to make a new commitment, a total commitment to Jesus of Nazareth.

4. From Torah-Centrism to Christo-Centrism

From his being a blameless Pharisee Paul started to live the life of a humble follower of Jesus. The basic difference between these two modes of existence was very conspicuous. The central focus of Paul's Jewish life was his conformity to the Torah and its various demands. With all the excellence and sublimity this Torah had, it was still a written code of dead letters. There was no personal touch involved in following the prescriptions of the Torah. It brought about only a personal satisfaction and complacency for those who observed theTorah that they were good persons before God and the people. It was more a question of not violating the prescriptions of the written law because the general tendency of everyone confronted by a law is to violate it. The law gives directives from outside about what is to be done or what is not to be done; but it never gives the inner energy and power to observe its demands.

Paul was a prisoner of this vicious circle. He wanted to excel all others in his devotion to the Torah and he did succeed in it to a great extent, as we have seen above. At the same time, he could not tolerate anyone who did not correspond to the kind of spirituality he owned for himself. He was zealous and at the same time intolerant. He was a martyr for the sake of the Torah. Since the Torah was dissociated from the reality of the covenant, especially from the time of the Babylonian captivity, Paul had not experienced any personal fulfillment in his blind following of the Torah. It was all a duty he had to fulfill, a burden placed on him for the simple reason of his being a Pharisee. His life was centered on the Torah and he would die for it and he would also make others die for the sake of the Torah.

It is from this Torah-centered religion that Paul made a radical shift to a person-centered religion. Once he realized the fact that Jesus of Nazareth was raised from the dead, his entire world-vision was changed. The fact that Paul was ready to believe in the resurrection as something in tune with his Pharisaic background made a real change in his understanding of religion. It is true that Paul never regretted his being a Pharisee; but his commitment to the Torah did not give him his ultimate sense of fulfillment. Conformity to a written law can never give a sense of personal fulfillment. It is only a question of accommodating to a norm of life. Once that goal is reached, there remains nothing to be further added. This is not the case when a person becomes the controlling power of one's religious experience. As one tries to understand a person, his or her personality is challenged by the one who wants to be in communion with him or her. It is all the more so when it is question of a divine person. In his Damascus encounter Paul had come to understand that Jesus of Nazareth was the Son of God and further it is said that he went straight to the synagogues and began to preach that Jesus was the Son of God (Acts 9:20). This new commitment to the person of Son of God would mean that Paul would never come to a stage where he would have reached the goal of his new religious commitment.One can never exhaust knowing and loving a person. The more Paul knew the mystery of Jesus, the more he realized that he is far removed from that goal.

5. Paul's Jnana and Bhakti Marga According to Phil 3:5-14

It is this new centre of gravity now fixed on the person of Christ that we read in Phil 3:5-14, an auto-biographic passage, in which Paul describes what had happened to him in his encounter with the risen Christ on the way to Damascus. After having explained his excellence as a Jew and Pharisee (Phil 3:5-6), Paul went on to say that all that excellence he now considered as a loss for the sake of Christ. His *dharma* according to the Torah gave way to a new *dharma* based on faith in Jesus Christ. Consequently, he reckoned everything as complete loss for the sake of what is so much more valuable, namely, the knowledge (*gnosis*) of Jesus Christ, whom he had now accepted as his Lord. For the sake of this Christ Paul threw everything away and considered all things as mere refuse.

As a Jew, Paul never had to know the Torah; he knew it thoroughly well. His learning it in the school of Gamaliel gave him ample opportunity to know the details of the Torah and also to teach it to others. But, now, as one who believed in Christ, it is now a question of gaining the knowledge about the whole mystery of Christ. From his being an ordinary person walking through the towns and villages of Palestine to the time he was considered a culprit and was crucified and then the unheard of things that he rose to a new life and that he continues to be one with his followers - all these meant alot for Paul to know about. Consequently, he undertook an ongoing process of knowing and devoting, of *jnana* and *bhkati,* -of knowing Christ and knowing the power of his resurrection, of sharing in his sufferings and of becoming like him in his death in the hope that one day he would also be raised from death to life. This *jnana* of Christ naturally leads to a *bhakti* towards Christ, to an unconditional commitment to Christ, to absolute devotedness to the person of Christ. It is a whole process of entering into the mystery of Christ, the mystery of his life, death and resurrection. It is a process of knowing and committing oneself to the object of one's knowledge.

Paul was aware of the magnitude of this effort to reach the goal of his new religious commitment. Hence, he wrote: "I do not claim that I have already succeeded or have already become perfect. I keep striving to win the prize for which Christ Jesus has already won me to himself. I really do not think that I have already won it. The one thing I do, however, is to forget what is behind me and do my best to reach what is ahead. So I run straight towards the goal in order to win the prize, which is God's call in Christ Jesus to the life above" (Phil 3:12-14). Paul uses an athletic language to describe his efforts to reach the goal of his call. Basically it is his commitment and dedication to the person of Christ, which prompted him to forget the past and run towards the goal. The goal is the perfect union with Christ in the mystery of his life, death and resurrection.

6. Paul's Karma Marga According to 1 Cor 9:19-23

Paul was no academician. Nor was he a silent mystic. His training in Judaism, through which he was made a Rabbi, did not prevent him from being a parson committed to the society. That is the reason why he not only opposed the new religious movement started by Jesus but also did everything in his power to destroy it, not only in Jerusalem out also in the far-off Damascus where he knew the followers of Jesus had gone for fear of him. He was a witness to the stoning of Stephen and he it was who took care of the cloaks of those who stoned Stephen, meaning thereby that he had a direct role to play in the execution of Stephen. It was part of his conviction about his faith and his commitment to his parent religion.

Paul's acceptance of Christ as the new principle of life only deepened his commitment to work for him. His *jnana* of, and *bhakti* to Christ prompted him to a way of action, a *karma marga,* the proof of which are the three missionary journeys he undertook during the ten years of his active apostolic life. At the end of all these adventures he had planned to go to Spain because he had no more place to work in the eastern part of the Roman Empire (Rom 15:23-24). He was a tent-maker by profession (Acts 18:1-2) and he worked hard night and day to take care of his needs and of those of his companions (1 Thes 2:9; 1 Cor 9:6). In his Farewell Speech to the Elders at Ephesus Paul explained the reason why he worked so hard for himself and his companions: By working hard one must help the weak, remembering the words that the Lord Jesus himself had said: "There is more happiness in giving than in receiving" (Acts 20:34-35).

The underlying principle of this altruism of Paul is beautifully explained in his letter to the first Corinthians (I Cor 9:19-23). On the one hand, he was aware of the meaning and importance of being a free person, and he did not want to be anybody's slave, meaning thereby a person with a slavish attitude to others. At the same time, Paul decided to make himself everybody's slave in order to win over to Christ as many people as possible. His work for Christ was not a strategy, much less a spiritual conquest. It was more a question of availability to others by which he could be at home with the Jews and the Greeks, with the strong and the weak. For Paul, it was all a matter of accommodating himself to others, always aware of the fact of his being under Christ's law of love (Gal 6:2). He was conscious of his being free from the Law of Moses, but he did not want to be like those who found satisfaction in being subject to that law. He could very well be like a Gentile who did not have anything to do with the Jewish law, and this was one way of winning them over to Christ. It was not any kind of diplomacy, but his ability to adapt himself to others, his readiness to make a compromise in secondary matters and. above all, his love for Christ and his yearning to make Christ known and experienced by others as well.

7. Paul's Yogic Experience Summarized in Gal 2:20-21

It is in the light of the above reflections on Paul's encounter with Christ and his total commitment to the cause of Christ that we have to analyze the classical passage about Paul's Christ experience which is presented in a yogic perspective in his letter to the Galatians. After having explained his total independence from all human agencies for the inner quality of his faith commitment to Christ and also to his gospel (Gal 2:1-14), Paul goes on to summarize the inner content of his gospel, stating that a person receives divine acceptance only through faith in Jesus Christ and not by obeying the Torah. Paul says that he himself took this courageous step, which for the average Jews would have been impossible. For such Jews, Paul was a renegade, one who denied the Torah and became a sinner and started favoring the cause of sin. But, Paul admits that, as far asthe Torah is concerned, he is dead to it, killed by the Torah itself, in order that he might live for God. His being killed by the Torah is nothing but his dying with Christ on his cross in order that hemight start a new life with Christ for God.

It is in this context of Paul's reflection on death and life together with Christ that he gave expression to that unique and courageous reference about his religious experience: "It is no longer I who live; it is Christ who lives in me" (Gal 2:20). The encounter which Paul had with the risen Jesus on the way to Damascus did not remain an isolated event in his life; rather it made a real metamorphosis in his person and life in such a way that he could conclude there from that he ceased to live, while Christ started living in him fully and totally. It would be impossible for us to fathom the profound implications of this statement of Paul. In fact, it was not that Paul ceased to live his physical life. He had a life of his own, but it was totally and definitively transformed by the person of Christ. Consequently, the life which he continued to live was a life of "faith in the Son of God, who loved Paul and gave his life for him" (Gal 2:20). The entire life and activities of Paul, as we know it from his letters and the Acts of the Apostles were an articulation of his commitment to Christ, his *karma, jnana* and *bhakti* were fused into a new relationship with Christ through which he allowed Christ to live in him. It was a *yogic* experience for Paul.

There are scholars who try to analyze the moment which prompted Paul to articulate this mystical union with Christ, this perfect *yoga* with Christ. Some are of the view that it is Paul's way of understanding his baptismal experience when he received baptism at the hands of Ananias (Acts 9:18). It might appear to some that here we are reading too much into a text of Paul. But, when we analyze the Pauline teaching on baptism in Rom 6:3-11 and Gal 3:26-29, which are Paul's own reflection about the meaning of baptism, we can see how they are both a sharing of his own experience which he gave to his readers. In Rom 6:3-11 Paul understands baptism as a dying and rising with Christ, a death to sin and a new life with Christ. Baptism, for Paul, is an entering into the very mystery of Christ. He writes: "By our baptism we were buried with him and shared his death, in order that, just as Christ was raised from death by the glorious power of the Father, so also we might live a new life" (Rom 6:4). Paul understands baptism as becoming one with Christ in his dying and in his being raised to a new life. The old being is put to death with Christ on his cross in order that the power of the sinful self might be destroyed and a new life be inaugurated. The same can be said about Gal 3:26-29 whereagain Paul speaks about the effect of baptism as a "putting on Christ" (Gal 3:27), as a result of which all discriminations, such as religious, racial and sexual, are removed and all become one new humanity in Christ: "There is no longer Jew or Greek, there is no longer slave or free, there is longer male and female; for you are all one in Christ Jesus" (Gal 3:28).

As we have seen above, the person of Christ totally captivated Paul and his name had become almost a secrete slogan (*mantram*) for Paul. Christ permeated Paul's life and action, his theology and world-vision. Proverbs 18:10 speaks about the name of Yahweh as a strong tower. For Paul, this was true about the name of Christ and he saw Christ more real to himself than all others, including himself. Christ was the *OM (AUM)* for Paul, the beginning of everything (Eph 1:3-4) as well as the goal of everything (Eph 1:10). We may call it the Christ-mysticism of Paul; but more than the name it was all a case of profound life-experience. What Paul wrote to the Corinthians holds good for the experience of every Christian: "All things are yours, and you belong to Christ, and Christ belongs to God" (1 Cor 3:21). Paul realized that he did not belong to himself, but to Christ and this explains how he could speak about a termination of his own life when he fully committed himself to Christ.

8. The Vine and Branches: A Paradigm of Yogic Experience (John 15:1-11)

What we have analyzed above as Paul's mystical and *yogic* experience is clearly illustrated by the evangelist John in the allegory of 'the vine and the branches (John 15:1 -11). A branch is united to the stem of the vine in such a way that at any given moment a branch can say: 'I live not I, the stem lives in me; the life that I live now is the life that is transmitted to me by the stem". The branches cannot live without the stem and the stem operates itself through the branches. In a certain sense, we can say that the stem needs the branches to reveal its creative power. But, this does not in any way cause the branches to forget their dependence on and the need of the stem. The stem without the branches lacks its perfection and the branches without the stem lack their vitality and life. The branches need pruning to be meaningfully united to the stem, especially to bear fruit. The branches which wither away are cut off and thrown away. Paul as a branch bearing much fruit was pruned in different ways, as we know it from his own letters.

Through his letters Paul gives to his readerstwo types of theological information: one of his own profound theological reflection and the other of his sharing of his own religious experience with his readers. Whereas the former has a ring of authority about it insofar as it is the result of his meditation and reflection on the meaning of the Christ event and Christian life, the latter is Paul sharing with his readers the inner insights of his own religious experience, and consequently it has its own power of persuasion about it. The core of this experience was Paul's life in Christ, a life which he began in his encounter with the risen Lord on the way to Damascus. It was this life which he treasured as his most cherished reality and it gave him the impetus to face the challenges of life. So he could write: "When I am weak, then I am strong" (2 Cor 12:10), meaning thereby that he could do everything with the power of Christ who strengthened him (cf. Phil 4:13). It is this same conviction of abiding union with Christ which prompted him to challenge all the enemies of Christian life and ask the readers: "Who can separate us from the love of Christ?" (Rom 8:35).

The above analysis of the close union Paul had with Christ shows that it is a relationship anyone can have in his or her life. It is not the unusual or the impossible. What is required is one's total commitment to Christ, a commitment that prompts the believers to break away from all other commitments. As a Jew, Paul had his total commitment to the Torah. When he realized that there is a greater and better way of religious commitment, he gave up his loyalty to the Torah and surrendered himself to Christ. This commitment was radical and definitive for Paul throughout his apostolic career and it enabled him to face all the challenges of his apostolic life. Consequently, Paul is a model for everyone who wants to get into a close relationship with Christ and he invites everyone to have this experience of oneness and togetherness with Christ, which we can call a *yogic* experience.

9

Mysticism without Bounds

Jacob Boehme, William Blake and Jung's Psychology

Dr. Patrick Menneteau

University of Toulon, Toulon, France

It may seem paradoxical to *talk* about mysticism, because the term is usually connected with theme of forbidden knowledge (as symbolized by the tree of Eden). Mystics generally insist on the inaccessibility of the mystical experience to thought and language: such is the case with the *Deus absconditus* of Master Eckhart, but also with Grégoire de Nisse, or again with Pseudo Denys, in his *Mystical Theology*. From the anonymous 17[th]century *Theologia Germanica*, we may catch a glimpse of this ineffable overwhelming moment:

> But, if the 'One', who is also the 'Whole', seizes a creature and submits it, if this creature seems to him well-disposed and adequate for him to recognize himself in it, being a will and a love, a light and a knowledge, he learns by himself that he must desire nothing but the "One" whom he is.[1]

Jacob Boehme, in the 17th century, describes the ultimate "reality" of God in terms of nothingness: "He is the One who is also the

[1] *Théologie Germanique*, ed. M. Windstosser, Paris: Arma Artis, 1911, 175: Mais si cet «Un», qui est en même temps le «Tout», s'empare d'une créature, s'il se la soumet et si cette créature lui paraît bien disposée et convenable pour qu'il se reconnaisse lui-même en elle, étant une volonté et un amour, étant une lumière et une connaissance, il apprend de lui-même qu'il ne doit rien désirer que cet «Un» qu'il est.

eternal Nothing [...] he is incommensurate"[2] ; "the eternal and divine intelligence is a free will [...] she is the Whole and yet is only, so to speak, Nothingness"[3]. Hence, the possibly disheartening observation of 20th century philosopher Guy Lardreau, who sums up the problem in the following terms, by reference to the writings of 6th century mystic Philoxène de Mabbourg:

> The paradox of spiritual literature: about that on which this 'life', the subject of long and well-codified discourses, is ordered and qualified by; about the end of these practices that are constantly fed by the numberless mass of apophthegms, lives of saints, rules, lectures and directories, in one word, about contemplation, nothing can be said: so many speeches, so ordered and constrained, to reach nothing but silence. The ineffable character of this experience – ineffable in as much as it is precisely an experience, for who has not lived it can endlessly talk about it: this is the definition of the philosopher -, there lies [...] in the end, the essential. A singular experience which each spiritual man lives next to the others, and which is so radically singular that it is properly through it that he becomes himself a singularity: what did they see, and how, we will never know.[4]

---

[2] Jacob Boehme,*Mysterium Magnum,* Plan de la Tour: Editions d'aujourd'hui, 1978, vol. I, 55 and 57: « Il est l'Un qui est en même temps le Rien éternel [...] il est incommensurable. »

[3] Jacob Boehme, *Mysterium Magnum*, vol. II, 336: « L'intelligence éternelle et divine est une libre volonté [...] elle est Tout et pourtant n'est pour ainsi dire qu'un Néant. »

[4] Guy Lardreau, *Discours philosophique et discours spirituel: autour de la philosophie spirituelle de Philoxène de Mabbourg,* Paris: Seuil, 1985, 99:Paradoxe de la littérature spirituelle: de cela même à quoi cette 'vie', dont on peut si longuement parler, et de manière si codifiée, est ordonnée, et qui la qualifie; de la fin à quoi tend cette pratique qu'inlassablement instruit la masse incalculable des apophtegmes, des vies des saints, des règles, des conférences et des directoires; bref, de la contemplation, on ne peut rien dire : tant de paroles, et si réglées, si contraintes, pour aboutir au silence. Le caractère ineffable de cette expérience - ineffable dans la mesure même où elle est une expérience, car qui ne l'a point faite en peut parler indéfiniment : cela s'appelle un philosophe -, là est bien [...] en fin de compte, l'essentiel. Une expérience singulière, que chaque spirituel fait *à côté* des autres, et si radicalement singulière que

Through this echo to the archetypal theme of forbidden knowledge, man does not seem to be meant to know about divine matters: indeed, Adam and Eve were punished for eating of the apple of the Tree of knowledge in Eden; Icarus burnt his wings while trying to approach the sun; Semele died when Zeus appeared to her in his splendour; Actaeon was devoured by his own hounds for having caught sight of Artemis in her nakedness, and similar misadventures befell Tantalus, Phaeton, and Bellerophon. In all these cases, the hero was punished for attempting to reach some kind of divine prerogative. Does such a difficulty imply that mysticism is to remain totally unconnected from everyday life? I would like to suggest that one means of going round this difficulty is to read mystical texts in psychological terms, bearing in mind a fundamental distinction between Sigmund Freud and Carl Gustav Jung.

Indeed, it would sometimes be tempting, in a Freudian vision, to read mystical texts as mere "projections" of our own subconscious, thus reducing every kind of mysticism to matters of sexual fantasies. The description of the first manifestation out of "nothingness", the primal matrix, by 16th century German theosopher Jacob Boehme does lend itself to such an interpretation: Will, the first manifestation of divine nothingness, is desire. And this desire begets within itself a thorn which, as it grows and swells, starts to oppose the desire that begot it in a contradictory movement, the account of which would equally suit a sexual act: a symbolic phallus exciting a desiring matrix[5]. In the same

c'est en elle, proprement, qu'il advient comme singularité : que voyaient-ils, comment voyaient-ils? Nous ne le saurons jamais.

[5] Jacob Boehme, *De la Triple vie de l'homme*, Plan de la Tour: Editions d'Aujourd'hui, 1982, 26-36: « Il y a deux volontés dans un seul être, et elles occasionnent deux principes ; l'un est l'amour, l'autre est colère […] La volonté du Père est la première dans l'éternité […] or telle est le propre de la volonté ou du centre, c'est particulièrement de désirer d'engendrer la parole ou le cœur : car autrement il n'y auroit rien […]. Le désir est astringent et attirant car il est la force serrant le large en étroit […]. Ainsi le désir attire à soi […] et l'attiré est l'empressement du désir, et le désir fait plaire, et là cependant il n'y a rien qu'un ténèbre ; […] la volonté mince est comme un rien et entièrement tranquille ; mais le désir la rend pleine, et cet attiré dans le désir est les essences ou l'aiguillon de la sensibilité qui combat l'enfermement, lequel le désir ne peut pas supporter, et attire d'autant plus fort à soi ; ainsi l'aiguillon en devient plus grand et s'emporte contre l'attiré, et ne peut cependant pas en sortir car le désir

way, it would be easy to read William Blake's description of the moment of the final resurrection in terms of sexual projections:

> The Grave shrieks with delight & shakes
> Her hollow womb & clasps the solid stem:
> Her bosom swells with wild desire,
> And milk & blood & glandous wine
> In rivers rush & shout & dance,
> On mountain, dale and plain.[6]

Jung, as to him, refused to limit the libido to the sexual definition given by Freud and sought to explain the power of fascination of these writings and illustrations in terms of the manifestation of a "reality" that lies much deeper within human nature, beyond the varieties of religious discourses or ideological values, and beyond the concerns of the individual subconscious: an objective psyche in which the images of a collective subconscious form the legacy of the fundamental experiences of the human species, the libido being a form of psychic energy at play in moments of inspiration[7]. I would like to propose, therefore, that we

---

l'engendre, et ne peut cependant pas l'endurer, car c'est une inimitié comme le chaud et le froid. Alors l'attract devient aussi astringent et fortement attirant pour contenir l'aiguillon, d'où il donne la mobilité comme une vie en mouvement […] car dans l'angoisse de l'attract, dans le dur attirant, il s'élève une forte froideur, et ce tiré est son aiguillon astringent amer, de façon qu'il donne une puissance effroyablement forte que l'aiguillon ne peut pas souffrir, […] et comme il ne peut pas s'échapper au dessus de soi, il devient tournant comme une roue, et disperse l'astringent d'où résultent les essences de la multiplicité. L'éclair du feu fait la troisième forme dans la nature […] et l'âme ou l'éternelle vie est la quatrième forme. […] Ainsi les quatre formes de la nature ne s'appellent plus le centre, quoiqu'elles aient le centre en elles dans leur original […] et l'angoisse fait une seconde volonté en soi, de façon que les quatre formes ont en elles-mêmes une éternelle volonté qui leur est propre. »

[6] William Blake, *Complete Writings*, ed. Geoffrey Keynes, London: Oxford University Press, 1972, 248: *The Song of Los*. See also his illustration « Christ in the Sepulchre, guarded by Angels », in which one can easily identify the picture of a phallus.

[7] See C.G. Jung, *Le Divin en l'homme*, Paris: Albin Michel, 1999, 481: « La langue prophétique n'[a] pas selon moi sa source dans l'imagination personnelle mais dans les représentations collectives. Comme dans les grandes œuvres littéraires, les expériences religieuses et les visions prophétiques, la source originelle est à chercher ici [dans le cas d'Osée] dans des représentations archétypiques qui n'ont que peu de rapport avec la disposition individuelle du poète. »

study what his theories have to say about mysticism, along the following lines: (1) some parallels between Jung and mysticism, (2) mysticism without bounds: a possibility or a danger: the psychological dimension of mysticism, and (3) the mystical dimension of psychology: "mysticism unbound".

1. Parallels between Jung and Mysticism

To Jung, mystical discourses are the only empirical elements we can take as objects of study if we have no access to any direct mystical experience. And in the course of the analysis, many striking parallels appear between Jung's ideas and mystical themes. For instance, one of the main themes that are common to mystical authors is the complaint about the shortcomings and inefficiencies of human language. William Blake talks of the English language as "the rough basement" and complains:

> O, how can I with my gross tongue that cleaveth to the dust
> Tell of the Four-fold Man in starry numbers fitly order'd,
> Or how can I with my cold hand of clay![8]

Jacob Boehme, as to him, observes that in the wake of Adam's fall, our language became "coarse and beastly"[9]: this is why he can only invite his reader to some kind of spiritual reading that reaches beyond the words of a deliberately obscure language[10]. Thus, it becomes apparent that the difficulty in reading Blake's prophetic poems or Boehme's theosophical treatises finds its source in a common conviction in mystical authors, according to whom nothing can replace experience itself: mysticism is primarily a matter of inner experience.

It should be noted thatJung's rational approach is based on his clinical experience, and that a number of empirical clues point to the validity of this working hypothesis: dreams may reveal archetypal

[8] William Blake, *Complete Writings*, 668 and 502.

[9] Jacob Boehme, *Mysterium Magnum,*vol. I, 82: « Nous avons posé avec l'esprit de notre connaissance un solide cadenas devant la compréhension de la folie [de ce monde], afin qu'elle ne comprît pas notre idée. [...] Chacun n'a donc qu'à voir ce dont il est capable, et chacun en tirera son profit. »

[10] Jacob Boehme, *Mysterium Magnum*, Vol. I, 53-4.

manifestations, but, as his works abundantly show, archetypal forms can also be found in many types of discourses belonging to various cultures and fields: mythology, alchemy, mysticism, metaphysics, and sciences. Events of synchronicity can be experienced by everyone of us and rest on the same ground as the ancestral practice of the Chinese Yi-King: the concept of a dual reality, both material and supra-material, an echo of which is to be found in the *Unus Mundus* of the alchemists. As soon as he started to explore these perspectives, Jung no longer met the scientific requirements to which Freud wanted to submit the new theories of psychoanalysis. Why did Freud, although he had found in a myth the perfect illustration of his Oedipus complex, refrain from studying mythologies and the field of the "occult"? It does seem as though he was under the influence of the scientific model, which, phenomenologically speaking, and from a Jungian point of view, stands for the prevalence of "sensation" and "reflection" at the expense of the other two faculties of the mind: feeling (which is not acknowledged as the ultimate ground for even our "rational" choices, despite David Hume's considerations on subjectivity), and intuition (which is nevertheless regarded as the gateway towards the unconscious). Whereas Freud was keen on keeping a scientific *persona*, Jung focussed on inner experience as a guide, as he acknowledged particularly in his later writings:

> This is why the conversations with the dead, the « Seven Sermons », are a kind of prelude to what I had to communicate to the world about the subconscious: They are a kind of ordering pattern and an interpretation of the general contents of the subconscious. (…) I can state today that i never distanced myself from my initial experiences. All my works and all that I have created in the field of the mind spring from the original fancies and dreams.[11]

---

[11] C.G. Jung, *Ma Vie*, Paris: Gallimard, 1973, 223: C'est pourquoi les conversations avec les morts, les « Sept sermons », forment une sorte de préludeà ce que j'avais à communiquer au monde sur l'inconscient : ils sont une sorte de schéma ordonnateur et une interprétation des contenus généraux de l'inconscient. […] Je puis dire aujourd'hui que je ne me suis jamais éloigné de mes expériences initiales. Tous mes travaux, tout ce que j'ai crée sur le plan de l'esprit proviennent des imaginations et des rêves initiaux.

The focus on inner experience, despite the paradox of mystical discourses, leads us to face once more the question: what can be said about this inner experience? William Blake first invites his readers to distinguish Locke's concept of experience (that is, empirical experiment, based on the observation of the outside world) from the inner experience of the subject, which he calls "the faculty which experiences": "As the true method of knowledge is experiment, the faculty of knowing must be the faculty which experiences. This faculty I treat of" (K98).

In so doing, he symbolizes a turning point in the history of ideas which is equally exemplified, in the field of philosophy, by David Hume's criticism of empiricism. Indeed, in his *Treatise on Human Nature*, the philosopher establishes that in the last analysis, even a discourse such as that of empiricism (with it claim to objectivity, and which was to become the basic method of modern science) is steeped in subjective roots:

> [...] an opinion or belief is nothing but an idea, that is different from a fiction, not in the nature, or the order of its parts, but in the *manner* of its being conceiv'd. But, when I wou'd explain this *manner*, I scarce find any word that fully answers the case, but am oblig'd to have recourse to every one's feeling, in order to give him a perfect notion of this operation of the mind. An idea assented to *feels* different from a fictitious idea that the fancy alone presents to us: And this different feeling, I endeavour to explain by calling it a superior *force*, or *vivacity*, or *solidity*, or *firmness*, or *steadiness*. This variety of terms, which may seem so unphilosophical, is intended only to express that act of the mind, which renders realities more present to us than fictions, causes them to weigh more in the thought, and gives them a superior influence on the passions and imagination.[12]

Hume's concept of the feeling of truth was to be taken up by Husserl's phenomenology, and finds an echo in Guy Lardreau's experimentum mentis:

[12] David Hume, *A Treatise of Human Nature*, Oxford: Clarendon Press, 1983, 628: footnote intended for page 96.

> All this can, it seems to me, be confirmed in yet another way, and at another level: by asking whence comes to the philosopher, when meeting with some truth, the certainty of being in front of a truth? He may hold this link firmly because he is sure of having tested the strength of a previous one, and because that one was yet again confirmed by a first: it is nevertheless necessary that at the very end the entire chain originate in an *experimentum mentis* which it cannot account for, since reason started from it, and whose insistence should legitimately be tested, although it grows weaker and weaker with every link, yet being taken up in each of them, at every moment. This experience, from which, in the last analysis, spring all philosophical statements, why should we not give it the name, which it too clearly claims, from Descartes to Nietzsche, of an *illumination*? [13]

This moment of illumination (which can be compared to the scientist's "insight" as studied by Rudolph Carnap in the Vienna school of the philosophy of science[14]), establishes the similarity between the subjective roots of all discourses alike (whether religious, mystical,

---

[13] Guy Lardreau, *Discours philosophique et discours spirituel*, 142-3: Tout cela se peut, il me semble, confirmer encore d'un autre biais, et à un autre niveau : à demander d'où vient au philosophe la certitude où il est de se trouver, lorsqu'il la rencontre, devant une *vérité*. Il peut bien tenir ce maillon assuré d'avoir éprouvé la solidité du précédent, et que celle-ci lui est encore par un premier garantie : il faut bien qu'à la fin des fins la chaîne entière trouve son origine dans un *experimentum mentis* dont elle ne rend pas raison, puisque la raison est à partir de lui, et dont l'insistance, en droit, doit pouvoir s'éprouver, même si de fait elle s'affaiblit de maillon en maillon, en chacun d'eux pourtant, à tout moment ressaisie. Cette expérience, dont tout philosophème relève en dernière instance, pourquoi ne pas lui donner le nom que, de Descartes à Nietzsche, trop clairement elle réclame, d'une *illumination*?

[14] See Rudolph Carnap, "Theories and Nonobservables" in J. Fetzer, ed. *Foundations of Philosophy of Science*, New-York: Paragon House, 1993, 107: It must not be forgotten that, both in the history of science and in the psychological history of a creative scientist, a theory has often first appeared as a kind of visualization, a vision that comes as an inspiration to a scientist long before he has discovered correspondence rules that may help in confirming his theory. When Democritus said that everything consists of atoms, he certainly had not the slightest confirmation for this theory. Nevertheless it

philosophical or indeed scientific!). Hume's subjectivism thus opened the questioning of Locke's over-simplistic view of perceptions leading to impressions (ideas) in the *tabula rasa* of the mind:

> Thus all probable reasoning is but a species of sensation. 'Tis not solely in poetry and music, we must follow our taste and sentiment, but likewise in philosophy. When I am convinced of any principle, 'tis not only an idea, which strikes more strongly upon me. When I give the preference to one set of arguments above another, I do nothing but decide from my feeling concerning the superiority of their influence.[15]

Today, this criticism has even spread to the field of economics, which also has claims to scientific truth (via the cult of mathematical models), but which some economists expose as being under the determinant influence of irrational factors[16]. Thus, all systems of human knowledge, all systems of explanation of the world, all claims to objective truth are liable to this radical questioning. Whereas Locke rejected past metaphysical systems as mere matters of opinion[17], Jung is now in a position to expose Locke's empiricism as prejudice:

> A general form of prejudice has it that (\[…] the ultimate ground for our knowledge be exclusively given from outside, and that *nihil esse in intellectu quod non antea fuerit in sensu.* And yet […) all those who know the old science or old natural philosophy know what part of psychic data is projected onto the unknown of the outside phenomenon. This part is so great that in the end we can never tell how the world in itself is

---

was a stroke of genius, a profound insight, because two thousand years later his vision was confirmed.

[15] Rudolph Carnap, "Theories and Nonobservables,"103.

[16] See le *Manifeste d'Economistes Atterrés*, by a number of distinguished economists and academics analysing the roots of the last recession (www.assoeconomiepolitique.org), or André Orléan's lecture on youtube.

[17] John Locke, *An Essay concerning Human Understanding*, London: Penguin, 1997, 89, Livre 2, chapitre 1 (« of Ideas in General, and their Originals » §1-5): "I know it is a received doctrine that men have native ideas […]. This opinion I have at large examined already".

> eventually made, for we are indeed compelled to transpose the physical element into a psychic process, as soon as we mean knowledge. [...] It is the soul that provides us with these images and these shapes, the only ones, in the last analysis, that make it possible to know the object.[18]

On the grounds of his own inner experiences, the psychologist then chooses to go back to the very notions which Locke had discarded from his philosophical investigations, the supra-material and the innate:

> In my opinion, it is grossly mistaken to suppose the soul of a new-born baby to be a *tabula rasa*, in the sense that it would not contain anything. [The child] does not bring to the impressions coming from outside *any kind* of disposition, but *specific* dispositions, which obviously supposes a particular choice and a certain shaping of the process of perception. These dispositions can be proved to be instincts and inherited pre-formations. Pre-formations are conditions of the process of perception that are grounded in instincts. They are *a-priori* and formal. They are the *archetypes* which define specific ways for any activity of the imagination.[19]

---

[18] C.G. Jung, *La Réalité de l'âme*, 684-5: Un *préjugé général* veut [...] que le fondement essentiel de notre connaissance soit exclusivement donné de l'extérieur, et que *nihil esse in intellectu quod non antea fuerit in sensu* (il n'y a rien dans l'intellect qui n'ait été auparavant dans les sens). Et pourtant [...] tous ceux qui connaissent l'ancienne science ou l'ancienne philosophie de la nature savent quelle part de données psychiques se trouve projetée dans l'inconnu du phénomène extérieur. Cette part est en fait si grande, qu'en fin de compte nous ne sommes jamais en mesure d'indiquer la manière dont, en définitive, le monde lui-même est fait, car nous sommes bel et bien contraints de transposer l'élément physique dans un processus psychique, du moment que nous voulons parler de connaissance. [...] C'est l'âme qui nous offre ces images et ces formes, les seules qui, en définitive, rendent possible la connaissance de l'objet.

[19] C.G. Jung, *La Réalité de l'âme*, 694-5: C'est à mon avis une grossière erreur de supposer que l'âme d'un enfant nouveau-né est une *tabula rasa*, en ce sens qu'elle ne contiendrait rien.[L'enfant] n'apporte pas aux impressions venant de l'extérieur *n'importe quelles* dispositions, mais des dispositions *spécifiques*, ce qui suppose évidemment un choix propre et un modelage de l'aperception. On peut prouver que ces dispositions sont des instincts et des préformations hérités. Les préformations sont des conditions de l'aperception fondées sur des instincts, *a priori* et formelles

Of the collective subconscious, indeed, we can only observe the diverse manifestations in dreams, synchronicity, mythologies, alchemy, mystical discourses, etc. Its supra-material dimension places Jung at the heart of a debate of tremendous consequences in the history of ideas, that which finds its archetypal literary expressions in Hamlet's famous monologue "To be, or not to be", or in Stevenson's novel *Dr Jekyll and Mr Hyde*, for instance. In modern times, yet another manifestation of this archetypal opposition is to be found in the confrontation between spiritualists like William Blake, who claim that "Mental things are alone real" (K617), and the advocates of a purely materialistic definition of reality, such Jacques Monod, who asserts that science is grounded on "the postulate of the objectivity of nature."[20] We are faced with an aporia. But, beyond this duality, the solution of which will necessarily be grounded in a mere feeling of truth, what is truly at stake is, according to Jung, nothing less than a collective neurosis on the scale of western civilization:

> Nothing is more likely to alienate man from the fundamental field of his instincts than his capacity for learning, which turns out to be truly an impulse towards a progressive transformation of human behaviour. [...] [this capacity for learning] is also the source for numerous psychic difficulties and troubles, the cause of which lies in the fact that man grows more and more distant from his instinctive bases: thus uprooted, he identifies himself to the conscious knowledge he has of himself, and consequently to his conscience only, at the expense of the subconscious. [...]. He is thus led to forget himself, that is, to lose sight of his original instinctive nature, and [...] he

[...] :ce sont les *archétypes* qui assignent leurs voies déterminées à toute activité de l'imagination...

[20] See Jacques Monod, *Le Hasard et la nécessité*. Paris : Seuil, 1970, 37-8: La pierre angulaire de la méthode scientifique est le postulat de l'objectivité de la Nature. C'est-à-dire le refus *systématique* de considérer comme pouvant conduire une connaissance «vraie» toute interprétation des phénomènes donnée en termes de causes finales, c'est-à-dire de projet [...]. Postulat pur, à jamais indémontrable, car il est évidemment impossible d'imaginer une expérience qui pourrait prouver la *non-existence* d'un projet, d'un but poursuivi, où que ce soit dans la nature.

substitutes the conception he has built of himself for his real essence.[21]

With this statement, Jung puts forward a deeply grounded criticism of western civilisation as it was defined in the wake of the so-called "Enlightenment". This is where the study of mysticism does have a bearing on our everyday lives. To put it in a nutshell, the scientific model of investigation has long been associated with the notion of progress (particularly in the wake of the industrial revolution), and David Hume himself aimed at making it the model for his own investigations on human nature[22]. But, the model rests on the a-priori denial of elements that belonged to a long-standing tradition (since Socrates and Plato), and, from a psychological point of view, on a lack of balance between the four faculties of the mind[23].

This point is a new occasion for observing parallels between mystical discourses and Jung's psychology. In a striking echo to Jacob Boehme's four primal forms of nature acquiring their own will, Blake's vision represents the fall of universal man as caused by the separation of his four "emanations", called the four Zoas: Urizen stands for Reason, Tharmas for sensation, Luvah for Love & emotions, Urthona for Imagination. The prophetic poems describe at length their battles and further emanations (the fall into the many), and eventually their

---

21 C.G. Jung, *Présent et avenir*, Paris: Buchet-Chastel, 1962, 76-7: Rien n'est plus susceptible de rendre l'homme étranger au plan fondamental de ses instincts que sa capacité d'apprendre, qui se révèle être en propre une impulsion à une transformation progressive des comportements humains. […] [Cette capacité d'apprendre] est aussi la source de nombreuses difficultés et perturbations psychiques qui ont pour cause le fait que l'homme s'éloigne de plus en plus de ses bases instinctives : déraciné, il s'identifie avec la connaissance consciente qu'il a de lui-même, et par conséquent avec sa seule conscience à l'exclusion de l'inconscient. […] Il en arrive à s'oublier lui-même, c'est-à-dire à perdre des yeux sa nature instinctive originelle, et […] il substitue à son essence réelle la conception qu'il s'est fabriquée de lui-même.

22 See David Hume,"Introduction" to his book, *A Treatise of Human Nature*.

23 See Patrick Menneteau, « La Sensation et la réflexion selon John Locke, ou la rhétorique au service de la séduction », colloque international « la séduction » de l'université de Paris IV, janvier 2008: published in *XVII-XVIII*, n°65 (2008), 131-153.

return to unity through the symbolical figures of Christ and Jerusalem[24]. Now, these spiritual entities match exactly the four faculties of the mind which Jung identified much later on the basis of his clinical evidence: “Sensation tells us what really exists. Thought enables us to know the significance of what exists; feeling, what is its true value; and intuition at last points to the possible origins and ends that lie in what exists now.

From a psychological point of view, cases of lack of balance between these faculties can be seen in Plato (with the dominance of Reason); Locke (dominance of reason and sensation); romanticism (dominance of feeling); madness or religious fanaticism (dominance of uncontrolled intuition). From a mystical point of view, to William Blake in particular, given the occult theosophical mathematics according to which $4 = 4 + 3 + 2 + 1 = 10 = 1 + 0 = 1$, the figure 4 bears in itself the potentiality of a return to the One, symbolized by Jerusalem.

But, Jung's considerations go even further into the phenomenological perspective: the subjectivity which is inherent to all systems of human knowledge leads him to regard the human psyche as intrinsically bound up in a world of psychic representations of the world. He is thus led to regard each representation as a phenomenon of conscience to be studied, whether it be a mystical vision, a religious discourse, a political ideology, a philosophical system, or a scientific explanation (much in the same way as Blake defined spiritual progression through “states” as materializations of errors[25]). If Jung never said “God exists”, it is because, to him, as for many mystics, ultimate “reality” definitely escapes our grasp, except in experiences of a particular kind, the so-called “numinous experiences” that lie beyond words.

As a direct philosophical consequence, he relinquishes Plato's search for a definitive discourse on universal truth. But, more importantly, he acknowledges that all discourses are ultimately grounded on a feeling

---

[24] See Patrick Menneteau, “William Blake & Carl Gustav Jung” in *Problèmes actuels de Philologie: procédés méthodiques de l'enseignement des langues étrangères*, actes du colloque international scientifique et pratique de l'université pédagogique de Novossibirsk, Faculté des Langues Etrangères, November 2006.

[25] See William Blake, in *A Vision of the Last Judgment*: «Whenever any Individual Rejects Error & Embraces truth, a Last Judgment passes upon that Individual» in *Complete Writings*, London: Oxford University Press, 1972, 613.

whose nature is similar to a mystical experience of illumination (that is, based on the faculty of intuition), which confirms that the original feeling of truth is what matters. The concomitant step is to go beyond the simple use of sensation and reason (as in Locke's materialistic perspective, or in Freud's scientific claim), and to open oneself up to these manifestations of the subconscious (whatever it may be it itself), thus re-establishing the legitimacy of the faculty of intuition which modern man has neglected. To Jung, the link with mysticism is natural:

> The man of religion enjoys a great advantage in that he is in a position to answer the present question which looms in front of us: he has at least a clear idea of the ground for and legitimization of, his subjective existence in its relationship to 'God'. I write 'God' between inverted commas to show that I mean an anthropomorphic representation the dynamics and symbolic values of which are transferred onto us through this medium which is the subconscious psyche. [...] It is no longer necessary to prove that there exist experiences of a truly religious kind. *But, is the ground for these experiences really what metaphysics or human theology call God or gods?* This is the question that will always remain unanswered. [27]

Beyond these philosophical or religious considerations, what matters, therefore, is to focus primarily on the original inner experience of the subject. Jung adds on:

> But, this question is vain at the bottom and carries its answer within itself, thanks to the subjectively upsetting numinosity of the experience. Anyone who has lived through such an experience is as it were 'seized' by it, and consequently cannot indulge in sterile considerations of a metaphysical order or related to any theory of knowledge.[26]

[26] C.G. Jung. *Présent et avenir*, 86: L'homme religieux jouit d'un immense avantage en ce qu'il peut apporter une réponse à la question actuelle qui plane menaçante sur nous: il a au moins une idée claire du fondement et de la légitimation de son existence subjective dans sa relation à 'Dieu'. J'écris 'Dieu' entre guillemets pour indiquer par là que j'entends une représentation anthropomorphe, dont la dynamique et la symbolique nous sont transmises par ce milieu qu'est la psyché inconsciente. [...] Il n'est plus

Thus justified in passing from the strictly materialistic frame of empiricism and science to the acknowledgement of inner experience as a grounding factor, we must now try to determine how far our new perspective may reach.

2. Mysticism without bounds: A possibility or a danger? The psychological dimension of mysticism

In other words, does madness necessarily lie beyond the bounds of mysticism? The next step consists in asking whether inner experience can provide sufficient guidance for man's values and behaviour. John Locke's warning against the possession of the mind by gods, the distance sought by the philosophers of the Enlightenment to avoid the dangers of "enthusiasm", have not kept a Hitler from harbouring a deep conviction that he was right, nor prevented modern confrontations between Protestants and Catholics, Muslims, Hindus, and Jews, which fuel our daily news reports.[27] The challenge to avoid the phenomenon

nécessaire de prouver qu'il est des vécus qui sont des expériences religieuses. *Mais est-ce que le fondement de ces expériences est bien toujours réellement ce que la métaphysique ou la théologie humaine appellent Dieu ou les dieux ?* Voilà ce qui restera l'objet d'un éternel point d'interrogation. Mais cette question au fond est vaine et comporte elle-même sa réponse, de par la numinosité subjectivement bouleversante de l'événement vécu. Quiconque a vécu une telle expérience est comme 'saisi' par elle et c'est pourquoi il n'est pas en état de s'abandonner à des considérations stériles d'ordre métaphysique ou de l'ordre de la théorie de la connaissance.

[27] See, David Hume, *Dialogues Concerning Natural Religion*, London: Penguin Books, 1990, 131: "Factions, civil wars, persecutions, subversions of government, oppression, slavery; these are the dismal consequences which always attend [religion's] prevalence over the minds of men." See also John Locke,*An Essay Concerning Human Understanding*, Glasgow: Collins, 1984, 429-30: *Rise of Enthusiasm.* Immediate revelation being a much easier way for men to establish their opinions and regulate their conduct than the tedious and not always successful labour of strict reasoning, it is no wonder that some have been very apt to pretend to revelation, and to persuade themselves that they are under the peculiar guidance of heaven in their actions and opinions, especially in those of them which they cannot account for by the ordinary methods of knowledge and principles of reason. *Enthusiasm.* Their minds being thus prepared, whatever groundless opinion comes to settle itself strongly upon their fancies is an illumination from the Spirit of God, and presently of divine authority; and whatsoever odd action they find in themselves a strong inclination to do, that impulse is concluded to be a call or direction from heaven, and must be obeyed; it is a commission from above, and they cannot err in executing it.

of religious fanaticism (which, in some cases, leads to the negation of human life), madness and solipsism remains, hence the need for a certain degree of rational control, that is, for keeping a balance between the four facultiesthat act as sources of information for conscience.

This is indeed the central stake in the process of individuation as a life-long attempt at confronting the subconscious [the 'not-yet known'], and reconciling conscience and the subconscious; integrating the subconscious into a wider conscience: the Self. David Hume initiated the rational enquiry into the original subjective experience which grounds a man's belief. He thus made it possible and necessary to acknowledge the part of subjectivity, even in those discourses that claim to objectivity, and this operation was developed in the phenomenology of Husserl,[28] which renews the Socratic "know thyself" precept.

Jung often insists on the need to exert the control of reason over the sometimes intrusive images coming from the subconscious, for the risk of being overcome by madness is real. Indeed, he finds the substance for this attempt at rationalisation in alchemy, in mythologies, religions, and, more particularly, in mystical discourses. As soon as he tries to keep a trace of his experience casting it into comprehensible linguistic forms, the mystical author starts performing a rational task.

In this respect, the absence of an overwhelming mystical experience in a subject may even be regarded as an advantage, for it enables one to keep a certain critical distance, and to compare various experiences without being overwhelmingly 'seized' by them. Mystical discourses provide a rich set of accounts of such 'numinous' experiences, and we may look for what they can teach us about ourselves. Our response to a mystical discourse, the echo it will awake in us, is an indication as to what we are, or more exactly as to our state. As Jacob Boehme

---

[28] See, Edmund Husserl, *The Crisis of European Sciences and Transcendental Phenomenology*, Evanston, IL: Northwestern University Press, 1970, 90: Through Berkeley's and Hume's revival and radicalization of the Cartesian fundamental problem, «dogmatic» objectivism was, from the point of view of our critical presentation, *shaken* to the foundations. This is true not only of the *mathematizing objectivism*, so inspiring to people of the time, which actually ascribed to the world itself a mathematical-rational-in-itself (which we copy, so to speak, better and better in our more or less perfect theories); it was also true of the *general objectivism* which had been dominant for millennia.

wrote: "I must exhort the intellect to have a good look into the mirror of intelligence and to contemplate what it is; and to accept to renounce its plan for the senseless building of Babel; it is high time it did so."[29]

In the renewal of the "know thyself" Socratic precept, many examples of readings and responses can be seen as depending on the subject's predisposition. In the perspective of Lockian materialism, for instance, mystical discourses are a simple matter of illusion (Freud belongs to this interpretative trend).[30] In the religious perspective, mystical discourses are genuine testimonies of direct encounters with God. In the Jungian perspective, mystical discourses are allegorical exemplifications of the process of individuation. According to Steve Melanson, Jung's reading of mystical authors may even lead to the definition of a modern form of mysticism that addresses each and every one of us.[31] Through such common notions as "detachment" (from sensation and intellect), divine incarnation as God's birth in the soul, and the mirror, mystical discourses can be read as allegories for the process of individuation, much in the same way as Jung interpreted the discourse of alchemy.

One result is that even when faced with civilisation or global problems, one should prefer individual "progress" to solutions of general systems, whether ethical, religious or metaphysical, political or economic. The confrontation with our own inner experience enables us to become aware of a deeper self: "such an experience will prove to some the truth of Christ, to others, the truth of Buddha, and this to the utmost violence."[32]

[29] Jacob Boehme, *Mysterium Magnum*, Vol. I, 104: Je dois exhorter l'entendement à regarder une bonne fois dans le miroir de l'intelligence et à contempler ce qu'il est; et à bien vouloir abandonner son projet de construction insensée de Babel; il en est grand temps.

[30] See what Freud has to say about it in *L'Avenir d'une illusion*; and remember Marx, to whom religion was the opium of the people.

[31] Steve Melanson, *Jung et la Mystique,* Vannes: Sully, 2009.

[32] C.G. Jung, *Psychologie et Alchimie*, Paris: Buchet-Chastel, 1970, 23 (quoted in Steve Mélanson, *Jung et la mystique*, 63): « une telle expérience prouvera, pour les uns, la vérité du Christ, pour les autres, la vérité du Bouddha, et cela jusqu'à la plus extrême évidence. »

In this second stage of phenomenological reflection, we can become aware of the reason why mystical discourses may vary and even contradict one another (which, in the eyes of the philosophers of the Enlightenment, for a matter for disqualification): "it is only a question of the phenomenology of so-called psychic dominants, whether they be named God, Allah, Buddha, Purusa, Zeus, Planets, the Zodiac or sexuality."[33] Thus, as was pointed out before, there is no longer any quest for a universal truth: "[…] what is valid for oneself is absolutely not so for other individuals with a different psychology. We are in any case far removed from a system of explanation that would be universally valid."[34]

In particular, Jung takes into account the fundamental differences between the Western and Eastern conceptions of mysticism:

> The Christian western world regards man as totally submitted to God's grace, or at least to the church as the only earthly instrument of redemption acknowledged by God. The East, by contrast, remains strong it its belief that man himself is the sole cause for his development; for the East believes in 'self-deliverance'. (…) For us, man is infinitely small, and grace is everything; in the East, man is God and delivers himself.[35]

To Jung, we are indeed prisoners of our own psychic world, in which our perceptions and thoughts are determined by innate archetypes

---

[33] C.G. Jung, *Le Divin dans l'homme*, Paris: Albin Michel, 1999, 209 (quoted in Steve Mélanson. *Jung et la mystique*, 68):« c'est uniquement une question de phénoménologie des dominantes dites psychiques, qu'elles se nomment Dieu, Allah, Bouddha, Purusa, Zeus, Planètes, Zodiaque ou Sexualité. »

[34] C.G. Jung, *L'Ame et le Soi*, Paris: Albin Michel, 1997, 177: «… ce qui vaut pour soi ne vaut absolument pas pour d'autres individus possédant une psychologie différente. Nous sommes donc en tous les cas fort éloignés d'un schéma d'explication qui serait partout valable ».

[35] C.G. Jung, *Psychologie et orientalisme,* Paris, Albin Michel, 1985, 136 et 137 (quoted in Steve Mélanson, *Jung et la mystique*, 155): L'Occident Chrétien considère l'homme comme tout à fait soumis à la grâce de Dieu ou du moins à l'église, seul instrument terrestre de la rédemption qui soit reconnu par Dieu. L'Orient, en revanche, persiste à croire que l'homme lui-même est la seule cause de son développement ; car l'Orient croit en 'l'auto délivrance'. (…) Chez nous, l'homme est infiniment petit, et la grâce est tout; en Orient, l'homme est Dieu et se délivre lui-même.

in us, hence the commons forms in the multiple mythologies of the world. Beyond the apparent variety and contradictions between the different mystical discourses, there exists a deep underlying unity. They can all be seen as manifestations of the collective subconscious through an individuation process that leads to the "Self" (sometimes called "God")... In the course of this rational analysis, phenomenology defines the concept of the *regard constituant* (which is taken up by C.G. Jung when he observes that our conscience is enclosed in a world of psychic representations): there is no longer such a thing as an outside object of study. Every system relies, in the last analysis, on a "constituting outlook" which reflects the subject's inner being and "reality": in this sense, every mystical discourse is a projection, a manifestation of the inner deep-seated "reality" of its author. "Every Eye Sees differently. As the Eye, Such the Object," as William Blake said.[36]

Yet, in the end, the choice between the readings of a mystical experience as a manifestation of God or as a projection of the human subconscious is itself a matter of subjective response and constituting outlook: mystics are not academics, and vice-versa! Just as it might be dangerous to lose control over a mystical experience, imposing too strict a restraint over it can reduce it to merely human dimensions. It is time to ask whether psychology reduces mysticism to its own earthly dimensions, or whether mysticism should be left to lead one to madness.

3. The mystical dimension of psychology: "mysticism unbound".

The boundaries between the two fields seem to disappear, thus leading to the final questions: are we, in the end, to give prevalence to the mystical or to the psychological discourse? Are Jung's psychological considerations a mere imitation of the themes of mysticism (Gnostic, in particular), to which he frequently refers? Or are they an invitation to beware of alluring illusions? Our working hypothesis will be that both discourses proceed from the manifestation of the same archetypes (the "reality" of which cannot spoken of), for instance, that of our spiritual desire to overcome death, because death is the negation of all meaning to material life (in which sense the tragic universe of astronomy can be read as a projection of the despair of materialist scientists). More

[36] William Blake, *Complete Writings*, 456.

fundamentally, all these discourses end up in displaying the conception of man as a mirror to a manifestation that vastly outgrows human dimensions.

Jacob Boehme, for instance, wrote: "There is not one thing that can be God, but God's formed and expressed being, a mirror to the spirit that is called God, in which the spirit manifests itself and, in the joy of his own image, plays with this manifestation which is his created being."[37]Angelus Silesius echoed the idea in the following words: "I carry God's image: if He wants to contemplate Himself. He can only do so in me, He that resembles me.[38]

And we can also read in the *Theologia Germanica*:

> When one acknowledges that Perfection is only the Whole, above everything, it necessarily follows that one ascribes all good, such as being, life, knowledge, power and everything, solely to this Perfection and not to creatures. This is when true inner life begins. In this process, God Himself becomes man, so that there is nothing that be from God, nor God's, nor nothing that take possession of something. It is only God, the eternal, unique and perfect Good, who is there, who lives there, who knows there, loves, can, wills, does and forgets.[39]

This typically mystical idea William Blake condensed in a much shorter formulation: "God only Acts & Is, in existing beings or Men"[40]. And, since archetypes also shape the scientist's ideas, we also find

---

[37] Jacob Boehme, *Mysterium Magnum*, Vol. I, 103: « Il n'y a aucune chose qui soit Dieu mais bien l'être formé et exprimé de Dieu, un miroir de l'esprit qui s'appelle Dieu, où l'esprit se manifeste et, dans la joie qu'il a de lui-même, joue avec cette manifestation qui est son être crée. »

[38] Angelus Silesius, *Le Pèlerin chérubinique*, (premier livre, distique 105, 40, as quoted in Steve Melanson, *Jung et la mystique*, 127): Je porte l'image de Dieu: s'Il veut se contempler/ Il ne peut le faire qu'en moi, Celui qui me ressemble.

[39] *Théologie Germanique*, éd. M. Windstosser, Paris: Arma Artis, 1911, 214:Lorsqu'on reconnaît que le Parfait est uniquement le tout et au-dessus de tout, il en suit nécessairement qu'on attribue tout bien, comme l'être, la vie, la connaissance, le savoir, le pouvoir et toute chose, uniquement à ce Parfait et non aux créatures. C'est alors que commence la vraie vie intérieure.

[40] William Blake, *Complete Writings*, 155.

it manifested in the discourse of modern astronomy, as when Hubert Reeves, after describing the original chaos that followed the Big Bang, writes:

> The billions of billions of particles which compose us are associated, ordered and combined in an organism of a daunting complexity, the behaviour of which is still widely unknown. Thanks to this organization, we are in a position to perceive, and become aware of, our surrounding world. The history of the universe can be told as the tale of this extraordinary metamorphosis.[41]

In this discourse of science, astronomical events since the Big Bang and the evolution of the species on planet earth lead to the emergence of a conscience of the universe through man: this vision is a way of re-injecting meaning in an otherwise tragic universe bound for annihilation[42], by calling upon an archetype:

> This discussion leads to a paradoxical situation. As a product of biological evolution, man *is undoubtedly part of nature*. Yet, by comparison with all living beings, his extraordinary level of performance is an invitation to grant him special status. We can, in a certain way, regard him as standing *outside nature*. This dual situation is a source for ambiguity. Biologist Jean Dausset writes: 'Nature does not speak, it is man that speaks.'

---

[41] Hubert Reeves, *Malicorne, réflexions d'un observateur sur la nature*, Paris: Seuil, 1990, 153: Les milliards de milliards de particules dont nous sommes faits sont associées, agencées, combinées dans un organisme d'une complexité fantastique, dont le comportement nous échappe encore largement. Grâce à cette organisation, nous sommes en mesure de percevoir, et de prendre conscience du monde qui nous entoure. L'histoire de l'univers peut être racontée comme le récit de cette extraordinaire métamorphose.

[42] See, L. Wolpert, *The Unnatural Nature of Science*, London: Faber and Faber, 1993, 146-7: (In the vision of a universe bound for annihilation): the scientist, or anyone else without religion, has to face an indifferent chaos and has to accept that all human hopes and fears, all ecstatic joys and dreadful pains, all the creative torments of scholars, artists, and saints and technicians, are going to vanish for ever, without trace.

It would be equally justified to say that man gives a voice to nature.[43]

In the end, indeed, man is that through which nature becomes conscious: "[Nature] pervades the field of values. Through the advent of moral sense in man, its eyes are open and it becomes responsible. Man is the conscience of nature."[44] And C.G. Jung takes up the same image in psychological terms:

> By virtue of his faculties of reflection, man has raised himself above the animal world, and through his spirit, he is proof that, precisely in the fact of the development of conscience, nature has invested a lot in him. Thanks to this development, he takes possession of nature, acknowledges the existence of the world, and, in so doing, confirms it to the Creator. Thus, the world becomes a phenomenon, which it could not be without a conscious reflection. If the Creator were Self-conscious, he would not need conscious creatures. [...] This is where the miracle of reflected conscience creeps in, the second cosmogony. Conscience matters so much that one cannot help supposing that the element of meaning probably lay hidden in all the drama of this monstrous and apparently senseless biological evolution. Meaning at last has found, as if by chance, a means of self-manifestation at the warm-blood level of the differentiated brain, not in any intentional nor predicted way, but in a fashion that was foreshadowed through an 'obscure impulse', both intuitive and tentative.

---

[43] Hubert Reeves, *Malicorne*, 157: Cette discussion nous mène à une situation paradoxale. En tant que produit de l'évolution biologique, l'être humain *fait indubitablement partie de la nature*. Pourtant, en regard de l'ensemble des êtres vivants, son extraordinaire niveau de performance nous invite à lui accorder un statut spécial. On peut, d'une certaine façon, le considérer comme *hors de la nature*. Cette double situation est une source d'ambiguïté. Le biologiste Jean Dausset écrit: 'La nature *ne parle pas*, c'est l'être humain qui parle.' Il serait tout aussi défendable de dire que l'être humain *donne une voix* à la nature.

[44] Hubert Reeves, *Malicorne*162: « [la nature] investit le domaine des valeurs. Par l'avènement du sens moral chez les humains, elle ouvre les yeux et devient responsable. L'homme est la conscience de la nature ».

[…] The hypothesis of a latent meaning provides man with a cosmogonic significance, a true "raison d'être".[45]

In the end, Jungian psychology finds in mysticism further ground for taking into account of experience of intuition, while acknowledging that this faculty is only one among four, the balance of which should be respected. Mysticism also provides an opportunity for reasserting the legitimacy of supra-materialism in the face of Locke and his followers (and modern western civilization). Rational analysis enables the phenomenologist psychologist to account for the contradictory multiplicity of mystical discourses in terms of the subject's disposition or state; and rationalizing mystical experiences makes it possible to integrate the archetypes of the subconscious into conscience, thus opening the way towards the larger personality of the "Self". This is making the fruits of mysticism accessible even to those who do not receive "grace": there is no "elitism" in Jungian psychology, much in accordance with Blake's prophetic poetry when it stated: "Every honest man is a prophet"[46]. Jung reasserts the legitimacy of mystical discourses and their link with everyday life, without reducing them to the dimension of projections of sexual fantasies: if he calls "God": the "Self" or the "subconscious", the meaning is the same, and the life-long process of individuation reintroduces meaning into life by acknowledging the co-existence of its two dimensions, corporeal and spiritual.

[45] C.G. Jung, *Ma Vie*. 384-5 et 427: En vertu de ses facultés de réflexion, l'homme s'est élevé hors du monde animal et, par son esprit, il démontre que, précisément dans le fait du développement de la conscience, la nature a investi un grand prix en lui. Grâce à ce développement, il s'empare de la nature, reconnaît l'existence du monde, et, par cela même, le confirme en quelque sorte au Créateur. De ce fait, le monde devient un phénomène, ce qu'il ne serait pas sans réflexion consciente. Si le Créateur était conscient de Lui-même, il n'aurait nul besoin de créatures conscientes. […] C'est ici que se glisse le miracle de la conscience réfléchie, seconde cosmogonie. L'importance de la conscience est tellement vaste que l'on ne peut s'empêcher de supposer que l'élément sens gisait probablement caché dans toute la mise en scène biologique, monstrueuse et apparemment insensée, sens qui a enfin trouvé, comme par hasard, à se manifester à l'échelon du sang chaud et du cerveau différencié, non pas de façon intentionnelle ni prévue, mais comme pressentie à travers une 'impulsion obscure', intuitive et tâtonnante. […] L'hypothèse d'un sens *latent* confère à l'homme une signification cosmogonique, une véritable 'raison d'être'.

[46] William Blake, *Complete Writings*, 392.

To conclude, contrary to what a Freudian psychoanalytical interpretation could suggest, sexual imagery in mystical texts is not necessarily a projection of man's sexual fantasies, but may symbolically refer to the primal spiritual realities of creation (which by all accounts escape our apprehension). To Jacob Boehme, indeed, the visible world is a symbol for the invisible[47], hence the determining character of the choice between materialism and supra-materialism, which will determine our reading of the world, on the ground of a feeling of truth.

The main contribution of mythologies, religions, and attention paid to the subconscious generally (as the "not yet known") is that they can provide efficient antidotes against the tragedy of modern conscience, which, according to Jung, is severed from its roots. Being a source for meaning, these roots can be a source for ethics, and as such point to the shortcomings of the techno-scientific vision of the world, economic globalisation, the consumer society with its inbred lack of respect for "mother nature", and the widening gap between rich and poor (which is the antithesis of a humanity in quest of a unified whole!).

The Jungian reading of mythological and mystical discourses is not an attempt to reduce them to the dimensions of psychology: rather, it aims at reasserting their value and legitimacy in a world that tends to disregard them as "disconnected" with reality, and is apparently unable to stop its meaningless race towards catastrophe. The archetype of the mirror, at play in mysticism and psychology (and even in science) implies that man, even if he is a necessary instrument for a manifestation of cosmic dimensions, can no longer claim to be the focal point of creation, nor an end in himself. Individuation enables the subject to reach beyond the individual, towards the universal in which he is no longer the same individual.

In the end, may I humbly suggest that talking about mysticism in a country in which human misery can still be seen in its most cruel forms is not beside the point: for it is in countries such as this, in which immemorial traditions are still at hand, that lies the last possibility

[47] See Jacob Boehme,*Mysterium Magnum*, Vol. 1, 49: Si nous considérons le monde visible avec son être et que nous considérons la vie des créatures, nous y trouvons alors un symbole du monde invisible selon l'esprit qui est latent dans le monde visible comme l'âme dans le corps, et nous voyons que le Dieu caché est proche de toit et compénètre tout, tout en restant parfaitement caché à l'être visible.

for modern mankind to find the means and the strength to give a new orientation to the western model of development, even as it claims to become global, bearing in mind the supra-material stakes defined by mysticism (without bounds), as expressed for instance in these lines about God: "Nowhere is he far from something or close to it, He is everywhere and in everything, his birth takes place everywhere, and outside him nothing exists. He is time and eternity, cause and absence of cause, and only true intelligence which is none other than God himself may grasp him."[48] This task, which aims at the level of civilization, mirrors the main stakes of the process of individuation on a personal level: it also requires the mediation of reason, which is why Jung preferred the concept of the subconscious to that of God: "I prefer the term « subconscious », perfectly knowing that I could as well speak of 'God' or 'demon' if I wanted to express myself mythically."[49]

Works Cited

1. Blake, William, *Complete Writings*, ed. Geoffrey Keynes, Oxford: Oxford University Press, 1972.
2. Boehme, Jacob, *De la Triple vie de l'homme*, Plan de la Tour, Editions d'aujourd'hui, 1982.
3. Boehme, Jacob, *Mysterium Magnum*, Plan de la Tour: Editions d'aujourd'hui, 1978.
4. Carnap, Rudolph, "Theories and Nonobservables" in J. Fetzer, ed. *Foundations of Philosophy of Science,* New-York: Paragon House, 1993.
5. Cazenave, Michel, *La Science et les figures de l'âme,* Monaco, éd. Du Rocher, 1996.
6. Hume, David, *A Treatise of Human Nature*, Oxford: Clarendon Press, 1983.
7. Hume, David, *Dialogues concerning Natural Religion*, London: Penguin Books, 1990.
8. Husserl Edmund. *The Crisis of European Sciences and Transcendental Phenomenology*, Evanston, IL: Northwestern University Press, 1970.
9. Jung, C.G., *Le Divin en l'homme*, Paris: Albin Michel, 1999.
10. Jung, C.G., *Ma Vie*, Paris: Gallimard, 1973.

[48] Jacob Boehme, *Mysterium Magnum*, Vol. I, 57: Nulle part il n'est loin ou près de quelque chose, il est par Tout et en Tout, sa naissance est partout, et en dehors de lui il n'existe rien. Il est le temps et l'éternité, la Cause et l'Absence de cause, et seule peut l'étreindre l'intelligence véritable qui n'est autre que Dieu lui-même.

[49] C.G. Jung, *Ma Vie,* 382-3: « …je préfère le terme d''inconscient', en sachant parfaitement que je pourrais aussi bien parler de 'Dieu', ou de 'démon', si je voulais m'exprimer de façon mythique ».

11. Jung, C.G., *Présent et avenir*, Paris: Buchet-Chastel, 1962.
12. Jung, C.G., *Psychologie et Alchimie*, Paris: Buchet-Chastel, 1970.
13. Jung, C.G., *Psychologie et orientalisme*, Paris, Albin Michel, 1985.
14. Jung, Carl Gustav, *L'Ame et le Soi*, Paris: Albin Michel, 1997.
15. Lardreau, Guy, *Discours philosophique et discours spirituel: autour de la philosophie spirituelle de Philoxène de Mabbourg,* Paris: Seuil, 1985.
16. Locke, John, *An Essay concerning Human Understanding*, London: Penguin, 1997.
17. Melanson, Steve, *Jung et la Mystique*, Vannes: Sully, 2009.
18. Monod, Jacques, *Le Hasard et la nécessité*, Paris: Seuil, 1970.
19. Reeves, Hubert, *Malicorne, réflexions d'un observateur sur la nature*, Paris: Seuil, 1990.
20. *Théologie Germanique*, ed. M. Windstosser, Paris: Arma Artis, 1911.
21. Wolpert, L., *The Unnatural Nature of Science*, London: Faber and Faber, 1993.

10

'Cosmo-theandric' Mysticism

Contemporary Scientific Views

Dr. Thomas Manikkam
Department of Philosophy
Faculty of St. John Vianney Seminary, Pretoria, South Africa

1. Contemporary Scientific Cosmology- 'The Expanding Universe'

According to the scientific observations of astronomer Edwin Hubble (1889-1953) with the concurred support of Albert Einstein, Stephen Hawking and many others, this universe is a "continuously expanding multi-billion galaxy system." In the light of this scientific cosmology of the "Expanding Universe" the contemporary theologians interpret this fantastic expanse of the universe as set in motion by a "designer" God who governs it with immanently interacting laws of rhythmic motions, and as such this universe indicate intrinsic values for all subsystems including our planet Earth together with all its living and non-living components. Just as every part of the human body is important so also every part of the universe is important for its smooth functioning as set by God's all comprehensive and all enveloping presence in every cosmic unit. Each part inherits an organic value from the value of the whole system of the universe. So observes ecologist Freya Mathews:

> Our world is an expression of a selfhood, of a cosmic will-to-exist, and as such has a meaning, and a value, that would not attach to a purely `blind' and contingent world. There is in this sense an element of affirmation and fulfilment in the

> existence of every physical thing. Even the rocks call forth a certain reverence in the light of their participation in this great act of self-realization on the part of the cosmos.[1]

According to ecologist, Arne Naess, even non-human life forms have values in themselves and contribute to the flourishing of the manifold life forms in the universe and on earth. Natural entities are to be respected for their own sake instead of regarding them only as means to achieve our individualistic goals. We lose friends when we use them as means for our selfish interest; we lose the pristine quality of nature by regarding it only as a means for our own personal utility. Naess is happy to give Nature its due role and respect. He assigns an ontological status to tertiary qualities in things. He feels that if all the qualities are projections of the human subject then we would get "the thing in itself" about which nothing is known, may be interesting but not informative. Hence, what St. Paul wrote to the Corinthian Community- "All things are related to you and meant for you, while you are related and meant for Christ, and Christ is related to God, His Father, and God will be all in all (I Cor.15:28).This is the holistic picture of relationship and interrelationship of the whole universe to humankind and finally to God. This vision should inspire us to love and respect all creation in their respective roles in the "*Harmony of God's Hymn of the Universe,"* to borrow a phrase from the beautiful book of Teilhard de Chardin - *The Hymn of the Universe.*

2. Scientific Bases for a Holistic Vision of the Universe, Planet Earth and Human Mind

Quantum physics rewrote the classical physics' conception of a static, fixed container like universe with ultimately separable constituents. According to the observed findings of biological and ecological world views emerging from Quantum physics, the universe is no longer seen as a machine, made up of a multitude of objects, but has to be viewed as one indivisible, dynamic whole whose parts are essentially interrelated and can be understood only as patterns of a cosmic process.

[1] Freya Mathews, *The Dancing of Wu Li Masters: An Overview of the New Physics,* New York: Bantam Books, 1980, 281.

The universe as whole including our planet earth generalized under the common term "The Nature" is a dynamic web of relations with its own overall self-consistency that compels us to recognize that, our human consciousness is, after all, an essential aspect of the universe. According to G. Bateson, the author of *Mind and Nature: A Necessary Unity* (1988), ourmental process is always a sequence of interactions between the various elements of reflection and awareness, what is generally called as 'Human Consciousness'.The explanation of our mental phenomena must always reside in the organization and interaction of multiple parts. The mental function is immanent in the interaction of parts, and the "wholes" are constituted by such combined interaction of differentiated parts.[2]

Life and mind are inbuilt in the dynamics of the self-organization of this universe. Human individual minds are only subsystems of larger manifestations of Mind at the cosmic level. There are levels of mind corresponding to the stages of cosmic evolution. When the mind-matter dichotomy lingers on, it is difficult to see the world as having any mental wave to qualify it as `mindful'. But, in the stratified order of Nature, individual human minds are embedded in the larger Mind of the Cosmos, and these are integrated into the planetary mental system which in turn must participate in some kind of Universal or Cosmic Mind.[3]

Fritjof Capra, an eminent ecologist andauthor of some bestsellers – *The Turning Point*[4], *The Tao of Physics,* etc., sees no hitch in associating this Cosmic Mind with the traditional idea of God. He reflects that God is 'the mind of the universe'.[5] Erich Jantisch, the author the controversial book, *The Self-Organizing Universe* (1980) has a very significant observation to make: "The God-idea does not stand above or outside of the evolution of the cosmos as an ethical norm, but it is placed in true mysticism unfolding into a self-realization of evolution."[6]

---

[2] G. Bateson, *Mind and Nature: A Necessary Unity,* New York: Bantam Books, 1988, 99.

[3] G. Bateson, *Mind and Nature,* 100.

[4] Fritjof Capra, *The Turning Point*, New York: Bantam Books, 1982,317.

[5] Fritjof Capra, *The Tao of Physics: An Exploration of the Parallels between Modern Physics and Eastern Mysticism,* London: Fontana Paperbacks, 1985, 11.

[6] Erich Jantisch, *The Self-Organizing Universe*, Oxford: Pergamen Press, 1980, 308.

Erich Jantisch in his more spiritually conceived book – *Origins of the Sacred: The Ecstasies of Love and War* (1993) makes a very pertinent observation that the scientific world is, at last, coming to see the intuition of the ancients. He observes that when a physicist says that matter doesn't exist, and is *really* just a mistaken epiphany of the energy-gods, he has almost come full circle, very close to the primitive animist who knows that everything is alive, and derives its liveliness from the winds of pneuma that blows through it.

For George Wald the physical and psychical are complementary aspects of the same reality. His views are serious and thought provoking:

> If I say the stuff of the world is mind-stuff that has a metaphysical ring. But, if I say that ultimate reality is expressed in the solutions of the equations of quantum mechanics, quantum electro-dynamics, and quantum field theory - that sounds like good, modern physics. Yet what are these equations? –indeed, what is mathematics, but mind-stuff? Virtually the ultimate is mind-stuff and for that reason deeply mysterious; [...] the universe of space and time and elementary particles and energies, is then an avatara, the materialization of primal mind.[7]

The new physics seems to chart a new course entering the domain of mysticism. Appreciating the Indian Unitary Vision of Reality, Michael Talbot, a scientist turned spiritual writer says, that matter is a condensed energy form of Consciousness (*chit*) itself. As it is written in *Mundaka Upanishad*, by Energy, Consciousness of God or the unbroken Ultimate Reality is meant; from that One is born life, mind and the worlds."[8]

Further, the cosmic law of unity and interconnectedness is echoed in the words of Richard Dawkins, the author of *The Blind Watchmaker* (1986):

---

[7] George Wald, "Life and Mind in the Universe," Paper presented in the Seminar of NCERT, New Delhi, February 1987.

[8] Michael Talbot, "Mysticism and New Physics," cited by Jitatmananda in *Complete Works of Sri Aurobindo,* Vol. 2, Pondicherry: Sri Aurobindo Ashram, 1993, 65.

> Natural Selection, the blind, unconscious, automatic process which Darwin discovered, and which we now know is the explanation for the existence and apparently purposeful form of all life has no purpose in mind. It has no mind…It does not plan for the future…It has no vision…If it can be said to play the role of a watchmaker in nature, it the blind watchmaker.[9]

Steven Weinberg, another great physicist, strikes a similar chord, when he says,

> We like to think that we are very special and that we are not the result of a series of accidents reaching back to the "big bang" but on the contrary we were within the cosmic plan. We don't realize that this homely earth is a tiny part in a really hostile universe and is destined to perish in extreme cold or heat. "The more the universe seems comprehensible, the more it also seems pointless.[10]

There are also critics like Riedel questioning the theories of chance-mutations. Can chance explain everything? Can an orderly universe be the result of mere chance mutations? In fact chance and necessity drive forward the evolution of organisms. Prospects of improvement lie in the realm of accidents, but its success, by necessity, depends on how well an organism adapts to a new situation and a new set up of alignments. When something is selected as normative from the realm of possibilities it enters the realm of necessity. Restricting the number of accidents will increase the prospect that a law of life is being successfully invented during the evolutionary process, restriction of accidents leads to a channelization of possibilities and to subsequent fixation. According to David Bohm, chance and necessary causal interconnections are two sides of every natural process. Neither causal laws nor laws of chance can be basic and final, rather they are approximations. He says:

---

[9] Richard Dawkins, *The Blind Watchmaker,* Essex: Lingman Scientific and Technical, 1986, 5.

[10] S. Weinberg, *The First Three Minutes: A Modern View of the Origin of the Universe*, London: Harper Collins, 1993,149.

> Just as a causal law can arise as a statistical approximation to the average behaviour of a large aggregate of elements undergoing random fluctuations, a law of chance can arise as a statistical approximation to the effects of a large number of causal factors undergoing essentially independent motions.[11]

3. The Universe is a "Divine Milieu"

Some of the foundational concepts we have about God as revealed to us from the Biblical sources are that *God is One Omnipresent,* All Conscious of everything that happens in the universe, almighty, all good, all true, all beautiful, all loving, all merciful, all compassionate, all forgiving, and all just. These are the transcendental qualities attributed in the super-eminent degree to the Ultimate Reality. Almost all human conceptions recorded in the religious annals of the various civilizations, cultures, literatures and scriptures, describe the essential characteristics of the Ultimate Causal Principle behind this universe in these terms of qualities, and this Ultimate Reality had been honored by certain appellations such as *Yahweh, Allah, Alaha, Brahman, Isa, Tao*, Lord, God, etc. The African Traditional Religions have most of the above mentioned transcendental qualities attributed to *Unkulunkulu* "Lord of the Universe." The sages, mystics and even common people of the ancient India, from time immemorial, visualized that this "moving universe is primarily indwelt by the Lord,"and hence this universe is a Divine Milieu, as intuited by the sage of the Isavasya Upanishad who rhymed: "*Isāvāsyam idam sarvam, yat kincha jagatyām jagat,tena tyagtena bhunjidha, ma gridha kasyaswidhanam*" (Isa Upanishad 1). ("This moving world together with all its minute particles is indwelt by the Lord;renouncingit, enjoy it; don't possess the wealth that belongs to somebody else.")

God's immanent presence in this universe makes the whole universe a Sacred Sanctuary, a "Divine Milieu." Since, this universe is primarily His Home, His indwelling habitat, we as His creatures are His "guests," invited to share His own home and his fellowship and hospitality. His invitation for us to share His fellowship, from the moment of our birth

---

[11] David Bohm, *Causality and Chance in Modern Physics*, London: Routledge & Kegan Paul, 1959, 145.

into this world, also includes a sharing of His fellowship with all other beings in His household. We are privileged to share His life with all other fellow beings. Every being/creature in the Household of God has a holistic placement in His immanent Wholeness. We cannot close our eyes pretending not having seen it, or understood it. That is why the Paleontologist turned theologian Teilhard de Chardin described this world as a *Divine Milieu.*

Our earth, and all that are in it, is not an empty space, nor is it a *"no-man's land."* As Raimond Panikkar has rightly argued in his book *the Cosmo-theandric Experience* (Orbis-1993) there cannot be a *"no-man's land in the Land of Being"* who is One and all pervading. The truth is that all that existhad been long - long ago occupied by the Lord of the universe from its foundation, and "His Almighty Power and Divinity are clearly manifested in the Creation of this Universe" as St. Paul wrote in his letter to the Romans (Rom.1:20). From the foundation of this planet, this earth so far explored by our scientists as the only life-sustaining planet had been the house of the "Living God". He is the all enveloping, pervading as well as indwelling "Parent-Principle," generating all life-forms and guiding their ongoing mutation and evolution in their progressive order of species generation, as to survive interdependently, as well as inter-relationally, i.e., holistically. He is constantly giving life and energy to every new "seedling" or "sibling" born into this world, both as its paternal and maternal generative source of life, fertilizing and begetting it into a family of numerous fellow living beings with a right to live and fulfill a set goal of its "being in this world." When a new life is born into this family of living beings, all existing living beings are supposed to welcome the new-comer warmly into their family and "accommodate" it giving its due place in the network of the web of life in the lap of Mother Earth, and Panikkar rightly observes: *It is in the birth of a new life that the Heaven and Earth embrace in a communion of love.*

4. The Cosmotheandric Vision of the Unity of Reality

The "Cosmo-theandric" vision of unity of reality and harmony of God-experience by humans in the universe is a corollary of the reality of the immanent presence of God in the Universe and in the human persons. Although in the western mechanistic world view our universe is generally qualified as a vast space in a process of expansion, meant for the humans to explore, occupy, operate and control, in the Biblical revelation as well as in the ancient world-visions of our forefathers, this universe is a *visvam*, a manifestation of God's presence, and further, as *Bhagavad Gita* says, it is the 'Form of God' - *visvarupam* (*Gita* 11:6). In such a unified and holistic vision of the universe, our human life is also understood as aliving participation in the life of the Divine in close affinity with the Universe, the living environment of mankind and other fellow beings. This is in essence the Cosmo-theandric experience as described by Raimond Panikkar about the unity of Reality – a three dimensional co-existence of the wholeness of One Being in the modes of *cosmos-theos-andronos,* i.e., cosmo-theandric harmony of the wholeness of one Reality in three co-relational modes of existence. Since all life emerge from one source of life, that is the Divine Creative Power, we have to relate ourselves to this divine source (*theos/thea*-divinity) and the *cosmos* (universe) in a harmonious communion of a holistic inter-subjectivity without having any conceptual conflict in our understanding of the unity of the Creator and His Creation, the universe and the humans. In Panikkar's own words the Cosmo-thea-ndric unity is articulated as follows:

> It is neither a merely diving affair, nor a purely human endeavor, nor a blind cosmic process, it is human, divine, and cosmic, all in one…It is cosmic-theandric. God, man and the universe are correlates. God without man is nothing, literally "no-thing". Man without God is exclusively a "thing," not a person, not a real human being, while the world, the cosmos, without man and God is "anything", without consistency and meaning, it is sheer unexisting chaos. The three are constitutively connected.[12]

The Cosmo-thea-andric vision (Universe-God-Humankind Configuration) of the unity of Reality is further highlighted by Scriptural testimonies about the enveloping and indwelling presence of the "*Spirit*

[12] Raimundo Panikkar, *The Vedic Experience: Mantramanjari*, Delhi: Motilal Banarsidass, 1994, 73.

of God hovering over the waters"(*Gen.*1:2), and the same Spirit as *Sophia* (Wisdom) empowered every creature being the dynamic force of everything (Wisdom 7:28-8:1 ff), and the same Spirit according to St. Paul indwells in the heart of every human being (Rom.8:9-11;14-16), empowering us to pray to God, calling God *Abba* – Father.

The same Spirit of God claims to have entered into the heart of everything -- *Sarvasya chāhamhrdi sannivishti. "*And I have inserted myself into the heart of everything"(*Bhagavadgita* 15:15) one of the classical spiritual synthesis of the Vedic and Upanishadic traditions of the ancient seers of India, and this insight is very experiential and highly motivational even for people of contemporary India, may be, the same is very inspiring for all spiritually oriented people all over the world. The divine person Krishna, the Spiritual preceptor of *Bhagavadgita*, identifying himself as the all pervading Divine Spirit, motivates Arjuna, his disciple, to boost up his dwindled spirit and empower himself to do his duty of fighting for righteousness (*dharma*). He was given the insight to feel that the almighty God himself is dwelling within him energizing him. God is said to have not only an overall command over the whole universe, but He has entered into the heart of everything, energizing and enlivening everything from within.

5. Cosmotheandric Experience as a Mystical Contemplation

The Cosmotheandric experience described above is also our contemporary Christian spiritual experience in our life in an "expanding universe," and our mystic experience of its harmony is a spirituality of a lifelong integrating process of our relationship with God in His creation, which is groaning for its progressive unification with the "*Omega point"* of the whole universe which is ever expanding and growing into greater perfection and unification.[13] It consists in the ongoing process of seeking after the wholeness of the truth of this "Divine Milieu" and getting enlightened of it at all the times while we contemplate on its progressive revelation of the truth of this Universe, the "Divine habitat" of our life and that of our fellow beings. This contemplation on the inner mysteries of the universe would motivate us to collaborate with every being in

---

[13] Raimundo Panikkar, *Cosmotheandric Experience- emerging religious consciousness,* New York, Orbis Books, Maryknoll, 1993.

this universe for improving their lot in this process of the liberation of the universe from its decaying deterioration. St. Paul describes this liberation process of the Creation through the collaboration of the 'Sons of God' as follows:

> All of creation waits with eager longing for God to reveal his sons. For Creation was condemned to lose its purpose, not of its own will, but because God willed it to be so. Yet there was the hope that creation itself would one day be set free from its slavery to decay and would share the glorious freedom of the children of God. For we know that up to the present time all of creation groans with pain, like the pain of childbirth. But, it is not just creation alone which groans; we who have the Spirit as the first of God's gifts also groan within ourselves, as we wait for God to make us his children and set our whole being free (Rom.8: 19-23).

Our Cosmotheandric mystical experience of the Divine Harmony in the Universe is also related and open to a Holistic Eco-spirituality which is the spirituality of experiencing "wholeness" and "perfection" of our life lived in interdependence and interrelationship with the whole Creation, while enjoying the "Joy of the Holy Spirit" who is operative in the heart of the universe, in the heart of every human being, who simultaneously envelops and indwells this cosmic habitat while making it a Temple of the Divine, a true Divine Milieu. This vision has its miniature in our own bodies, as St. Paul writes in his first letter to the Corinthians: " Don't you know that your body is the temple of the Holy Spirit, who lives in you and who was given to you by God"(I Cor. 6: 19).

6. Practical Applications of the Cosmotheandric Mystical Experience

The Cosmotheandric vision of the unity of the whole Creation in the One Designer God is also well interpreted by *Ecosophy* and *Quantum Physics,* two of the most advancing philosophical and scientific interpretations of our times. Both as allied branches of cosmological sciences have discovered today numerous links of harmony of relationship of humankind to Nature, the living habitat of all beings, while being herselfremaining a Temple of God. These sciences have also discovered existential and intentionality-relationship of humankind with Nature, and together withher our common inter relationship with God, our common creator. There is an explosion of the spiritual possibilities opening up for humankind to aspire and activate in the future, respecting Nature and serving her like our mother; for in her is manifested the "Almighty Power and Divinity of God from the foundation of this world" (Rom 1:20) and the human consciousness is always awakened from its dormancy by every contact we make with our living habitat, the lap of our Mother Earth. Hence, we need a twofold spiritual awakening today:

a) Be honest and responsive to God's Designs in the Nature, because the divineforce in Nature is the full time active "Almighty Power" permeating the entire universe to activate it making it capable of producing everything that is needed for the sustenance of all creatures. The humankind has no right to arrogate to itself all the potentialities of this mysteriously evolving universe denying its motherly availability to all other creatures. Exploitation, domination, destruction and devastation of the resources of our "Planetary Common Wealth" are to be considered as expressions of arrogant selfishness, self-centeredness and crass negligence over the simple existential rights of all other beings however insignificant they are.
b) Be ready to respect the whole universe, as the house of the living God and our own planet as our own "Sweet Home" because we are invited by God the host of this house to be born into the lap of this Mother Earth which is just one of the fragile homes, which God created as the nurturing and nursing Mother. This Planet Earth nourishes us with all her wonderful life sustaining nutrients for our progressive growth into maturation and perfection as long as we are allowed to be here in this playful courtyard. We are brought to this temporary earthly home of the expanding universe to live here for a short while as playing children in the courtyard of the House of God. As invited guests to the House of God we are not supposed to do anything that is damaging to its sustainability and viability, rather we are obliged to keep this

> house in improved conditions reset for the next generation of the "Children of God" who are awaiting entry into the motherly bosom of our existential cradle of the "Cosmic Expanse." Our short "life is a transit from the womb to the tomb of our Mother Earth," through the mediation of our own beloved mothers; hence respectfully deal with our common Mother Earth just like we respect and honor our own biological mothers!

Cosmotheandric Mysticism, therefore, is based on some of the axioms of Nature's behavior keenly observed by the contemplatives of all times. Such meditative observations on the universe inspired the great masterminds of ancient times as well as of our own times, and they proposed to us to apply some of the basic laws of Nature in the manufacturing of herbal medicines, which are naturally preventive and curative means of holistic treatment of most of the illnesses caused by our estranged relationship with Nature and Natural elements which are supporters of life, such as air, water, moisture, light, and fire. These basic elements of Nature above all favour us to enjoy a peaceful life in harmony with Nature and its various forms of living and non-living beings. Some of the foundational rules of conduct that we should understand and observe in dealing respectfully with the Nature and her productivity and progress are expressed in the form of axioms, such as understanding the "Unity of Nature," "Interdependence of Nature and Atmosphere," "Co-relation of Elements," "Regularity of Species-generation," "Convertibility of energies," "Mutation of Geo-biospheres," etc.

7. Virtues to be practiced for our Harmonious Life on Earth

(i) Grow beyond the 'Culture of Violence' towards Nature, Humanity and God

Practicing non-violence *(ahimsa)* to Nature and natural realities is very basic to cosmo-theandric spirituality. This is also the inspiration behind the well-known three levels of transcending the culture of violence, namely, *manasa- vaca- karmana,* i.e., mental non-violence, verbal non-violence and non-violence in deed. Positively conceived and explained these are to be practiced on three levels of our human consciousness and behavour.

Firstly, mental non-violence is practiced by thinking positive about life and its variety of situations interacted with our living environment, and maintaining a 'feel good' attitude towards the opposite challenges of the various situations of Nature, and deciding in favour of taking 'face the challenge attitude' towards the opposite situations and never taking an escapist or 'damn it' attitude. Eventually, this positive mental disposition will tone us up to be more *tender, serene, compassionate, kind, gentle, friendly as well as to be 'attractive and affectionate' towards others with some extra charm and humor.*

This mental peace-oriented thinking is what is underlying our common expressions of console, like, "*Take it easy*," "*Never mind*," "*Forget it*," etc., and these often do a great psychological service-stroke to our wounded feelings and depressed state of personality. Sri Buddha, Sri Krishna and Jesus Christ, Francis Assisi, Mahatma Gandhi and many other great personalities this patient Mother Earth generated in the past are heroic examples of this great multi-faceted virtue called "non-violence": non-violence first towards ourselves, then towards our living environment consisting of the "lilies of the field," the "sparrows of the air," "the doves of the fields," "the snake peeping out of its hiding hole," the honey bees of our gardens, the dolphins of our oceans, the ant-lines of our roadways, the anthills of our lands, and all such curious creatures of God's Creative Word. They are all there as wonderful creatures of our Nature, teaching us inspiring lessons of being 'innocent,' 'simple,' 'humble,' 'wise,' 'loving,' 'co-operative', 'kind,' 'endearing,' 'charming,' 'self-reliant' and hard working, and yet depending on Somebody Who provides for them all day and night. Why should we think of doing violence to their habitats? Let us think of a policy of "live and let live" and never destroy anything that God has set in motion to play the dance of Nature in the wider Cosmic Expanse.

Secondly, verbal non-violence is avoiding angry words, abusive language, condemnatory or cursing expressions in our conversation with others, even when others may be using them against us. Positively described, verbal non-violence is speaking complimentary words about others in view of encouraging them and appreciating their goodness and achievements, not as flattery but as sincere expressions of regards and well wishing. It consists also in soft speaking to other human beings and not shouting at them, even if they are our subordinates, babies or children. Verbal non-violence has to be practiced by observing the niceties of courtesies and etiquettes in social interactions. Non-violence in words also implies to engage in edifying discourses and never enter into quarrelsome arguments with our fellow humans. Such heated arguments generate disturbing waves of "sound pollution" in our living environments, domestic as well as working places disturbing the mental peace of all others. Angry words of superiors and higher officers generate 'fear complexes,' 'phobias' and hatred in the minds of the subordinates and these destroy spontaneity, creativity and enthusiasm for doing their prescribed duties.

Thirdly, non-violence in deedsis avoiding all forms of violent actions, such as physical attacks, blows, beating, hitting, shooting, looting, raping, murder etc. Positively described, whatever we do to promote good relationships between persons, environments, families, communities and assemblies as well as maintaining "law and order" in chaotic situations, are all deeds which promote peace and harmony in the Nature and in the Society of human transactions and interactions.

Our practice of *ahimsa* is not to be compromised with the western materialistic ideology of exploitation of Nature under the pretext of "progress and development." The western industrialists, who have de-sacralized and irreparably polluted their own countries' geographical areas of this planet, have recently started polluting the natural environments of the developing countries' water ways, forests and their plain lands by dumping toxic wastes like atomic reactor's waste loads, chemical and other industrial discharges from their factories. This is institutionalized sins against humanity under the pretext of global development and global marketing. The right word for this kind of atrocities of the industrial giants is 'exploitation' of the patience of the larger populations the developing nations and "gross violation of the patience" of Mother Earth. They are also insensitive to the human rights of the peoples of the developing countries.

Already some of the world class manufacturing giants like Coco-Cola and Pepsi Cola have exploited, spoiled and polluted the water resources and the living environments of millions people of the developing countries, endangering their sane and safety means of healthy life– all under the tantalizing banner with the confusing slogan of "industry for progress"! Is consumerist industry alone to be considered progressive? If it is so, then we are blindly led to the tragedy of a catastrophe of suffering from the "Poverty of the Spirit".

To prevent this catastrophe we need challenge these industrial giants and their behaviour in the court of Law as the people of the village of Plachimada, in north Kerala, India, have done recently. These people could legally stop the Coco-Cola giant from continuing polluting the drinking water wells of the local people by means of proper court orders. They have shown effectively the values for good living and right ways of sustainable development, in tune with the "values of sanity and sanctity" as well as values of "sparing and sharing," in the true spirit of "non-violence in deed" towards Nature, our motherly habitat, as well as to our own homes and their neat and tidy environments.

(ii) Practice the Spirituality of Renunciation (*tyagtena bhunjeedha)*

From the vision of this world as 'God's dwelling place' both in and out, there emerges a spirituality of *balanced enjoyment* of the goods of this world, and not an exploiting consumerism at the expense of the less privileged. The instruction, *tyagtena bhunjeedha* (enjoy (this world) while being ready to renounce the excess) is a wise exhortation given by the sage of *Isavasya Upanishad* quoted above. It is a spiritual maxim as well as an ethical norm of using this world, and it derived logically from our vision of the world as a "Divine Milieu." It is God's world offered to us to enjoy moderately sharing with all its inhabitants. Since this world belongs to God, and we are all His invited guests to His home, we humans have to see that we share the blessings of the House of God always*with a spirit of renunciation of something for the benefit of our fellow beings.* This renunciation is not a negative attitude to the goods of this world but a positive decision to share the goods with a community sensitivity. Because as guests we are all equals before the host who brought us all to this "House of His Being" sharing his Beingness with all his creatures.

It is interesting to note here, that this instruction of the *Isavasya* Upanishad was first imparted to the students of ancient schools which were the houses of great masters *(Gurukulas)*, where all students irrespective of their family ancestry or caste differentiation were instructed to treat each other with equal respect and share everything of the *Gurukula* with a sharing and sparing fraternal concern. This was the ideal of good egalitarian education backed up by a concern of fraternity lived and experienced in the Gurukulas of ancient India, where the invisible Real *Guru* was the Lord of the Universe, who was represented by the person of the teaching *Guru* of the *Gurukula.*

(iii) Practice the Ethics of Non-possessiveness (*mā gridhā kasyaswiddhanam)*

Just like there developed a Spirituality of renunciation and sharing on the basis of the Eco-theology explained above as is evident from the *Isavasya Upanishad* and *Bhagavad Gita*, there is also derived an *Ethics of Non-possessiveness and Non-aggressiveness*. A good eco-theology generally highlights a goodmorality and an ethics for practical life in harmonious relationship with the entire creation. This is so because the interrelationship between theory (*theorea)* and practice (application of the vision in life) has been considered to be flowing logically and spontaneously making the theory as the fountain of the practice. Faith and morals had been understood as so integrally connected from the beginning of human culture. Hence, we have the foundation of a non-possessive and non-aggressive ethics. Transact the wealth of the house of God without having any possessive attitude over it. Because the whole world all that is in it belong to the Lord of the universe. Hence, *ma gridha kasyaswiddhanam* – don't arrogate or possess the wealth that belongs to somebody else. We are only allowed to use it in as much as we need it and not to possess it as to feed our greed on it. It is an "ethics of need" and not an "ethics of greed" that is propounded in the Upanishads in general, especially in *Isavasya Upanishad.* Thus, a good Eco-theology paves way for a balanced economic transactional system based on the needs of everybodyand not controlled by the greed of somebody.

8. To be Kind toward our 'Mother House', the Planet Earth

Imaging earth as mother can be helpful to stop our conflict with nature and to nurture an ecological worldview. The capacity to generate and nurture all forms of life makes earth eminently feminine. But, today for some people earth is *material and not yet maternal.* The earlier mother-offspring relation turned into one of resource-exploiter; respect and veneration gave way to greed andthe urge to conquer and possess. It is ironical to view humankind, the one-time offspring of Mother Earth now aggressively trying to be the lord of the same Mother!! This attitude has resulted in the rape and pillage of the earth and her degradation to be waste land, as if she is a "No-Man's Land". But, it must be an all time truth that in the "Land of God, there is no 'No-man's land'.

Therefore, in the wake of the ecological crisis today, it will be good for us to retrieve our lost consciousness about this universe. This expanding universe is a fully God- occupied space that is enveloping us around. It is in "His Holy, Mysterious and Silent Presence" which is always "expanding" not under the controlling power of any human agency. We are privileged to gaze and even telescope into this wonderful Cosmic Expanse of more than two billion galaxies (recent pictures taken by Hubble's Telescope) and enjoy its grandeur and magnitude and be taken up again and again by the great "Wonder" our ancient visionaries were having. This is an aspect of the Cosmotheandric Mystical vision of the Universe which any human being of good fantasy can visualize and contemplate to experience the glory of God shown up there in the Expanding Universe as well as enjoying the smiling face of our own Planet Earth in every turn of her Seasons, and this must be our true "Cosmotheandric Experience."

9. Respect Feminine Characters of Earth as Generating *Shakti* or *Gaia*

Feminization of Nature implies the idea of *Shakti* or creative energy and its inherent power of synergy according to Indian mythological and aesthetic traditions. The same feature had been visualized by the ancient Greek cosmic mythologies under the symbol of *Gaia*. The concept of *Sakti,* as the primordial creative power, is the feminine potency of mother earth. This has been variously described in some of the Indian

Puranas like *Devi-Mahatmyam*, and philosophically interpreted in the Vedantic school of *Saiva Sidhanta.* Behind the nature- personification is the insight into the law of nature as the force of *rta* that sustains the world. It provides humans with a sound norm for environmental ethics. Human culture must be integral with the laws of nature. Feminization of nature also shows the feminine dimension of reality, a dimension, the patriarchal culture of some dominant civilization had lost long ago. Recovery of this dimension can enrich our lives. It will imply the appreciation of the feminine dimension of reality in all its different realms: divine, human and natural. In order to recover the feminine principle of the Divine Harmony active in the progressive evolution of the expanding universe we have to perceive Nature as alive represented by our motherly women as co-creatrix with the divine Shakti bringing forth new babies into the house of the Divine *Shakti,* who is equally describable as motherly *Gaia* encompassing and indwelling the whole universe rather than remaining as a transcendental supervisor far away from the accessibility of the Creation.

Maternity of Nature is not just a mythological or cultural symbol but a scientific truth. A tree cares for the seed with great precaution surrounding the embryo with layers of protective substances and storing around it the first nutrients it needs when a seed breaks out of its shell as a living sapling. In the lower levels of nature motherhood exists in humble forms. In the mammalian stage there is a strict bond of communion between the mother and child. The universe itself appears to have a feminine dimension. For, in the so-called barrenness or emptiness of atmosphere there are the microscopic seeds of the *phyktoplantans* which germinate in the steady waters or pools making the whole base green; and these little micro-plants cluster to form algae, hair like net work of water lilies which form a webof interrelated organic life-system which becomes the breeding ground for many other fungus kinds. The profound mysteries of life are handed down to us through symbols; and symbols give rise to thoughts. The mother symbol engenders in us visions of harmony and peace, and it also evokes respect. Our human task is to respond appropriately to the feminine dimension of Nature which is another dimension of the Cosmotheandric Mysticism.

10. Shift from Anthropocentrism to Cosmotheandric Holism

We have to develop our consciousness more and more eco-friendly, a consciousness which will involve a transition from anthropocentrism to eco-centrism, an awareness of our rootedness in the *womb of mother earth* much more than our dominating 'headship' over her. Our consciousness of our situatedness in the bosom of Mother Earth must be that of an infant, as we were all once infants playing in the lap of our own mothers, were sucklings of the breasts of our mothers, so are we all doing even as we have become adults, sucking the life-giving and nourishing "nectar of Mother Earth," drilling deep into the under-earth storage reservoirs. So, we owe much to our Mother Earth and we have to acknowledge this life-indebtedness to her in all humility, respect and honour, for nurturing us like a foster mother once we are out of our own mothers' womb. Our life journey, then, is to be understood as a holy pilgrimage from the womb to the tomb of Mother Earth.

Hence, let us not be so cruel to poison, contaminate or adulterate this nectar of life, filtered through the numerous porous silt strata of our Mother Earth. The Earth stores the rain water filtered through her silts in her interior rocky cellars, as if in reservoirs well protected from contaminating elements from outside. This is the precious drink we drill out from the womb of Mother Earth; this becomes our new umbilical cord, our life-line connected to this Earth for our survival as long as we are here in her lap. Water is the most energizing life-sap of all living beings. We should not forget the simple biological fact and truth about ourselves, humans, that about 90% of our own body is filled with water and our whole body functions like a sponge soaked in water which lubricates every tissue of our body, making it alive and continuously refreshing it round the clock. So, the water we drink should be pure, safe and uncontaminated with toxic elements from the land surface or from the atmosphere during rainy season. Our drinking water should not be a carrier of disease causing bacteria. This is one of the important warnings ofthe cosmo-theandric vision of Nature to which our life is holistically connected for its survival. This is what is meant here by suggesting to our own options to have a decisive shift from our "anthropocentric adventures on Earth" to a more cosmo-theandric participation in the maintenance of our Mother Earth, by means of our services towards the preservation and replenishment of the life-supporting resources of our Planet Earth, the only life-sustaining habitat in the entire Universe explored so far, which should be scrupulously maintained as a safe home for numerous little infants of our own successive generations who are on the waiting line to be born into this temporal milieu of "The Eternal Divine."

11. Conclusion: Make this World a 'Sweet Home' for all Beings

Most religious traditions sometime exhibit an ascetic undercurrent for self-purification, and when it is overemphasized it goes to the extent of denial or disparagement of the world. It is presupposed that the self and the world are essentially separate and that the one can be heeded ignoring the other. Dubbed as a *maya* or a shadowy realm, the world turned out to be a transit point and ceased to be a real home. It is considered as a battlefield where the forces of good and evil face each other. In this battle any kind of domination can be misinterpreted as God's will because each one thinks that he is on God's side battling the evil. Then, the world is just a background, a proving ground for humans who only matter. The world was also understood as a trap wherein we may get caught up and enslaved. To affirm a transcendental reality in the material realm was looked upon with contempt by negativist spiritual visionaries. But, the sense of detachment from the world does not achieve often the intended sense of detachment from the ego or selfishness of ambitious people. Trying to escape from something that we are dependant on, breeds a love-hate relationship with it. This love-hate relationship with Nature is permeated in our present day consumerist culture, and it inflames a twofold desire: to destroy or possess, crave foror avert from, and this is a conflict inflaming us in a kind of vicious circle of confusion, and yet in our new eco-friendly and "cosmo-theandric" attitude to the Universe we have to resolve it with prophetic vision and wisdom.

Hence, we have to consolidate all our available wisdom today in order to make this planet (*griham*) a "sweet home" for all beings, living and non-living, to live in fellowship and familial partnership, and never get tempted to turn it into a battlefield of aggression, exploitation and possession, nor a prison of locked relationship; but a real household of free-beings, having rights to exist, live and flourish in a God-set environment of freedom, a freedom not to be suppressed by the ego-centric aggressiveness of a few humans, but preserved by all humans with a good sense of stewardship, which God seems to have set in the heart of mankind as the primary precept (*Genesis* 2:15) of the primal partnership of humans in the "Garden of Eden" which God appreciated as "good", "very good"(*Genesis*1:31). Let us also practice the great virtue of generosity (*udarata)* which is the characteristic virtue of those who make this world a home (*kudumbam)* for all beings to live in the freedom of the family of God's creation, remembering the wisdom of our great teachers who defined a home as *udaracharitanam tu vasudhaiva kudumbakam,*"a home, indeed, is the good earth of generous people"(*Hitopadesha* 1:70).

This must be a guideline for living the new cosmo-theandric vision of human life in close co-existential relationship with all other fellow beings in the lap of Mother Earth, our "Sweet Home" on this shore of the flow of time, where we have to strive to grow in loving all beings as "to become perfect as the Heavenly Father is Perfect" (Mt.5:48). This is possible when we expand our love relationship with all beings beyond our private intimacies and personal hatreds, swimming over to the "Further Shore," into the Expanse of God's Holy Presence of timeless Immensity and Mystery, glimpses of which can be only experienced by us if we can open our mystical eyes to see the wonders of this Expanding Universe which is equally extensive to the overwhelming Presence the God who is beyond all astronomical boundaries, as He is Mysteriously and Silently so close to us all that the truth is that "It is in Him we live, we move and have our being" (Acts.17:28).

Select Bibliography

1. Bateson, G., *Mind and Nature: A Necessary Unity,* New York: Bantam Books, 1988.
2. Bohm, David, *Causality and Chance in Modern Physics*, London: Routledge & Kegan Paul, 1959.
3. Cannato, Judy, *Radical Amazement*, Notre Dame, Indiana: Sorin Books, 2006.
4. Capra, Fritjof, *The Tao of Physics: An Exploration of the Parallels between Modern Physics and Eastern Mysticism,* London: Fontana Paperbacks, 1985.
5. Capra, Fritjof, *The Turning Point*, New York: Bantam Books, 1982.
6. Coyne, George V. and Omizzolo, Alessandro, *Way Farers in the Cosmos*, New York: Crossroad Book, 2002.

7. Dawkins, Richard, *The Blind Watchmaker,* Essex: Lingman Scientific and Technical, 1986.
8. Delio, Ilia, *Christ in Evolution,* New York: Orbis Books, 2008.
9. Garon, Henry A., *The Cosmic Mysticque*, New York: Orbis Books, 2006.
10. Jantisch, Eric, *The Self-Organizing Universe*, Oxford: Pergamen Press, 1980.
11. Mathews, Freya, *The Dancing of Wu Li Masters: An Overview of the New Physics,* New York: Bantam Books, 1980.
12. O'Murchu, Darmuid, *Quantum Theology- Spiritual Implications of the New Physics,* New York: A Crossroad Book, Crossroad Publishing Company, 2004.
13. Panikkar, Raimundo, *Cosmotheandric Experience- emerging religious consciousness,* New York: Orbis Books, Maryknoll, 1993.
14. Panikkar, Raimundo, *The Vedic Experience: Mantramanjari,* Delhi: Motilal Banarsidass, 1994.
15. Schoenborn, Christoph Cardinal, *Chance Or Purpose*, San Francisco: Ignatius Press, 2007.
16. Talbot, Michael, "Mysticism and New Physics," cited by Jitatmananda in *Complete Works of Sri Aurobindo,* Vol 2, Pondicherry: Sri Aurobindo Ashram, 1993.
17. Wald, George, "Life and Mind in the Universe," Paper presented in the Seminar of NCERT, New Delhi, February 1987.
18. Weinberg, S., *The First Three Minutes: A Modern View of the Origin of the Universe*, London: Harper Collins, 1993.
19. Wells, Harold, *The Christic Center*, New York: Orbis Books, 2004.

11

Mysticism and Apophaticism without or within Bounds?

Four Contemporary Challenges for Christian Theology in a Western Context

Dr. Lieven Boeve
Faculty of Theology
Katholieke Universiteit Leuven, Leuven, Belgium[1]

It is in his *Mystical Theology* that a Syrian monk, living at the end of the fifth and the beginning of the sixth century, and hiding behind the pseudonym and authority of Dionysius Areopagita (Denys the Areopagite, – the name of the Athenian disciple of Paul [Acts 7, 34]) made a strong connection between mysticism and apophaticism, and, so doing, mystical theology and negative theology – a connection which will influence theology up until today. In his reflection on our naming of, and relationship to God, Pseudo-Denysforges a link between the speculative Neo-Platonism of late antiquity (Proclus) – and its intensive concern for the way in which philosophical language meets its limits in addressing the absolute, the one, the good, the cause of everything –, and traces of apophasis from the Jewish-Christian belief in God (as was reflected

[1] This paper rehearses some of the ideas and texts which I have developed over the last few years. Where appropriate, I will refer to the original publications. For the overall argument, see especially my *Negative Theology and Theological Hermeneutics:The Particularity of Naming God*, in I. Dalferth, K. Schmid & P. Stoellger, eds., *Gott Nennen* (Religion in Philosophy and Theology, 35), Tübingen: Mohr Siebeck, 2008, 191-207.

upon by some of the Patristic Fathers, including Gregory of Nyssa).[2] All names and titles which are predicated of God – theological names such as Trinity, Father, Son, Spirit; intelligible or conceptual names as the good, one, beauty, truth, life, love; representations of the experiential world as sun, rock, water, wind –, all have a strictly 'symbolic' nature: they do not exhaust the divine essence, or make God knowable. They are names referring to what is beyond all names, beyond all naming. Only through the negation of these names can one create a space for God. Not a single name can be spared: neither images borrowed from everyday experience, nor abstract concepts, nor revealed divine names or titles. In the end, only negations can be true. For sure: at stake in this never ending process of negating, is not the negation of God, but the affirmation of the impossibility of naming and conceiving God. In the negation and in the negation of the negation, Pseudo-Denys attempts to evoke what cannot stand evocation through language. Finally, what should be observed hereis that, for Pseudo-Denys, negative theology stands not on its own, but belongs intrinsically to the mystical (non-) experience of God.[3] It therefore "is not merely *apophasis* but *aphasia*, a devout and learned silence."[4] Negative theology serves the cause of the mystical relationship of human beings to God.

Ever since, at many instances negative theology and/or its procedures have been called upon whenever both theologians and philosophers engage in a reflection on knowledge of, and/or relationship to 'God', 'Transcendence', 'Being', 'Otherness', 'Difference' – to that what surpasses creation, world, being, language, etc. Also today the link between mysticism, mystical experience, relationship to transcendence, otherness, difference, and negative theology is made again. In the

[2] Cf. D. Carabine, *The Unknown God. Negative Theology in the Platonic Tradition: Plato to Eriugena*, Leuven: Peeters, 1995, 279-300. See also J. Hochstaffl, *Negative Theologie. Ein Versuch zur Vermittlung des patristischen Begriffes*, München: Kösel, 1976; and R. Mortley, *From Word to Silence. II. The Way of Negation, Christian and Greek*, Bonn: Hanstein, 1986. For *The Mystical Theology*: *Pseudo-Dionysius. The Complete Works*, trans. C. Luibheid, New York: Paulist Press, 1987.

[3] Cf. D. Turner, *The Darkness of God: Negativity in Christian Mysticism*, Cambridge: Cambridge University Press, 1995.

[4] F. O'Rourke, *Pseudo-Dionysius and the Metaphysics of Aquinas* (Studien und Texte zur Geistesgeschichte des Mittelalters 32), Leiden: Brill, 1992, 61.

following we will shortly elaborate on four different constellations in which mystical experience and negative theology would seem to appear today: (a) philosophical dealings with negative theology, (b) cultural dealings with religion and spirituality, (c) interreligious comparative dealings with mysticism, and (d) scientific dealings with mystical experiences. We will reflect on these four cases from a Western cultural-theological perspective, and investigate how Christian mystical experience and the accompanying negative theology can face the challenges coming forth from them in view of an appropriate contemporary theological assessment of both.

1. The Rediscovery of Negative Theology in 'Post-Ontotheological 'Philosophy: Beyond Christian Faith?

After decades in which mainstream philosophy showed a lack of interest in religion, a wide range of philosophers, belonging to the phenomenological and/or hermeneutical tradition – denoted as 'continental philosophy' across the Atlantic – have placed the theme of religion on their philosophical agenda, and this often in relation to their attempts to overcome 'ontotheology,' namely, the philosophical attempt to ground (and signify) the whole of being in an ultimate being, a first cause which is its own cause, God.[5] It is noteworthy that in this turn to religion, these philosophers often introduce negative-theological thinking patterns, sometimes with explicit reference to Jewish-Christian apophatical traditions. Some pertinent examples in this respect include: Jean-Luc Marion,[6] Richard Kearney,[7] Jacques Derrida, John Caputo, etc. We briefly present some of the latter's ideas in this regard.[8]

---

[5] A fine introduction in this subject is to be found in J. Schrijvers, *Ontotheological Turnings? The Decentring of the Modern Subject in Recent French Phenomenology*, New York: SUNY Press, 2011.

[6] J. L. Marion, *In the Name: How to Avoid Speaking of 'Negative Theology'*, in J. D. Caputo and M. J. Scanlon, eds., *God, the Gift, and Postmodernism*, Bloomington, Indiana University Press, 1999, 20-53.

[7] R. Kearney, *The God Who May Be: A Hermeneutic of Religion*, Indiana: Indiana University Press, 2001

[8] For these paragraphs, and an elaboration of other examples, see my *Negative Theology and Theological Hermeneutics*, and *The Rediscovery of Negative Theology Today: The*

Deconstructionist thinkers such as Derrida try to radicalise the hermeneutical turn of philosophy. For him, only a hermeneutics that deconstructs all signification to an originary differential space ('différance'), which is presupposed by and makes possible all discourse, is radical enough.[9] The later Derrida, herein emphatically accompanied by John Caputo and others, expresses the dynamics of deconstruction, and the corresponding critical consciousness, in explicitly religious vocabularies. This results in a so-called 'radical hermeneutics of religion' that seeks to determine the 'religious' in terms of 'religion without religion,' which reduces religion to a universal structure of religious desire. As another way of expressing this structure of religious desire Derrida and Caputo indicate the 'messianic structure' recognised in, but at the same time distinguished from the various particular messianisms.[10] As a matter of fact, this radical hermeneutics results – at least in Caputo's reception – in a kind of (philosophical) negative theology that expresses, beyond concrete discourse and particularity, a 'religiously being related to' that which lies at the origin of every particular religious discourse, but is betrayed in every attempt to name it. Caputo indeed strives to uncover the structure of 'pure prayer,' that is, a relation of the subject to a 'You' while at the same time deferring the question whether this 'You' in effect exists.[11] He is concerned, as it were, with retrieving a form of spirituality uncontaminated with particularity and narrativity to the point of dropping (reducing) the presupposition that there is a 'You' to whom or to which the prayer is

Narrow Gulf between Theology and Philosophy, in M. Olivetti, ed., *Théologie négative* (Biblioteca dell' 'Archivio di Filosofia', 59), Rome: CEDAM, 2002, 443-459.

[9] Cf. J. Derrida, *L'écriture et la différance*, Paris: Seuil, 1967.

[10] Cf. J. Derrida, *Comment ne pas parler. Dénégations*, in J. Derrida, *Psychè. Inventions de l'autre*, Paris: Galilée, 1987, 535-595; *Sauf le nom*, Paris: Éditions Galilée, 1993; *Foi et savoir. Les deux sources de la «religion» aux limites de la simple raison*, in J. Derrida & G. Vattimo, eds. *La religion. Séminaire de Capri sous la direction de Jacques Derrida et Gianni Vattimo*, Paris: Éditions du Seuil, 1996, 9-86; J.D Caputo, *The Prayers and Tears of Jacques Derrida. Religion without Religion*, Bloomington: Indiana University Press, 1997; *More Radical Hermeneutics: On Not Knowing Who We Are*, Bloomington: Indiana University Press, 2000.

[11] Cf. J. D. Caputo, *Shedding Tears Beyond Being: Derrida's Experience of Prayer*, in Marco Olivetti, ed., *Théologie négative* (Biblioteca dell' 'Archivio di Filosofia', 59), Rome: CEDAM, 2002, 861-880.

directed. Pure religion makes praying '*etsi Deus daretur,*' not knowing whether there is a God 'at the other side' of the address. This results in a complete doing away with all positivity, Christian narrativity and even negative theology's ultimate 'limit-affirmation' that there is an Other, albeit ineffable and incomprehensible. At other occasions, I have called this movement a kind of 'committed agnosticism.'[12] The passion for unknowing amounts to a passionate refusal to choose between theism – an option for a relation with God – and atheism.

Despite this passion, however, Caputo is also aware of the fact that neither Derrida nor he himself escapes from linguistic contamination. In the end, he avows that the distinction between the 'messianic' and the diverse messianism "cannot be rigorously maintained [...]. We are always involved with structures whose historical pedigree we can trace if we read them carefully enough [...]. That is no less true of deconstruction itself [...]. If we search it carefully enough, we discover that it, too, is another concrete messianism, which is the only thing livable."[13]

It is not so much the fact that prominent philosophers still – or better: again – speak of God that matters to us here, although it surely is, as we will observe in our second part, consonant with the revival of the 'religious' in contemporary Western societies. It is rather the manner in which they speak of God that is of importance to the theological reflection we undertake here. Very often they tend to place the basic structure of the religious desire and truth claims outside or beyond particularity of religious expressions and practices, and deem language as contamination. Definitely in the case of Derrida and Caputo, the religious desire and truth claim appear to be entertained at the expense of its rootedness in a particular discourse. And in view of our discussion in this paper: it is above all the extent to which their accounts of religion remain dependent upon negative theology that is symptomatic. Such philosophical theologies display a formal messianic structure that forever remains to be kept open. Moreover, because of its incurable

[12] Cf. Lieven Boeve, *(Post)Modern Theology on Trial? Towards a Radical Theological Hermeneutics of Christian Particularity*, in *Louvain Studies* 28 (2003), 240-254.

[13] *What Do I Love when I Love my God? An Interview with John D. Caputo* (by B. Keith Putt), in J.H. Olthuis, ed., *Religion With/out Religion: The Prayers and Tears of John D. Caputo*, London/New York: Routledge, 2001, 150-179, 165.

predicative nature, language is considered as a contamination, even as a betrayal to a kind of original religious purity. In concrete prayers, the purity of the religious address at work in 'pure' prayer cannot be maintained. Because of the fall of, and in, language (language both as and in a fall), religious desire and truth must be beyond language – even though both Caputo and Derrida would be the first to avow that, on the epistemological level, there is no 'beyond language.' Thus, in the end, language and narrativity differentiate and divide. Religious desire and truth are finally to be situated in what is radically beyond language, beyond narrativity. Radical hermeneutics then becomes a tool to evoke and point at 'this beyond.'

However, is it legitimate to equivocate language with contamination? Since language seems to be our condition, does the irreducible particularity of religion always already contaminate religious desire and truth claims? If this would be the case: Is Christianity, then, with its Christocentric and thus incarnational approach, not doomed to be always too particular, too historical, too positive? Is Christianity, therefore, to be deconstructed in the name of a more originary desire to, experience of, and/or relationship to God, or if this name remains too particular, to the Transcendent, Otherness, Difference? And, are all particular religions today to be evaluated with such standard?

2. Cultural Apophaticism: Negative Theology as the Outcome of the Transformation of Religion in Western Europe?

Perhaps one could say that this renewed philosophical interest in religious apophatic thinking patterns constitutes the reflective counterpart for equally strong, culturally motivated apophatic tendencies apparent in the religious revival in contemporary European society. Indeed, kind of a 'cultural apophaticism' would appear to be the product of the processes of detraditionalisation and pluralisation which have changed the religious landscape of Europe over the last half century.[14] Both processes seem to foster the development of a broadly-spread, vague religiosity that does

[14] For an elaboration on these processes and the resulting post-secular and post-Christian religious landscape, I refer to my *God Interrupts History: Theology in a Time of Upheaval*, New York: Continuum, 2007, Chapter 1.

away with some particular beliefs of Christian faith.[15] In this second part, I will elaborate on the process of detraditionalisation, in the following on the effects of religious pluralisation.

In Western-Europe, the process of detraditionalisation has not led to the disappearance of religion, but to its transformation (which explains why we rather speak of detraditionalisation than of secularisation).[16] The continuing institutional and mental dechristianisation of Europe has not led to a merely secular culture and society, but resulted also in a new kind of vague religiosity. A new religious consciousness has grown that 'there is something more' to life than facts and figures. A lot of Europeans, claiming no longer to believe in God or to belong to Christian communities, still hold to the religious intuition 'that there is something more.' That is the reason why in Dutch this phenomenon sometimes has been labelled 'ietsisme' – translated in English 'something-ism.'[17] Some claim that this religiosity is an infantile waste product of contemporary secular culture, to be overcome when secularisation will be fully realised. Others, on the contrary, consider it as the new shape of humanity's religious consciousness, resulting from the disenchantment with secular rationality and utopia, and reacting against the nihilism in post-secular society. Confronted with the contingency and meaninglessness of their existence, post-secular people develop a new type of religiosity with special attention to personal experiences and responsibility, while being averse to traditional orthodox religions. It is the expression of a religious longing, adequate to the contemporary context, for the hope that there is more to life than what scientific worldviews maintain.

As a matter of fact, what is apparent in these strains of religiosity is *a kind of culturally motivated negative theology*. It strives at relativising elements of the Christian tradition, especially those aspects it denounces

[15] For this and the following part, I also refer to a longer treatment in my *God Interrupts History*, Chapter 7.

[16] Cf. Y. Lambert, 'A Turning Point in Religious Evolution in Europe', in *Journal of Contemporary Religion*, 19 (2004), 29-45.

[17] Cf. S.W. Couwenberg, 'Onttovering van het geloof en het 'ietsisme' als eigentijdse uiting van religieus verlangen', *Streven* (Jan. 2004) 10-20; G. Groot, *Geloven en geluk: over het krediet van een religieuze cultuur* (Alfrinklezing 2004), Vught: Radboudstichting, 2004, 5-22; G. Dingemans, *'Ietsisme' – Een basis voor christelijke spiritualiteit?*, Kampen: Kok, 2005

as over-determining, dominating and even oppressive of the religious openness of human beings. The result is a spirituality with ample attention for experience, diversity, freedom, power, energy, positivism, and so on. Religiosity then becomes a source of joy and happiness, and at the same time provides strength to cope with life's dark sides.[18] This apophatic move, one could say, prompts a scrapping of encumbering old religious images and ideas; it invites to make room for new and more fitting religious images and intuitions, in order to give shape to a religious longing for harmony, cohesion, etc.

This vague religiosity can be analysed as both the symptom of, and the solution to the crisis of the modern subject, who has become conscious of the fact that he/she is no longer the master of him/herself. In a search for identity, meaning, harmony, stability, security, the human subject engages in a movement of self-transcendence towards something other, the divine, which both reveals the limits of the subject as well as enables it to cope with these limits. The growing number of those who believe in life after death reinforces this line of thought.[19] Because of the fact that meaning is located in the auto-construction of the self, people cannot situate their own death. Religion, as a kind of 'self-divinisation' through the decentering of the subject, again seems to be first and foremost a mastery of contingency, the opening of a comforting and hospitable horizon in which everything finds its legitimate place, and everything is related to everything else. This would explain why this cultural apophasis sometimes swings in the direction of an overabundant religious imagination fed by the diversity of the religious market, leading to beliefs in angels, miracles, paranormal powers, and other phenomena, all of which, in some Christian theological circles, have been abandoned and demythologised in modern times.

It is, of course, a legitimate question to ask why people in their search for religion are not returning to Christianity, especially when one acknowledges that many of them are still nominally Christian. Due to detraditionalisation, however, there is no longer an immediate cultural link between such religiosity and Christianity: the factual overlap

[18] See also the analyses made by A. van Harskamp in *Het nieuw-religieuze verlangen*, Kampen: Kok, 2000.

[19] Cf. Y. Lambert, 'Turning Point in Religious Evolution in Europe,' 43.

between the Christian horizon of meaning and contemporary culture has faded away. Moreover, Christianity still suffers on many occasions from its own cultural-hegemonic past, and in this regard is called to account for seemingly still unsettled bills.

To be sure, this evacuation or 'deconstruction' of specific Christian beliefs, rituals and practices is not only visible with those who have taken leave of Christianity, but also manifests itself within and at the borders of the Christian churches. Some, for example, will venture that the language of the Christian tradition, the structures of Christian churches, etc., are outdated and should be renewed.[20] One may wonder, however, whether this is really the whole answer to the question. Maybe there is something about Christian faith itself that hampers those who are religiously longing from smoothly taking up this faith themselves. The question to be posed therefore, is whether this cultural apophaticism and its constitutive religious experience are an alternative to Christian faith, or rather should be analysed as its transformation: its liberation from old forms, beliefs and practices in order to speak liberative again to people of today.[21]

---

[20] Cf. J.A. van der Ven, *God Reinvented? A Theological Search in Texts and Tables* (Empirical Studies in Theology, 1), Leiden: Brill, 1998.

[21] This is a point particularly made by Erik Borgman in his *Metamorfosen: Over religie en moderne cultuur*, Kampen: Klement, 2006. Borgman is not so interested in the *content* of religious claims but rather in the *basis upon which* such claims are made. He thus hopes to find traces of what it is that fundamentally binds human beings together (before concrete religions and religious convictions separate them). According to Borgman, theologians today can only achieve this "not by presenting the Christian traditions and arguing in support of their enduring importance, but by reading the present situation […] as a religious situation" (23). Indeed, the metamorphosis our culture has undergone also leads us to understand God in a new way. Those who desire to find God, or traces of a relationship with the sacred, should reflect first and foremost on the way "'religion after religion' is taking shape in our culture" (32), how religion today is not secularised and absorbed into the world, but emerges rather from a secularised culture.

3. Mystical Experience and Negative Theology: Experiential and Epistemological Basis for Harmony in a Religiously Pluralised and Globalised World?

The pluralisation of religion is the other aspect under which the transformation of religion in Europe should be discussed. On closer inspection, it would seem that this consciousness of religious diversity also enforces a culturally motivated negativetheology, adding to the one discussed in part two. In the prevailing cultural consciousness, there seems to be a wide spread assumption that above, or underlying, the many forms of religiosity and spirituality, intra-religious as well as extra-religious, resides the same religious longing, the same mystical experience, the same relationship to the divine (or whatever name this transcendent reality is given), expressed in manifold ways, according to time, place and traditions. This assumption is often present in Christian as well as non-Christian circles.

Taken on its own merits, this kind of apophaticism relativises those aspects which make Christianity a particular, specific religion, and further that which distinguishes it or even separates it from other religions. The shared mystical experience, feelings of religious authenticity, or experience of longing for wholeness and harmony make people do away with what brings separation, conflict and difference: particular truth claims, specific practices and imagery, etc.

Likewise in pluralist-theological circles, many metaphors have been used to hint at such a structure to think about religious plurality: religions are paths to the same mountain top (mystically veiled in clouds); they are the many sides and limbs of the same elephant, the different perspectives one can take in looking at the same dew drop glistening at the break of dawn, the many colours of the same rainbow, and so on. Pluralist-theological thinkers such as John Hick and Paul Knitter would advocate such a position: religious plurality is the other side of religious unity – it concerns a manifold of particular expressions of a common mystical experience and/or relationship, beyond language, traditions, religions, while at the same time witnessed to in them. Moreover, at best religions are vehicles of an encompassing learning process towards religious harmony and peace.[22] Therefore, as regards Christianity, according to Hick, incarnation is to be considered as a myth or a metaphor, a Christian way to express our being related to the 'Real,' and definitely not a historical claim, or a claim to uniqueness and unrepeatability.[23]

In his contribution to the proceedings of the LEST IV Conference on religious experience and theological epistemology,[24], Sebastian Painadath, an Indian Christian theologian working at the Center for Indian Spirituality (Kalady, India) formulates a similar point. He proposes that we adapt the classical scheme of Paul Tillich, distinguishing between 'religion' and 'culture' ('culture is the form of religion; religion constitutes the substance of culture'[25]), in order to analyse and resolve religious plurality. Painadath, however, substitutes 'spirituality' for 'religion' and 'religion' for 'culture.' Religions then are particular symbolic expressions of spirituality, whereas spirituality constitutes the uniting kernel of cultural-historically differentiated religions. "The universal spiritual experience finds concrete expression in the diversity of religions."[26] Spirituality, rooted in a mystical involvement with the transcendent is, as a consequence, that which binds the various cultural-historical religions. Those who are unable to reach through and beyond religion to this more profound spirituality, run the risk of reducing religion to fundamentalism.

---

[22] Cf. J. Hick, *An Interpretation of Religion. Human Responses to the Transcendent*, London: Macmillan Press, 1989, 299-315, 380; P. F. Knitter, *One Earth Many Religions. Multifaith Dialogue & Global Responsibility,* Maryknoll: Orbis Books, 1995, 35-37.

[23] See e.g. J. Hick, *The Metaphor of God Incarnate*, London: SCM, 1993.

[24] LEST stands for 'Leuven Encounters in Systematic Theology', a biannual international congress organised by the research department of systematic theology, K.U. Leuven. For more information: http://theo.kuleuven.be/page/lest/.

[25] Cf. Paul Tillich, *Kirche und Kultur, in Die Religiöse Substanz der Kultur. Schriften zur Theologie der Kultur* (Gesammelte Werke, IX), Stuttgart: Evangelisches Verlagswerk, 1967, 42; *Uber die Idee einer Theologie der Kultur*, Stuttgart: Evangelisches Verlagswerk, 1967, 21-22.

[26] Cf. S. Painadath, *Diversity of Religions, Unity in Spirituality*, in L. Boeve, Y. De Maeseneer & S. Van den Bossche (eds), *Religious Experience and Contemporary Theological Epistemology* (BETL, 188), Leuven: Peeters Press, 2005, 141-151, 144-145.

One may wonder, however, whether the Hindu metaphor being referred to here, that of the nut from which one has to strip layer after layer in order to arrive at a harmonious kernel, is appropriate to imagine what particular religions are like, and to qualify the apophatic-theological strategies it instigates. It might be more appropriate to use the metaphor of the onion in order to imagine the outcome of such an apophatic move. After all, when one strips layer after layer of an onion, it is not a kernel which one obtains; one is merely left with the skins. Nevertheless, again the combination of mystical experience and negative theology puts serious doubts on Christian faith, its capacity for harmony and peace, in short: its future in a religiously pluralised and globalised world.

4. Evolutionary and Neurological Research in Religions and Mystical Experience: A Scientific Argument for Negative Theology?

Almost as an addendum to what we already said, we briefly mention the new scientific research into religions and religious experience. Do evolutionary, neurotheological theories of religion at last deliver the fatal blow to Christianity, and to religion altogether? Neo-Darwinistatheists as Richard Dawkins,[27] Daniel C. Dennett,[28] Samuel Harris and others are quite clear about this. Religion, analogously to all so-called 'higher' human virtues, conceptions, etc., is a mere product of evolution; a strategy of the species to enlarge its possibility to survive – a strategy also which has outgrown its use in an age of science and technology. Neurological research into religious experience, on the other hand, has been able to render religious experience to brain activity, by investigating experiences of both Christian and Buddhist nuns. Irrespective of their different religious backgrounds, the same brain activity could be detected during intense mediation and/or prayer. That is, according to one of the researchers, 'why God won't go away': God is located in our 'neurological hardware.'[29]

---

[27] Cf. R. Dawkins, *The God Delusion*, New York: Bantam Books, 2006.

[28] Cf. D. Dennett, *Breaking the Spell. Religion as a Natural Phenomenon*, New York: Penguin (Viking), 2006.

[29] Cf. A.B. Newberg, et al., *Why God Won't Go Away: Brain Science and the Biology of Belief*, New York: Ballantine Books, 2002.

Be it the atheistic apologetics of Dennett who explains religion in an evolutionary way as a 'meme,' or be it neurotheology, providing a neurological explanation for mystical experiences: a theological confrontation with such thinking should not let itself be tempted to an undifferentiated dismissal. Theology surely should criticise the seamless extension of methodological atheism to religious atheism displayed in such studies, but also – after dismissing such reduction – learn to appreciate attempts to uncover, scientifically, the historical-biological and neuro-physical basis of religion and religious dynamics. For, from a Christian theological perspective: how else could God reveal Godself but through the mediation of history and bodiliness?[30]

Obviously, any reductionist interpretation on the basis of these scientific findings makes of religion nothing more than an evolutionary epiphenomenon or brain activity, and advocates ideological atheism. However, also in a non-reductionist way scientific insights might stimulate a negative-theological dynamic, relativising the particularity and narrativity of concrete religious traditions, practices, communities, while pointing at their common neurological basis and/or evolutionary offspring. Are religious language, narrative, history, etc., then only instantiations of such historical-biological and neurological givens?

5. Negative Theology Today: Finally Going Beyond the Particularities of Christian Faith and its Incarnational Impetus?

In the four constellations I have briefly presented, it would seem that both negative theology and mystical experience no longer are at work within Christian faith, but rather go beyond Christian faith, and more generally beyond particular religions and religious traditions. (a) Philosophical hermeneutics of religion in terms of 'religion without religion,'(b) the cultural apophaticism engendered by post-secular and post-Christian 'something-isms,' (c) the appeal to an underlying mystical kernel by proponents of a pluralist-theological hermeneutics of religious plurality oriented at harmony and unity, and (d) new scientific insights into the evolutionary and neurological basis of religion and mystical experience

[30] Cf. L. Boeve, *Gooi God niet weg! Over hoe God weggegooid wordt in een pleidooi om God niet weg te gooien*, in D. Pollefeyt & E. De Boeck, ed., *Niet van God los? Geloof en wetenschap* (Nikè-reeks, 53), Leuven: Acco, 2007, 31-44.

– all of these appear to point to universal structures of religious desire, experience, etc., which would seem to be underlying to the particularity and diversity of religious traditions, beliefs, expressions, and practices, and on the basis of which the latter can be relativised. In as much as the insights stemming from all four constellations inform a contemporary religious consciousness which is quite pervasive in the West, negative theology seems to be considered as the stripping of all too particular instantiations from a more originary religious desire, mystical experience and/or relationship – to be conceived of beyond language, knowledge, religion, etc.

As mentioned before, the challenge for theology runs as follows: is such philosophical, cultural, interreligious and scientifically informed apophaticism and mysticism a new contemporary adequate religious way to deal with the contingencies and particularities of life? How does it relate to Christian faith? Is it in the West its successor? It's opponent? Is it the contemporary *modus* of appearance of Christian faith, even its fulfilment, or is it rather the expression of a post-Christian attitude of life? Can we still hold to concrete traditions, beliefs and practices, or are they to be relativised or treated ironically in view of these contemporary apophaticisms and mysticisms? And particularly in case of Christian faith: can we hold to the incarnation to conceive of the religious truth claim of Christianity? Or is the belief in the incarnation an a priori hindrance to religious truth and naming God, rather than the way to do so? In this last part, I address these theological questions, and deal first (1) with the differences between current cultural and Christian apophaticism and mysticism, and further (2) with the problem incarnation, characteristic for the latter, seemingly poses to the first kind of apophatic and mystical religious consciousness.

(1) First of all, I would like to evaluate *cultural apophaticism and mysticism*as *the exponent of a post-secular and post-Christian religiosity rather than the future of Christian faith itself.*[31] The same verdict applies to philosophical apophaticism as well in so far as it reflects this cultural sensibility, which is the result of detraditionalisation and pluralisation. In as much as the scientific insights are considered to further inform

[31] For these paragraphs, see again my: *God Interrupts History*, chapter 7.

such post-secular and post-Christian apophaticism and mysticism, such usage of these insights is included here as well.

In all of its diversity, this cultural negative and mystical theology takes leave of the Christian God. There appears to be *an embarrassment with God* as the Other who makes with us concrete history; and this under two aspects. (a) First, it experiences difficulties with the confronting otherness of God, of a God who, from Gods difference with history, comes towards history and engages it. They seem to be unable to conceive of (and accordingly believe in, or surrender to) a transcendence that is really distinguished from and anterior to the human subject. This inability only becomes stronger when conceiving of this transcendence implies the belief in a personal God making an appeal on people, challenging, perturbing, judging, loving them, etc. The embarrassment thus concerns the structure of faith, and the inability to come to faith, as an answer to an anterior and provocative appeal. (b) However, this embarrassment not only concerns God as Other vis-à-vis history, but also the way in which this God reveals Godself in the particularity of history. Christian knowledge about God is intrinsically linked with an interpretation of concrete events and stories, embedded in particular histories of interpretation, and lived by specific communities of interpretation. A number of contemporaries in search for spirituality appear to have many difficulties with the irreducible link between revelation and particular history, that is, with a faith tradition that makes concrete history and remains indissolubly bound to it. Christians indeed profess that God reveals Godself in a definitive and unique way, unrepeatably, in specific events on particular occasions. The culminating point here is the profession that the concrete human being Jesus of Nazareth is the Christ and that in this Jesus Christ, God has become known to us in an incomparable way. From the perspective of history, however, these events and occasions are as contingent and particular as any other historical matter.

As a matter of fact, these two intrinsically interwoven constitutive elements of Christian faith are underrepresented or absent in the present-day cultural negative and mystical theology. It is to these two elements that the living Christian tradition bears witness, in narratives and praxis, prayers and rituals, doctrines and reflections. Combined, they give rise to a specifically Christian critical-hermeneutical consciousness. Christian faith, then, is the option (made from a complex interplay of initiation, will and intellect) to look at history and society from the perspective of this God and to interpret them accordingly.

This precludes a very facile identification between cultural apophaticism and Christian negative theology. Indeed, some theologians do claim that precisely here, a close connection could be made again between culture and Christian tradition. Some would argue that through this vague religious apophatic sensibility a possibility arises to contextually anchor anew the relevance and plausibility of Christian faith. However, to my opinion, the cultural apophaticism indeed challenges Christian theology, but not to recuperate it because of a familiarity with its own apophatic consciousness. On the contrary, cultural apophaticism rather leads Christian theology to rediscover anew the specificity of its own position, including its apophatic-theological dimension. In a Christian radical hermeneutical consciousness, *apophasis* is not doing away with *cataphasis*, but is intrinsically at work in it. God's ineffability has nothing to do with vagueness, nor with something that leads away from the concrete. To the contrary, it leads immediately back to history itself. God as the Other of history is involved in it as determinate Love, as a prophetic challenge to all to make visible God's invisible presence and activity. In this regard, it is like the love between two human beings which is not an indeterminate given, but which is only realised and survives as something very concrete, tangible, life giving, inscribed in particular events and stories, even when the language of love does not have the words for it, even when all determination ultimately falls short, and never succeeds in grasping its mystery.

(2) What then about the Incarnation? As far as Christian theology is concerned, incarnation is not so much a hindrance, but the key to reconsider faith, experience, religious truth claims, the naming of God. For it is precisely the theological-epistemological concept of incarnation that takes into account the very particularity, not as a contamination of, but as a irreducible condition for religious truth – there is no religious truth claim without particular discourse. At the same time, this incarnational interpretation of the irreducible particularity of religious

discourse implies a critical and hermeneutical dynamic that already qualifies the religious truth claim.

This is at least what I would consider to be the epistemological kernel of the theological doctrine of Incarnation. Contrary to some of the philosophical, cultural and pluralist-theological criticisms, the incarnation, as the anchor point of a constitutive Christology, does not constitute the end of religious hermeneutics, but is the motor of very radical Christian hermeneutics. The all too particular is not an obstacle for the revelation of God, but its very condition. This is what a hermeneutical retrieval of the Christological dogma of Chalcedon points to: the affirmation that Jesus Christ is both God and human (unmixed, unchanged, undivided, unseparated) means proclaiming that in person, life, speech, and deeds, he was the definitive hermeneutics of God, but that he – himself being God – only can be approached in a radical-hermeneutical way. He is the definitive revelation of God, and this precisely in the paradoxical relation of God and humanity established in his person. In so far as Jesus Christ is a signification of the divine reality, the same religious hermeneutical-critical proviso applies to him as to all other religious discourse. In other words, God's superfluous love has been revealed in a particular life story that does not exhaust this love, but nevertheless signifies it in a definitive way. As a particular life story, Jesus' narrative bears, entangled in particularity, witness to the universality of grace, which as such can never be articulated.[32]

Indeed, incarnation presupposes an ongoing 'radical hermeneutics' that prevents one from lapsing into either a universalism without particularity or a closed particularism (fundamentalism). In this perspective, negative theology assumes a role very different from the one demonstrated in the aforementioned thinkers: its aim is no longer to take leave from the narrativity of religious discourse, but rather to raise one's awareness of this narrativity to the utmost. Apophatic theology does not abandon kataphatic theology, but qualifies it.

Put quite boldly: the truth of the incarnation is the incarnation of religious truth. From a Christian theological perspective, language does

---

[32] See my 'Christus Postmodernus: An Attempt at Apophatic Christology,' in: T. Merrigan and J. Haers, eds, *The Myriad Christ: Plurality and the Quest for Unity in Contemporary Christology* (BETL, 152), Leuven: Peeters Press, 2000, 577-593.

not need to be a contamination or a fall that would make any 'pure' religious desire, experience, relationship, truth claim in the end impossible and that would compel hermeneutics to leave its entanglement with particularity behind in the direction of a pure, but nonetheless untenable, religion without religion, something-ism, or mystical experience before and beyond language. A hermeneutic of religion does not lead 'beyond' or 'before', let alone 'behind', language, but to language itself: to the concrete stories, practices, texts and traditions in which religious truths are lived and experienced. Only in these can one find both the groundand the content of religious truth claims. It is only from the awareness of the entanglement of religious truth with this concrete particularity that religious believers can become more conscious of their being positioned in a context of religious plurality. As participants in the interreligious conversation, they venture, together with others, religious truth claims, each of which come from their own particular religious narratives and practices.

This may lead to a renewed, radical hermeneutics of religion that fully takes particularity as its point of departure, and that, in order not to fall prey to the pitfalls of a closed particularism or fundamentalism, develops a critical consciousness precisely *from within* particularity. It is because of the irreducible particularity of religious truth claims that an ongoing hermeneutical process is called for, a process that, in its determination of religious truth today, no longer abandons, but holds fast to precisely this very particularity.

Conclusion

From a Western cultural-theological perspective Christian the pair of mystical experience and negative theology face challenges coming forth from (a) philosophical dealings with negative theology, (b) cultural dealings with religion and spirituality, (c) interreligious comparative dealings with mysticism, and (d) scientific dealings with religion and mystical experiences. (a) The turn to religion in continental post-metaphysical thinking often results in a philosophical negative theology – a 'religion without religion' beyond the contamination of language; (b) cultural post-secular religious sensibilities lead to a widespread search for spirituality outside the realm of classical religions, often results in a vague religiosity, sometimes referred to as 'something-ism' ('I believe that there is something more') and very wary of all too determinative religious language; (c) for some comparative religionists and pluralist theologians mystical experience is the underlying core of religion as such, before or beyond the differentiation in the many (world) religions; and (d) scientific approaches point to the same biological and neurological basis of mystical experiences, irrespective of the different particular religions in which these experiences are made. I have argued that the attempt of most of these approaches to understand Christian apophaticism and mysticism from underlying generic patterns, thus reducing the very particularity and narrativity of Christianity to these structures, is missing what from a Christian theological perspective mystical experience and the negative theology stemming from it, really is about. Although, a lot can be learned from contemporary philosophical dealing with religion, from cultural religiosity, etc., I have argued that (a) Christian mystical experience and negative theology are first of all not about the contamination by language of pure religious desire, (b) nor are they about a vague God, leaving aside God's otherness as it is revealed in concrete history and narrative, (c) nor do they concern an experience which is common to religions rather than differentiating them, and (d) nor is the neurological basis of mystical experience an argument against particularity, let alone a contra-indication for its transcendent referent. In sum: Christian mysticism and negative theology do not lead away from the very particularity and narrativity of Christian faith but are at work right within them, qualifying their nature and stimulating their development.

12

The Mystical Strategies of St Teresa of Avila

Dr. Peter Mark Tyler
St Mary's University College, London, UK

1. Introduction

> When a number of books in Spanish were taken away from us and we were not allowed to read them, I felt it very much because the reading of some of them had given me great recreation, and I could no longer do so since they were only available in Latin. Then the Lord said to me: 'Don't be upset, for I will give you a living book'. (Teresa of Avila, V,26.6)[1]

In this passage in her *Libro de la Vida* ('Book of the Life', hereafter V) Teresa hints at some of the external and internal circumstances that led to her own writing career. In the passage we come across some of the key events that were influencing her: the prohibition of spiritual books in the vernacular following the Valdés decree of 1559, her own reliance on just such vernacular books of spirituality in her early life and finally

[1] The English translations of Teresa's works will be either my own or, unless stated, Kavanaugh and Rodriguez 1987. V = *El Libro de la Vida* (Book of Her Life), M = *Las Moradas* (The Interior Castle), CE = *Camino de Perfección* (Way of Perfection), Escorial Codex, CV =*Camino*, Valladolid Codex, CT = *Camino*, Toledo Codex, C = *Meditaciones del amor de Dios*, Exc = *Exclamaciones*. For a biographical sketch of Teresa, see Peter Tyler, The *Way of Ecstasy: Praying with St Teresa of Avila*, Canterbury: SCM, 1997.

the inspiration for her own writing found in the words she received: 'I will give you a living book'. Central to her own vision of her 'mission' is the next sentence:

> I wasn't able to understand why this was said to me for as yet I had received no visions. Afterwards, after only a few days, I understood very clearly. For what I saw presented to me gave me much to think about and recollect (*recogerme*), and the Lord showed me so much love and taught me in so many ways that I had little or hardly any need for books afterwards. (V, 26.6)

In this passage, Teresa seems to be making a move from 'saying' to 'showing', or, in this case, a move from the intellectual book-learning of the *letrados* to the 'vision' of 'what the Lord presents' 'in His love'. The key word here being *recogerme* – 'to recollect myself', a crucial term that links Teresa with the main spiritual currents of her time and especially the writings of the 'vernacular master' she refers to in the previous sentence and had already mentioned in Chapter Four of the *Vida:*

> When I was on my way, that uncle of mine I mentioned who lived along the road gave me a book. It is called *The Third Spiritual Alphabet*[2] and endeavours to teach the prayer of recollection... And so I was very happy with this book and resolved to follow that path with all my strength… For during the twenty years after this period of which I am speaking, I did not find a master, I mean a confessor, who understood me, even though I looked for one. (V, 4.7)

Before we now look at Teresa's own use of the *theologia mystica* it is necessary to give a brief word on the crisis of *alumbradismo* of mid sixteenth century Spain (and the prevalent cause of the Valdés Index) and how Teresa's work was a reaction to it.

---

[2] By Francisco de Osuna, hereafter TA.

2. *Alumbradismo,* 1559 and the Valdés Index

Writing on Teresa and *alumbradismo,* the North American Teresian scholar Gillian Ahlgren states: "Though Teresa never used the term *alumbrados*, the effects of the movement were probably the most important influence on her literary objectives. The suspicions of prophecy and of women's religious experience which the movement had inflamed affected Teresa's credibility" (Ahlgren, 1996, 29).

Contemporary scholarship differs as to the role, nature and scope of the *Alumbrados* (See especially Márquez, 1980), the term *alumbrado* (lit: 'enlightened', 'illumined') seems to have originally been one of mockery and abuse used to denote 'excessive piety and to suggest hysteria and hypocrisy and fraudulence' (Hamilton, 1992, 28). At the beginning of the sixteenth century it began to be associated in Spain with a loose-knit group who were condemned at various times by the Church and State. The propositions for which they were condemned were first collected together in the Edict of Faith issued by the Inquisitor General, Alonso Manrique (Archbishop of Seville) on 23rd September 1525. The edict contained forty-eight propositions directed against *'alumbrados, dexados e perfectos'* (lit: 'the enlightened, abandoned and perfect' see Bataillon 1982, 166) which consisted of a collection of questionable and heretical statements held by and attributed to the group. As well as certain apocalyptic statements they included propositions such as 'prayer must be mental and not vocal'; the denial of the necessity of any sacramental intermediary between God and humans – thus rejecting the efficacy of external works as well as the authority of the church to interpret scripture; contempt for the cult of the saints, the worship of images, bulls, indulgences, fasting and abstinence. Although, the Edict condemned what appeared to be a homogenous and coherent group scholars such as Bataillon and Marquez have concluded that the 'group' was a fragmentary assemblage of various collections of people with differing motives, ideas and spiritualities. It was the emphasis on the importance of personal prayer within these groups that caused the most problems for Teresa as one of the thrusts of her own life and work was the restitution of personal prayer as central to the life of the average Christian.

A key phrase used in the condemnations of the *alumbrados* was *dejamiento* (lit: 'abandonment') which was used to describe the type of prayer advocated by the *alumbrados*. It is unclear what exactly was meant by the term however it seems to have arisen as a variant of the prayer of *recogimiento* (lit: 'gathering together') alluded to above. The teaching of *recogimiento,* as Andrés Martin (1975) points out, placed an emphasis on the importance of withdrawing from activity once or twice a day, usually to a dark room, for quiet contemplation with lowered or closed eyes. The teaching of *dejamiento*, often ascribed to Isabel de la Cruz, suggested that such a withdrawal was unnecessary and the contemplation could continue in all states and places – even allowing evil thoughts and temptations to arise. After the Edict of 1525 an inquisitorial process was initiated against Pedro Ruiz de Alcaraz and Isabel de la Cruz of Toledo (See Márquez, 1980, 244-57) who were found guilty of the practices condemned. In 1529 Alcaraz was flogged, his property confiscated and both plaintiffs were condemned to 'perpetual reclusion and habit'. From this time any groups of laypeople, women and those associated with the Franciscan *recogitorios* were suspect of the heresy.[3]

It is notable that a number of the *alumbrados* groups were connected with *converso*[4] or 'New Christian' groups, a group to which Teresa herself belonged. It is clear, as Bataillon points out (1982, 166) that in the minds of the Inquisition, *alumbradismo* had to have somewhere a connection with the wider religious reforms of Northern Europe, even if, as appears likely, little such connection existed in reality.

The condemnation of the *alumbrados* by the Edict of Seville in 1525 marked in many ways the beginning of the end of the wave of openness and 'renaissance' within the mystical tradition in Spain initiated by Cardinal Cisneros at the beginning of the sixteenth century (See, Bataillon, 1982, 699 – 737). Teresa of Avila, born in 1515, was able to have access to many mystical works from the medieval tradition

---

[3] For a full list of the condemned propositions, see Marquez, Los alumbrados: orígenes y filosofía, Madrid: Taurus, 1980, 250.

[4] Literally 'converts' – recently converted Christians usually from Judaism but also Islam.

of *theologia mystica*[5]. As well as Osuna's *TercerAbecedario Espiritual* already mentioned, she read Bernardino de Laredo and the classical 'mystical' writers such as Augustine, Gregory and Bernard.[6] However, as her own spiritual life grew and developed, the political climate in Spain began to change again.[7] Following years of tension between the 'Erasmians' and the Inquisition, events in Spain came to a head in 1559 when many works of the 'Cisnerosian Spring' of the early 16th century (including Erasmus and Luther) were condemned in the Valdés Index. Valid only for Spain, it contained many of the writings of the people who had already fallen foul of Valdés and the Inquisition: Carranza, Luis de Granada, Juan de Avila and the works of Erasmus in Castilian and Latin. It also incorporated many of the writers and works who had contributed to the Cisnerosian revolution at the beginning of the century: as well as Francisco de Osuna's *TercerAbecedario* (but not the other *Abecedarios*), it included Herp's *Theologia mystica* and de Balma's *Via Spiritus* (de Bujanda, 1984, 303- 592).

As Hamilton puts it: "By forbidding so many books published with the approval of Cisneros, the Index could also be regarded as the first official statement condemning his spirituality, the coronation of the trials which had started in the 1520s and of which the *alumbrados* had been the first victims" (Hamilton, 1992, 111). Some works remained uncensored such as those of Alonso de Madrid and Bernardino de Laredo. In total it listed some 253 titles including fourteen editions of the Bible. In addition to the mentioned titles it also created a wider sense of alarm and caution on a whole range of areas.[8] In Ahlgren's words:

[5] For more on the medieval genealogy of this term see my forthcoming *The Return to the Mystical: Ludwig Wittgenstein, Teresa of Avila and the Christian Mystical Tradition*, London: Continuum.

[6] References to all four are found in her works.

[7] There are many good analyses of the reasons for these changes. In English good analyses are found in Ahlgren and Hamilton and in Spanish, Andrés and Marquez, all referred to above.

[8] Other entries included books by known heretics, partial or whole translations of the Bible, books in Arabic or Hebrew or that tell of Muslim or Jewish practices, books regarding witchcraft and superstition and manuscripts that mention biblical tradition or the sacraments of the church. See Ahlgren, *Teresa of Avila and the Politics of Sanctity*, Ithaca: Cornell UP, 1996, 17.

> In summary, the Valdés Index of Prohibited Books was not merely a list of books prohibited to the public; it was an edict intended to limit the scope of religious speculation and to define religious faith and practice very narrowly as the province of an educated elite whose task was not speculation but transmission of dogma. (Ahlgren, 1996, 17)

For Andrés, the Valdés Index 'tried to banish affective spirituality in its various manifestations, encouraging the traditional spirituality of the practice of virtues and the destruction of vices over other ways of spirituality considered mystical' (Andrés, 1976: 1:362). As Ahlgren notes:

As the new mystical pathways opened in the first half of the century narrowed to a dogmatic and disciplined orthodoxy, so did the range of subjects appropriate for theological debate… If the works were to survive intact, certain topics had to be handled with extreme care, and authors used language to hide rather than reveal their intent. (1996, 19)

> As most women did not read Latin, the Valdés prohibition of spiritual books in the vernacular posed a particular problem. However, as these ideological concerns impacted upon her, Teresa was able to respond, I argue here, largely because of the 'training' and 'education' she had received from 'her master' Fray Francisco de Osuna and his exposition of the *theologia mystica* in the *Tercer Abecedario Espiritual*. In this respect, her schooling in the mystical strategies of the *theologia mystica* were ideal preparation for the challenges of the environment within which her mature work would develop.

3. Teresa and the *Theologia Mystica*

One of the central arguments of my paper is that Teresa is heir to, and knowingly uses, the techniques of what I have called the tradition of *theologia mystica*. Although, as argued, she relies heavily on this tradition throughout her works she only makes three explicit references to the *theologia mystica* in her work, these occur in Chapters Ten to Twelve of her *Vida.* It is worthwhile spending some time on these references and their place in the text of the *Vida.*

The decision to write the text of the *Vida* coincided with Teresa's re-formation of the Carmelite houses in Spain. In 1561 the Inquisitor of Toledo, Francisco de Soto y Salazar suggested that Teresa present a description of her experiences and methods of prayer. The first draft was completed in 1562 and the final draft in 1565, which was then to be read by several learned *letrados*: Juan de Avila, her Dominican mentors and probably Balthasar Alvarez, one of her Jesuit mentors. In 1574 the work came under inquisitorial suspicion – due, amongst other things, to the vindictive malice of the Princess of Eboli, and the manuscript disappeared into the Inquisition's hands until after Teresa's death in 1582. It was later recovered by Ana de Jésus and edited by Luis de Léon.

The context of Chapters Ten to Twelve of the *Vida* is that they are preceded by Teresa's descriptions of how her life of prayer had gone astray once she had joined the Convent of the *Encarnación.* As she describes the sins into which her soul had fallen she makes a telling comment: "And helping this was that as my sins grew, I began to lose the pleasure and gift (*gusto y regalo)* in the things of virtue"(V, 7.1).

For Teresa, one of the most distressing things at this time in her life was the loss of the pleasure *(gusto)* of the life of prayer. Deprived of this *gusto*, this link to the affective, she became 'afraid to pray' instead resorting to 'vocal prayer'. She clearly practised the outward virtues 'So that the nuns had a good opinion of me' whilst retaining this 'inner dryness'. She contrasts at this time her outer shows of piety and holiness (including instructing others on prayer) with her own interior sense of alienation from the source of her being – God. The experience of this time is one of *recollection*, dryness punctuated by another state of which she finds it difficult to speak (V, 4.8). This period ('of some twenty years' V, 8.2) she tells us was a time of neither 'pleasure in God' nor 'contentment with the world'(*yogozaba de Dios nitraíacontentoen el mundo*)(V, 8.2) for she is adamant that prayer is the source of 'delights/ pleasures' (*gustos* V, 8.9) from the Lord, it is the place where 'the Lord takes delight in a soul and gives the soul delight/ *entrar a regalarse con un alma y regalarla'* (V, 8.9).

In this place of deconstruction – without intellectual concourse (V, 4.7, 9.4, 9.5, 9.9) Teresa enters into a place to which she gives the name *místicateología:*

> It used to happen, when I represented Christ within me in order to place myself in His presence, or even while reading, that a feeling of the presence of God would come upon me unexpectedly so that I could in no way doubt He was within me or I totally immersed in Him [...]. I believe they call this "mystical theology. (V, 10.1)

Teresa equates this 'mystical theology'with an indubitable sense of the presence of God:

> The will loves; the memory appears to me almost lost; the understanding does not discourse, so it appears to me – it is not lost, but, as I say, it does not work – however it is amazed at how much it can understand, because God wants it to understand how little it can understand of what God represents to it. (V, 10.1)

Using the classical scholastic/Augustinian typology of the memory-will-understanding Teresa presents here what I call a deconstructive-affective strategy in clear terms. The pull of the text is as though she wants to declare that the reason *(entendimiento)* ceases to work – the most extreme position of unsaying. Although her uncertainty allows her to interject the milder *no discurre* – 'does not discourse', only the affective/libidinal can function at this point as she makes clear in her short statement *ama la voluntad* ('the will loves'). The mystical strategies of the *theologia mystica* are clearly being employed here (See V, 12.5 too). As she describes in 12.5 this 'stopping of the intellect' is not something that is done by voluntary action, but something received from God, 'for otherwise we would be left like cold simpletons'. The intellectual should 'delight in God' (13.11) rather than 'wear themselves out in composing syllogisms'.

Her next mention of the 'mystical theology' in V, 11.5 is to distinguish it from the beginning stages of prayer (or as she calls it 'mental prayer') which will form a small discourse from Chapter Eleven to Chapter Twenty Two – the famous analogy of the 'four waters' (See Kavanaugh and Rodriguez, CW I, 470). In Chapter Twenty Three she returns to her 'mystical theology', this, she says, is distinguished by being the stage where we 'enjoy' God's presence: *'lo máses gozar/* the more to enjoy it'(V, 11.5). The beginning 'mansions', as she will later call them in the *Moradas*, are places lacking in *gustos y ternera*[9] – these are the special attributes of the *teologíamística* (see V, 8.5, 9.9. 10.2 and 25.11). At this earlier stage the 'understanding' continues to 'work' and for this she recommends books such as Alonso de Madrid's *Arte de servir de Dios* (V, 12.2). The great delight in the Lord's presence in the soul (V, 14.2, 14.9) reflecting the opening of the *Moradas*: "This quietude and recollection is something that is clearly felt through the satisfaction and peace bestowed on the soul, along with great contentment and calm and a very gentle delight in the faculties." (V, 15.1)

4. Strategies of Unknowing in Teresa

The climate, then, in which the mature Teresa was writing books of affective spirituality for her sisters was clearly one of *odium theologicum* towards an intelligent woman presuming to teach men, a daughter of *converso* stock and someone whose teachings came perilously close to that of *alumbradismo* (See Llamas Martínez, 1972 and Rivers, 1984). We remember the famous quote from the Inquisitor Fray Alonso de la Fuente, made in 1589, some seven years after her death:

The author of the said book passes it off and recommends it as a doctrine revealed by God and inspired by the Holy Spirit; but if in fact the author was that nun whose name is on the title page, it is a matter *praeternaturam* for her to have written something taught by an angel, because it exceeds a woman's capacity. In any case it could not have been a good angel, but a bad one, the same one that deceived Mohammed and Luther and the other leaders of heretics. This being the case, the so-called miracle of the nun Teresa of Jesus, that her body is today intact and uncorrupted, is a fabulous business, either the work of Satan or the invention of heretics (Llamas-Martínez, 1972, 396).

[9] The terms literally mean 'taste/savour/pleasure' and 'gentleness'. For more discussion see Tyler 2011.

Within this climate it appears to us now that Teresa deliberately used her own 'vulgar style of substandard written Spanish' (Rivers, 1984, 120) to survive. Indeed, within the context of the *theologia mystica* her 'anti-rational' style makes complete sense. Her style, as Rivers points out, deliberately avoids the syntax and style of the newly developing Romance Spanish then popular with Renaissance Spanish humanists such as Luis de Granada and Juan de Valdés: "Teresa's written Spanish is in fact hard for us to read and understand in a wholly rational way; it is comparable, within an American context, to something composed by a writer of Black English, who deliberately tries to avoid the academic sound of white bourgeois correctness (Rivers, 1984,121).

My argument in this paper is that taking her cue from Osuna and the tradition of *theologia mystica* she is engaging in her own form of 'unknowing' all the better to teach the truths of *theologia mystica* and in particular *recogimiento*. I will conclude the paper by highlighting six ways in which I believe she does this.

A. The Direction of Locution

After Teresa's death in 1582 the Discalced Carmelites, on the recommendation of St John of the Cross, approached the *converso* Augustinian friar and professor of Hebrew at Salamanca University, Fray Luis de León, to edit her texts for publication. Luis, as a theologian with a humanistic bent and from *converso* origins himself had also spent five years in the prisons of the Inquisition so knew something of the dangerous climate within which such mystical texts would be received and engaged in his task with perception and insight (see Rivers, 1984, 122).The first edition was published with remarkable speed in 1588 with a dedicatory letter to Ana de Jésus, Prioress of the Discalced in Madrid and close friend of John. Luis begins his letter by stating: "I never knew, or saw, Mother Teresa of Jesus while she lived on earth; but now that she lives in Heaven I do know her, and I see her almost continuously in two living images of herself which she left us – her daughters and her books (Peers, CW III, 368).

From the beginning Luis recognized how 'alive' Teresa's texts were and how dependent they were on the 'oral community' of Carmelites that she had created:

> I believe that your reverences are important witnesses, for you are quite similar models of excellence: I never remember reading her works without imagining that I am listening to Your Reverence's voices, nor, conversely, do I ever hear you talk without feeling that I am reading the words of the Mother. Those who have experience of this will know that it is the truth. (Peers, CW III, 372)

For Luis, Teresa's writings *must* be understood within the context of the oral community. They benefit from being read aloud and strive to repeat the patterns, rests and pauses of speech with which she was familiar. The texts are peppered with '*erss*', '*umms*' and '*puess*' as she seeks at headlong pace to transcribe the oral to the written. Take, for example, this breathless interruption to the exposition of the 'Prayer of Quiet' in Mansion Four of the *Moradas*:

> God help the mess I've got in to! I've already forgotten what I'm writing about as business and poor health have forced me to put this work on one side until things were better, and as I have a bad memory everything will come out confused as I can't return to read it all over again. Perhaps everything I say is confused – that's what it feels like anyway. (M, 4.2.1)

Writing on Teresa's style in 1941 (and possibly having in mind passages such as the above) the Spanish critic Menéndez Pidal wrote: "St Teresa does not really write, but speaks through writing; thus the excitement of her emotional syntax constantly overflows the restrictions of ordinary grammar" (*Menéndez Pidal,* 1942, 135). As De Certeau suggests, when we read passages such as the later ones from the *Moradas* where she has perfected her craft it is almost as though we can see the sisters round us, pressing nearer to hear what she has to tell us (see also M, 6.4, 3.1, 4.1, 4.2). Her discourse then presupposes and creates a community of discourse.

B. Contradiction

In his dedicatory letter Luis de León also defended Teresa's habit of 'failing to carry her argument to its conclusion, but introducing other arguments which often break the thread of her sense' (Peers, CW III, 373). Throughout her writings Teresa is not concerned to reproduce the classical Latin style of the new Renaissance humanism. Hers is a 'rough and ready' style whose directness is its appeal.

As befits the *stultasapientia*[10] of the *theologia mystica* Teresa, like Osuna, frequently employs paradox to shift meaning to the point where it begins to break down. The soul in the third degree of prayer in the *Vida* is: "Rejoicing in this agony with ineffable joy [...] the state is glorious folly [...] a heavenly madness [...] delectable disquiet [...] So, delectable is this distress that life holds no delight which can give greater satisfaction" (V, 24).

Menéndez Pidal writes of her style in a similar vein as Luis de León: "Her incessant ellipses; confused grammatical arguments; enormous parentheses, which cause the reader to lose the train of thought; lines of reasoning that are never completed because of interruptions, verbless sentences" (*Menéndez Pidal,* 1942, 135). I would argue that Teresa *deliberately* writes in this confusing way as a true daughter of the *theologia mystica* of de Osuna and *Los Recogidos*. The understanding, as for Osuna, must be thwarted to allow the soul's direct access to God through *recogimiento*. The tumbling morass of sentences, adverbs, meandering constructions and exclamations only helps to serve that purpose. Rivers again: "She refuses to accept the analytical or linear sequentiality of linguistic discourse, and she strives for simultaneity, for saying everything all at once, as it actually happens, "writing with many hands" (Rivers, 1984:127, see, for example, CV, 20:6).

C. Avoiding Conclusions: Humility

The whole groundwork of prayer is based on humility and that the more a soul lowers itself in prayer the more God raises it up. (V, 22.11)

In an important essay on Teresa's *Moradas* published in 1983 (Flasche, 1983) Hans Flasche points out the importance of the verb

[10] Literally 'foolish wisdom' – a medieval term for the *theologia mystica* ultimately taken from Dionysius (See, Tyler 2010).

parecer – 'it seems, it appears' in *Las Moradas. Parecer,* he writes, 'is one of the most important words in Saint Teresa's lexicon' (Flasche, 1983, 447). She uses the verb repeatedly in all her texts creating a deliberate atmosphere of uncertitude and provisionality which can only assist in the 'disguising' of Teresa's intentions with regard to her exposition of the 'mystical theology'. Pictures and suggestions are 'offered' to the reader as possible solutions and answers she has found: once again we have the familiar 'stammering, broken voice' of Teresa. In the *Moradas,* for example, it appears frequently: *'Parécemequeaun no osveosatisfechas/* It seems to me that you're still not satisfied' (M, 5:1), *'Parécemequeestáis con deseo de verqué se haceestapalomica/* It seems to me you have a desire to see what this little dove is doing' (M, 5.4), *'Parécemequeosestoymirandocómodecís/* It seems to me that I can see you asking' (M, 6.6). Once again the rhetorical strategies we identified above are coming into play. Accompanying this studied incertitude is Teresa's continual insistence that as an unlettered *'mujercilla'*[11] she is not qualified to talk on such lofty matters: "For the love of God, let me work at my spinning wheel and go to choir and perform the duties of religious life, like the other sisters. I am not meant to write: I have neither the health nor intelligence for it" (Peers, CW, 1.xxxix).

Frequently, she tells us she is unqualified and useless to the task: "God help me with what I have undertaken! I've already forgot what I was dealing with, for business matters and poor health have forced me to set this work aside just when I was at my best; and since I have a poor memory everything will come out confused because I can't go back to read it over again. And perhaps even everything else I say is confused; at least that's what I feel it is. (M, 4.2.1 immediately followed by a *Parece*: 'It seems to me I have explained the nature of consolations in the spiritual life').

It is notable that these linguistic devices become more evident when Teresa talks of the more 'inexpressible' elements of prayer such as in the Fourth Mansions quoted above. The phrase 'little woman' or 'stupid woman' was a typical theological attack on women's inadequacy when it came to questions of doctrine or theology. Bartolomé de Medina had

[11] Literally 'little woman'.

denounced her as *'mujercilla'* saying that her nuns would be better off 'staying in their convents and praying and spinning' (Weber, 1990, 36).

As Weber shows in her classic exposition of this tactic, Teresa's defense was to 'embrace stereotypes of female ignorance, timidity, or physical weakness but disassociate herself from the double-edged myth of woman as seducible/seductive' (1990, 36). For example in *Vida* 11, 14:

> As for a poor woman (*mujercita*) like myself, a weak and irresolute creature, it seems right that the Lord should lead me on with favours (*regalos*), as He now does, in order that I may bear certain afflictions with which He has been pleased to burden me. But, when I hear servants of God, men of weight, learning and understanding (*de tomas, de letrados, de entendimiento*) worrying so much because He is not giving them devotion, it makes me sick to listen to them... They should realise that since the Lord does not give it to them they do not need it.

As Weber remarks 'With disarming modesty she concedes to women's intellectual inferiority in a way that frees her to explore a new theological vocabulary' (1990, 38):

> I shall have to make use of some comparison, for which I should like to apologise, since I am a woman and write simply what I am ordered to writer. But, this spiritual language is so difficult to use for anyone who like myself has not gone through studies, that I shall have to find some way of explaining myself, and it may be that most of the time I won't get the comparison right. Seeing so much stupidity will provide some amusement for your Reverence. (V, 11.6)

As Weber comments: "In these passages, and in many others, Teresa concedes to women's weakness, timidity, powerlessness and intellectual inferiority but uses the concessions ironically to defend, respectively, the legitimacy of her own spiritual favours, her disobedience of *letrados*, her administrative initiative, her right to 'teach' in the Pauline sense and her unmediated access to scripture" (Weber, 1990, 39/40). For both reader and writer, then, humility is required. The opening sections of the *Moradas* stress the need for 'humility', not just morally but intellectually. Only by this *stulta* can the means be prepared for God to impart *sapientia.* Teresa's 'little woman' is thus the first cousin of the 'unlettered woman' presented by Gerson, Laredo, Osuna and the other masters of the *theologia mystica.*

D. Disorientation

In Luis de León's letter to Ana de Jésus mentioned above he points out that he does not feel it is necessary to amend the style with which Teresa presents her writing:

> I have neither amended them verbally nor adopted the considerable changes which copies now in circulation have made in the text of them either through the copyists' own carelessness or out of presumption or error... If her critics had a real understanding of Castilian, they would see that that of the Mother is elegance itself. For even though, in certain passages of what she writes, before she completes the sentence that she has begun, she contaminates it with other sentences and breaks the train of thought, often beginning anew with interpolations, nevertheless she inserts her digressions so skilfully and introduces her fresh thoughts with such grace that the defect itself is a source of beauty, like a mole on a lovely face (Peers, CW, III. 373).

As we have seen Luis, her first editor, recognised at the outset that the meaning of Teresa's message was inextricably bound up with the medium of the message: that rag-tag bag of flooding prose full of errors, inconsistencies, *puess*, *buts*and *errs*. The very same style that makes the whole work comes alive for the reader. Exclamations litter Teresa's text, as do lengthy repetitions and interpolations in the text. In the *Vida* in particular the sentences tumble out making it difficult for the reader, and the translator, to keep up:

At first these things did me harm - so it appeared (*me parece*) -, and it shouldn't have been her fault, but mine; for afterwards my own wickedness was bad enough, together with the servants we had, whom for every wrong they were able to assist; that if one had given me good counsel, to benefit me; rather self-interest blinded them as did desire me. And because I was never inclined to much wrong – because I naturally abhorred bad things - , but to the pastime of pleasant conversation; yet, placed in the situation, I was in the hand of danger, and would be placing my father and brothers in it as well. (V, 2.5)

Teresa seems to recognize that in order to maintain the vitality of the spiritual world she is trying to convey to her reader she must also retain the rough edged inconsistency of speech in real time. Her texts 'show' as much through what they do not say as through what they do. Accordingly, Teresa will often use pictures, metaphors and images to 'disorientate' the discursive intellect and take it to places it would rather not go.

As we have seen above, Teresa frequently uses the 'rhetoric of incompetence'. Thus in *Moradas* 1.2.7 we find the following passage:

> These interior matters are so obscure for our minds *(tan oscuras de entender)* that anyone who knows as little as I will be forced to say many superfluous and even foolish things in order to say something that's right. Whoever reads this must have patience, for I have to have it in order to write about what I don't know. Indeed sometimes I take up the paper like a fool (*unacosaboba*), for I don't know what to say or how to begin (M, 1.2.7).

Following Gerson and Osuna, the 'fool' (or 'little woman') is the one who is wise in the '*theologia mystica'*. Perhaps, she implies, all of us, writer and reader alike, must become fools before we can enter the strategy of the 'mystical theology'.

E. Humour

"The soul sometimes laughs to itself when it sees seriously religious and prayerful persons make a big issue out of some rules of etiquette which it has already trampled under foot" (V, 21.9).

As is attested by many of her contemporaries and is clear from her writing, humour was always an important part of Teresa's armoury in her struggles to establish the discalced reform. Although examples of this abound throughout her work perhaps the clearest examples are in the *Libro de Las Fundaciones* ('Book of the Foundations', hereafter F) describing in open fashion the recent events around the founding of her convents in Spain. As Weber points out (Weber 1990:126) the topics dealt with had to be done so with tact and care as many of the protagonists were still alive and the tension between the Discalced reform and the Carmelites of the Mitigated Rule remained high. She describes her style in the prologue to the book as *tan pesado* ('too heavy') and suffering from too much *grosería* ('coarseness'). Weber describes the history as 'picaresque': "She slyly reveals that in her determination to do God's work she must rely on her charm, ingenuity, and, at times, deception in order to outwit unenlightened souls, be they landlords, town councilmen, or archbishops" (Weber, 1990, 128).

A few examples will suffice:

- Chapter Thirty One describes the difficult foundation at Burgos. Here the Archbishop, Don Cristóbal Vela was initially enthusiastic, encouraging the sisters to come prior to his granting a licence for the foundation.[12] Teresa describes the struggles to get to Burgos, the rivers in full spate and her own illness. Having finally arrived Teresa describes how the Archbishop does not want them there and tells them if they do not have an income and a house of their own they should leave to which Teresa comments: 'The roads of course were charming and it was such nice weather!' (F 31, 21).
- Chapter 19 describes the foundation of Salamanca with the full vigour of the picaresque. The house they had chosen (which still presently stands on the Plaza de Santa Teresa) had previously been occupied by students and Teresa's description of the first night herself and an elderly sister, terrified of the evicted students returning on Hallowe'en is a masterpiece: "When my companion found herself shut up in the room, she seemed to be a little calmer about the students, though she did nothing all the time but look about her fearfully, first in one direction then in another… "What are you looking for?" I asked her. "Nobody can

[12] His uncle was Teresa's godfather, see Peers, CW III: 184 fn 2.

possibly get in here." "Mother", she replied, "I am wondering what you would do all alone if I were to die here." […] So I said to her: "Well, sister, I shall consider what is to be done if the occasion arises: now let me go to sleep" (F, 19:5).

- One of the most interesting depictions of humour occurs in Chapter Six which begins with Teresa back with her favourite topic of the *Vida* and the *Moradas* – vis. the spiritual life and how progress can be made in prayer. Almost immediately she reaches the 'point of unknowing': 'I wish I knew how to explain myself here, but it is so difficult that I do not know if I shall be able to do so' (F, 6.2). However, in this chapter she touches on the controversial subject of raptures and ecstasies, so easily associated with the *Alumbrados*. The chapter also deals with the controversial topic of the relationship between spirituality and sexuality and the proximity of sensual with spiritual delights. She gives clear guidelines that prioresses should beware these prolonged 'swoons' or 'raptures' and not encourage them in their sisters. To make her point with humour she refers to an incident that took place at Medina del Campo with a choir nun, Alberta Bautista and lay sister Inés de la Concepción (See Peers, CW, III.30 fn. 1). In their desire to experience ecstasy they asked for frequent communion from their confessor: 'the result was such an increase in distress that unless they communicated daily they thought they were about to die' (F, 6.10). Teresa realizes how unhealthy this attachment has become but has to deal with an obdurate confessor who refuses to believe this can cause anything but good for the sisters. Let Teresa complete the story herself:

I started to talk to the nuns and to give them many reasons, sufficient, in my opinion, to prove to them that the idea that they would die without this particular help was pure imagination. But, the notion was so deeply rooted in their minds that no argument could eradicate it and it was useless to reason with them further. So, seeing that it was in vain, I told them that I had those very desires myself and yet I should stay away from Communion, so that they might realize that they ought not to communicate except when all the nuns did so together: we would all three die together, I said (F, 6.11).

Potential heretics, timid and difficult nuns, and wavering clerics, Teresa encounters each with humanity and warmth allowing her humour to pepper the narrative and convince us, her readers, of the correctness of her remedies and solutions. Perhaps the key to her use of humour in the *Fundaciones*lies at the beginning of the prologue where she stresses the need for humility (*humildad*) in the enterprise (see 3. above). Humility, humour and grounded or ordinary language: all three rotate around each other to produce the necessary effect on the reader. As we read the accounts we realize that she is gently laughing at us the reader – with all our pomposities, obsessions with prayers, worldly concerns and judgemental attitudes. Yes, we can laugh at the targets of her humour in the *Fundaciones,* but we must always remember that her comments are directed equally at us, her readers.

F. Ordinary Speech

As we have seen Teresa herself is conscious of her style, she calls it 'my rough style rather than that of those more elegant' (*mi groseroestiloqueporotroselegantes)* (CVA, 16.9) full of 'imperfection' and 'poverty' (CVA, Prologue). As Allison Peers points out in his 1953 essay *Saint Teresa's Style: A Tentative Appraisal* (Allison Peers, 1953) the key note in her style is down-to-earthiness and naturalness. Here, again she appears to be a disciple of Osuna and the simple direct style of the *theologia mystica* of the *TerceraAbecedario*. She states that the manner of writing (like talking) adopted by nuns should be:

> Simple, frank and devout, rather like that of hermits and people who live in retirement. They must use none of the newfangled words – affectations, as I think people call them – which are current in a world always eager for newfangled things. In all circumstances let them give preference to common expressions rather than to unusual ones ('Method for the visitation of convents of the Discalced Carmelite nuns' in Allison Peers, CW, 3.251).

As Allison Peers points out, she avoids learned words (Allison Peers, 1953, 84) and her text is notable for the lack of precise theological terms especially concerning ‘mystical theology’. Indeed, as we have seen, the word ‘mystical theology’ is only used a handful of times in the *Vida* before it is dropped not to be used again in her work. The humility of ordinary language is close to the humility of humour and central to the effect she wants to produce in her readers.

In his study, *The Vernacular Mind of St Teresa* (Rivers, 1984), Elias Rivers points out how Teresa’s ‘vernacularism’ was a part of the sixteenth century Spanish humanist movement which deliberately sought to communicate to ‘ordinary people’ through Castilian rather than Classical Latin. Rivers suggests that in this, as we have seen before, the simple Latin of Augustine’s *Confessions*, an influential text on the young Teresa, was clearly an important influence (Rivers, 1984, 117): “Teresa of Jesus knew very little Latin, and she deliberately refused to imitate the new style of classical Spanish prose; in a true patristic spirit, she invented her own vulgar style of substandard written Spanish, a style that is clearly anti-academic and even anti-rational” (Rivers, 1984,120).

Thus, in her prose we find that ‘classical’ Castilian spellings are twisted and subverted, often using more phonetic spelling than grammatical. Thus, she uses *ylesia* and *yglesia* for *iglesia* (‘church’), *naide*for *nadie*(‘no-one’), *relisión* for *religion* (‘religion’) as well as a host of diminutives and familiarisations of words: *mariposita* (a little butterfly), *pastorcito* (little shepherd boy), *avecita* (little bird). Peers suggests that she creates words of her own invention ‘charging them with emotional content which another language can only approximately express’ (Peers, 1953, 85): *un disgustillo* (V, 12) ‘ a little annoyance’ / ‘a little feeling of frustration’; *estostemorcillos* (V, 31) ‘these little fears’; *centellicapequeñita* (V, 15) ‘the tiniest of tiny sparks’ – this latter being her appropriation of the classical phrase *scintilla* from the *theologia mystica* to describe the point at which the soul meets the divine.

Her conversational and immediate style, Rivers suggests, is deliberate and intentional:

> She learned to read Spanish fluently as a young girl and knew that she had an advantage there that she could never have in the official Scholastic language of the Western Church, with its exclusively male priesthood. Her Spanish was not structured, as Louis of Granada's and John de Valdés's was, by a familiarity with written Latin, whether ecclesiastical or neo-classical. When she wrote, she neglected, or perhaps deliberately avoided, the normal spelling and syntax of the Spanish texts that she had voraciously read (Rivers, 1984, 121).

Antonio Marcos (1997, 153) suggests that she deliberately uses the *'avulgarización intencionada'* of the *'estilo de ermitaños'*. If this is the case, Teresa in her 'rough speech' is deliberately positioning herself in her writings with her beloved *espirituales* of the *recogimiento* movement such as Pedro de Alcantara rather than the sophisticated *letrados* with their more polished and scholastic Latin rhetoric.Teresa's language, then, may be considered coarse, vulgar or stupid, but she is happy with this as it serves the purpose she wants, to 'change the aspect' of her reader:

> Your behaviour and language must be like this: let any who wish to talk to you learn your language; and, if they will not, be careful never to learn theirs: it might lead you to hell. It matters little if you are considered coarse (*groseras*) and still less if you are taken for hypocrites: indeed, you will gain by this, because only those who understand your language will come to see you (CVA, 20, 4-5).

5. Conclusion

I have argued in this paper that the context of Teresa of Avila's circumstances, especially inquisitorial pressure as a result of traces of *alumbradismo*, her status as a woman and her interest in mystical prayer means that her texts have to employ a particular 'mystical strategy' that I have termed the *theologia mystica*. This strategy, inherited from the medieval Dionysian tradition emphasizes both *affective* and *deconstructive* approaches to mystical writing. In this paper, I have concentrated on six so-called *strategies of deconstruction* in Teresa's writing, vis: direction of locution, contradiction, humility, disorientation, humour and ordinary speech. By employing these strategies, I conclude, Teresa of Avila shows herself to be a true heir to the 'mystical masters' she studied as a young woman. She also shows herself to be a true master of 'mystical strategy' in preserving the importance of personal affective prayer in times of great institutional pressure against these forms of prayer.

Bibliography:

Works by Teresa of Avila

1. *Obras Completas de Santa Teresa de Jésus*,ed. Efrén de la Madre de Dios and Otger Steggink, 9th ed. Madrid: Biblioteca de Autores Cristianos, 1997.
2. *Santa Teresa Obras Completas*, ed. T. Alvarez, 10th ed., Burgos: Editorial Monte Carmelo, 1998.
3. *The Collected Works of St Teresa of Avila*, trans. K. Kavanaugh and O. Rodriguez. 3 vols. vol. 1: 2nd ed.; Vols. 2 & 3; 1st ed. Washington: Institute of Carmelite Studies, 1980 -87.
4. *The Complete Works of St Teresa of Jesus*, trans. E. Allison Peers, 3 vols. London: Sheed and Ward, 1946 (Peers, CW).

Abbreviations

C	=	*Meditaciones del amor de Dios*
CE	=	*Camino,* Escorial Codex
CV	=	*Camino,* Valladolid Codex
CT	=	*Camino,* Toledo Codex
Exc	=	*Exclamaciones*
M	=	*Las Moradas*
V	=	*El Libro de La Vida*

1. Ahlgren, G., *Teresa of Avila and the Politics of Sanctity*, Ithaca: Cornell UP, 1996.
2. Bataillon, M., *Erasmo y España*. Mexico: Fondo de cultura económica, 1982.
3. de Bujanda, J.ed., *Index de L'Inquisition Espagnole 1551,1554, 1559/Index des Livres Interdit,* Vol. 6, Québec: *Éditions de* l'Université *de* Sherbrooke, 1984.
4. De Osuna, Francisco, *Tercer Abecedario Espiritual de Francisco de Osuna*, ed. S. López Santidrián, Madrid: Biblioteca de Autores Cristianos, 1998.
5. De Osuna, Francisco, *The Third Spiritual Alphabet*, trans. M. Giles, New York: Paulist. 1981.

6. Flasche, H., El Problema de la Certezaen el "Castillo Interior" in *Actas de Congreso Internacional Teresiano* ed. T. Egido Martínez, V. García de la Concha and O. Gonzalez de Caredal, Salamanca: Universidad de Salamanca, 1983.
7. Hamilton, A., *Heresy and Mysticism in Sixteenth Century Spain: the Alumbrados*, Cambridge: James Clarke, 1992.
8. Marcosn, Antonio, 'Recurrencias y Concatenadores: La Cohesiónen el Discurso Teresiano' in *La Recepción de los Místicos Teresa de Jesús y Juan de la Cruz*, ed. S. RosGarcía, Salamanca: Ediciones Universidad Pontificia, 1997.
9. Márquez, A., *Los alumbrados: orígenes y filosofía (1525 –1559)*, Madrid: Taurus, 1980.
10. Martin, Andrés, *LosRecogidos: Nueva Vision de la Mistica Española (1500 – 1700),* Madrid: Fundacion Universitaria Española, Seminario 'Suarez', 1975.
11. Martínez, Llamas, *Santa Teresa de Jesús y la Inquisición español*, Madrid: CSICm 1972.
12. *Menéndez, Pidal* R., "El estilo de Santa *Teresa*" in *Escorial* 2 (1941): 13-30. Reprinted in *La lengua de Cristóbal Colón*, Col. Austral No. 280 (Madrid, *1942*).
13. Peers, Allison E., 'Saint Teresa's Style: A Tentative Appraisal' in *Saint Teresa of Jesus and Other Essays and Addresses*, London: Faber and Faber, 1953.
14. Rivers, E., 'The Vernacular Mind of St Teresa' in *Carmelite Studies*, Washington: ICS, 1984.
15. Tyler, P.M., 'The Catholic Mystical Tradition as a Guide to Contemporary Pastoral Care' in *Keeping Faith in Practice: Catholic Perspectives on Practical and Pastoral Theology,* ed. D. Lonsdale, J. Sweeney, & G. Simmonds, Norwich: SCM-Canterbury, 2010.
16. Tyler, P.M., *The Return to the Mystical: Ludwig Wittgenstein, Teresa of Avila and the Christian Mystical Tradition* (London: Continuum), 2011.
17. Tyler, P.M., *The Way of Ecstasy: Praying with St Teresa of Avila*, Norwich: SCM-Canterbury, 1997.
18. Weber, A., *Teresa of Avila and the Rhetoric of Femininity,* Princeton, NJ: Princeton University Press, 1990.

13

Presence and Mysticis

Retrieval of Pseudo-Dionysius in Deconstruction and Theology

Dr. Sebastian Madathummuriyil
Duquesne University, Pittsburgh, USA

Introduction

The debate surrounding the "theological turn"[1] in French phenomenology and the *apophatic* theology (negative/mystical theology) of Pseudo-Dionysius is an important area of engagement in postmodern philosophy and theology. A fascinating outcome of this debate is that it has aligned thinkers into two camps based on the divergent routes that they take in the retrieval of negative theology. One of those camps is theistic, and the other is atheistic. The present article explores the influence of Dionysius in the theology of Jean-Luc Marion and argues that postmodern theology assumes a mystical dimension in the understanding of the sacraments. This task is undertaken as follows: The first part of this article introduces the debate on the relationship between deconstruction and negative theology, with special reference to Derrida. The second part examines the retrieval and reinterpretation of Dionysius in the theology of Marion, exploring some of the key notions of his phenomenology. The third part explores how God re-enters postmodern theology through the mystical

[1] Dominique Janicaud *et al.*, "Phenomenology and the 'Theological Turn': The French Debate," ed. John D. Caputo, *Perspectives in Continental Philosophy*, New York: Fordham University Press, 2000.

language of love rather than through that of being, highlighting the traces of mysticism that permeate contemporary understanding of God and sacramental presence with special reference to Marion.

1. Deconstruction and Negative Theology

The postmodern interest in negative theology can be traced back to Jacque Derrida's lecture *Différance* in 1968.[2] In what follows, we will briefly examine the "third way" of Dionysius and its relationship with deconstruction as exemplified in the notion of the 'impossible' and the *tout autre* (the Wholly Other), highlighting its collision and coherence with negative theology in terms of its theistic intent.

1.1. The "Third Way:" Beyond Affirmation and Denial

The classical theme or scheme of apophatism is attributed to the sixth century monk Dionysius the Areopagite, who is known as Pseudo-Dionysius. Negative theology characterizes a mystical tradition that tries "not to speak" of the trace of God.[3] It basically affirms that it cannot say something affirmatively about God. In other words, it says nothing other than saying: "There is no speaking of it, nor name, nor knowledge of it" (MT 1048B).[4] We cannot speak of God, because, the cause of everything is perceptible in the things of the world, while God remains himself imperceptible (MT 1040D). In the same way, although he is the cause of conceptual things, he himself is not conceptual (MT 1045D). The higher we fly upward, the more we find ourselves falling short of words. Language falters, and when we pass further and beyond,

[2] It may be traced even further back to his 1964 lecture on the ethical phenomenology of Emmanuel Levinas. In this essay, entitled "Violence and Metaphysics," Derrida argues that Levinas' thought on ethics is largely metaphysical, with citations from mystical theologians such as Meister Eckhart, Dionysius and Nicholas of Cusa. Jacques Derrida, "Violence and Metaphysics," in *Writing and Difference*, ed. Alan Bass, Chicago: University of Chicago, 1978, 76.

[3] In the trajectory of the orthodox tradition, Dionysius emphasizes the paradoxical nature of God's revelation retaining the hiddenness (mystery) of God (essence) and the manifestation of God (energies – powers, names, etc.). See John D. Jones, "An Absolutely Simple God? Frameworks for Reading Pseudo-Dionysius the Areopagite," *The Thomist* 69 (2005): 387-388.

[4] All references to the Dionysian corpus are from Pseudo-Dionysius, *Psuedo-Dionysius: The Complete Works*, trans. Colm Luibheid, New York: Paulist Press, 1987.

our language ends up in silence, since we finally become united with the indescribable (MT 1033B). Therefore, Dionysius advises Timothy to leave all of his perceptions and understanding, and instead to strive to achieve union with the one who is "beyond all being and knowledge" (MT 1000A). We must not apply concepts or words to the hidden divine because he is beyond being and speech. We can only look upward to the light of the sacred scripture. As he observes, "It[God] is beyond assertion and denial. We make assertions and denials of what is next to it, but never of it, for it is both beyond every assertion, being the perfect and unique cause of all things, and, by virtue of its preeminently simple and absolute nature, free of every limitation, beyond every limitation; it is also beyond every denial" (MT 1048B). Therefore, negative theology holds that the yearning for naming God who is the cause of everything cannot be expressed in the language of affirmation. However, this yearning takes the theologian to a third way or mystical moment in theology which is beyond affirmation and negation.

Furthermore, "the negations are not simply the opposite of the affirmations, but rather that the cause of all is considerably prior to this, beyond privations, beyond every denial, beyond every assertion" (MT 1000B). The unique contribution of Dionysius to the history of mysticism is to think of the divine beyond the categorical alternatives of affirmation and negation which is characterized by an "illogical logic" of neither/nor, beyond this/beyond that, which explains the hyperessence of God as Goodness. Hence, apophatism is not the affirmation of the negative, e.g., God is not this, but rather it is affirming the 'not being' of God. In other words, it is affirming that God is beyond being as at Mount Sinai where Moses enters into a complete union with God (Ex 19 and 20:18-21), renouncing all knowledge, and knows beyond knowledge by knowing nothing (MT 1001A). Moreover, negative names or the apophatic mode of theology overrides the positive or kataphatic names in speaking about God for Dionysius, although none of these would suffice to explain the divine essence. Over and above the affirmative and negative language, the mystical moment or the third way is flooded with hyper-terms. Marion's notions of excess, saturation, etc., are founded on this hyper notion of Dionysius.

1.2. Hymnic Language

Negative theology is more eloquent when it is not saying any words. It is a particular way of doing God-talk by retreating or withdrawing from saying anything, which involves a tension between silence and speech. This makes speech both necessary and impossible, originating the language of praise. The language of praise is not only addressed to God, but also says something about God. In this sense, negative theology is "theology" or a discourse about God.[5] For instance, Dionysius opens *The Mystical Theology* by praying "Trinity!! Higher than being" (MT 997A). Here the Trinity is addressed as *hyperousie* (higher than or beyond being). The prayer has a double function of praising as well as speaking of the One to whom the praise is addressed. Praise involves a discourse by addressing the One who is praised. It is essentially a Christian prayer, as it is addressed to the Trinity. Hans Urs von Balthasar has tried to retrieve the Dionysian mode of thinking into his theology. As he puts it, "[w]here it is a matter of God and the divine, the word *hymnein* (to praise), almost replaces the word '*to say*'."[6] Thus, the language of praise predicates (says) something without speaking about God.

The third way of Dionysius is significant since it goes beyond the way of conceiving God in terms of Being, where language and concepts play a central role. The priority of the Good opens a way for theologians to speak of the divine in a language that is different from the framework of concepts and language. In this sense, Dionysian language, the language of praise, has been accepted widely in postmodern discussion on God. Furthermore, for Dionysius, the purpose of hymnic language is not to reveal the superessence of the divine or to unravel the mystery of the divine, but rather it is necessitated by the encounter with the divine, who is beyond thought and language, and is invoked in the mystical moment of prayer. As Dionysius points out, "[t]he purpose of this discourse is not to reveal that superessential essence as superessential, for this is something beyond words, something unknown and wholly unrevealed [...]. What I wish to do is sing a hymn of praise for the

---

5 John D. Caputo, *The Prayers and Tears of Jacques Derrida: Religion without Religion*, Bloomington/Indianapolis: Indiana University Press, 1997, 32.

6 Hans Urs von Balthasar, *The Glory of the Lord: A Theological Aesthetics*, trans. Erasmo Leiva-Merikakis, 2 ed., vol. 1, San Francisco: Ignatius Press, 1982, 173.

being-making procession of the divine Source" (DN 816B). Negative theology speaks about God while trying not to speak about God. This is done through prayer. Even though prayer is a form of addressing God, it also says something about God in the form of address. Of various forms of prayers, the prayer of praise, "not only speaks to God, but *of* God, so that prayer preserves a relationship with a predicative content, a constative."[7]

1.3. The Transcendence and Immanence of God

Mystical theology upholds the transcendence and immanence of God. According to Dionysius, the universe proceeds from, and returns to, a transcendent God who is beyond the universe as the superessence. Within this scheme, God is the cause or *aitia*. As the cause of the procession, God is immanent in everything, and everything manifests God. At the same time, God, the cause of everything, reveals himself in the cosmos while concealing and being transcendentally above it. The hidden cause manifests itself in and through its procession into creation. It/God stands outside and beyond everything that manifests it/God. As the Divine Cause transcends everything, it is different from beings that manifest their cause (DN 593C). As Jeffrey L. Kosky put it, "[t]he universe can be seen as the manifestation of the unmanifest or hidden divine cause, a manifestation in which divine transcendence is manifest precisely and paradoxically as unmanifest."[8] The notion of the procession and return of the universe to its cause alludes to the symbolic function of the universe in representing or manifesting a relationship between the transcendental God and the material universe. As Bernard McGinn puts it, "[a]ll things both reveal and conceal God. The 'dissimilar similarity' that constitutes every created manifestation of God is both a similarity to be affirmed and a dissimilarity to be denied."[9] Thus, the universe is, in a way, understood as the procession of God out of Godself and into the cosmos. Therefore, the cosmos actually manifests the divine cause

---

[7] Caputo, *The Prayers and Tears of Jacques Derrida*, 38-39.

[8] Jeffrey L. Kosky, "Contemporary Encounters with Apophatic Theology: The Case of Emmanuel Levinas," *Journal for Cultural and Religious Theory*, no. 1.3 (2000). http://www.jcrt.org/archives/01.3/kosky.shtml [accessed December 2010].

[9] Bernard McGinn, *The Foundations of Mysticism*, New York: Crossroad Press, 1992, 174.

that transcends the universe. Things, although manifesting God, are not like God. Therefore, manifestation coincides with concealment. The dynamics of the dissimilar similarity existing in the universe become radical and complete in the incarnation. Thus, the revelation of the transcendent is concealed in its very manifestation in Christ (Letter 3). In the incarnation God puts aside God's hiddenness to make manifest in Christ, but even after this revelation, the mystery of Jesus remains hidden in a way that escapes our words and understanding.

1.4. The "Cause" as the Call

In mystical theology, the notion of the cause functions outside of the scheme of causality. For Dionysius, the cause is not causality. As he observes, we "call it [the transcendent] Cause of beings since in its goodness it employed its active creative power to summon all things into being" (DN 592A). Thus, creation is understood in terms of a summons or command that brings everything into being. Therefore, in mystical theology, the Cause is understood as the Good and Beautiful in comparison with the Being of onto-theology. As Dionysius expresses it, "[e]verything looks to the Beautiful and Good as the cause of Being" (DN 704B). When the Cause summons everything into being, the beings are gifted with a longing for the Cause (Good) which makes them what they are (DN 696A) and makes the response possible.[10] Dionysius goes on to say, "From this beauty comes the existence of everything….It is the great creating cause which bestirs the world and holds all things in existence by the longing inside them to have beauty… It is ahead of all as Goal, as the Beloved, as the Cause toward which all things move, since it is the longing for beauty which actually brings them into being" (DN 704A). Therefore, the relationship between God and creatures, as both the origin and teleos of creatures, is understood in terms of Goodness, and not in terms of ontology. As Kosky puts it, "[b]eings' way to be is at first thoroughly determined by the Good and Beautiful which marks their origin in the form of a summons and their end in the form of the

---

[10] The prevenient desire of beings can be compared with prevenient grace, and has Thomistic and Rahnerian overtones, although they function in a metaphysical framework. However, more similarity can be found in the "givenness of the call" in Marion, as it is both originary and outside of the metaphysical scheme.

desirable. Beings both come from and head beyond Being – namely, to the Good. Their desire might therefore be thought of as endless yearning insofar as what they desire is the source of their desire."[11] Thus, in the theology of Dionysius, the name Good (Beauty) occupies the central place as the origin and destiny of everything. Mystical theology uses the term beyond Being for explaining the cause of everything, and not to explain their causal relationship with the divine. Therefore, ultimately speaking, it is not the Being that causes, but rather God that explains the cause of everything. Thus, it can be argued that the postmodern quest for reimagining God outside of being is incipiently present in the thought of Dionysius. Derrida and Marion are two important figures who engage Dionysius in their thinking, although with differing intents.

1.5. Derrida and the Wholly Other

Derrida had made a radical retrieval of negative theology in his deconstructionist thought.[12] Although the linguistic strategy of negative theology could be identified in deconstructionist thought, its theistic intent is less evident as compared with the explicitly theological character of negative theology. However, attempts have been made to explore the quest for the *tout autre* and the use of binaries as incipiently theological in nature.

The theologians who take seriously the death-of-God thinking of Nietzsche, Hegel, and the linguistic turn taken by Wittgenstein and Heidegger generally lay emphasis on the incapability of language in theological discourse for explaining dogmatic or transcendental certainties.[13] The dynamic potential of language is open to an endless slippage of hermeneutics and meaning, because meaning is derived by a series of signifiers moving toward a future, which is open to different meanings and interpretations. The meaning that the

---

[11] Jeffrey L. Kosky, "Contemporary Encounters with Apophatic Theology: The Case of Emmanuel Levinas," *Journal for Cultural and Religious Theory*, no. 1.3 (2000). http://www.jcrt.org/archives/01.3/kosky.shtml [accessed December 2010].

[12] Deconstruction is a method of literary analysis based on the principle that by the very nature of language, no text can have a fixed or coherent meaning.

[13] Graham Ward, "Deconstructive Theology," in *The Cambridge Companion to Postmodern Theology*, ed. Kevin J. Vanhoozer, Cambridge, UK: Cambridge University Press, 2003.

signifiers communicate is always deferred and different. Différance is a philosophical term coined by Derrida to explain this difference and deferral of meaning within language. As a result, the meaning at which one arrives is going through a continuous displacement or dissemination of meaning. Since there is an endless hermeneutics and transition of meaning, dogmatic claims can be deconstructed. This linguistic or hermeneutical claim of deconstruction has its implications for theology.[14]

According to Derrida, every discourse involves an allegory of *différance*. Therefore, the signification or the meaning of language can never be finalized. The language is not used to say something or to convey meaning, but rather the meaning of a term is deciphered by its use in different contexts in which they are used repeatedly.[15] This indeterminacy of meaning finds expression in Derrida's works as binary of oppositions/non-oppositions such as "impossible possibility," "religion without religion," "community without community," etc. According to Derrida the text enters into a discourse with what is outside of and other than the text, originating a diversity of meanings in different contexts. Therefore, what is rejected is a fossilized or a frozen meaning attributed to all discourse. In this sense, *différance* involves a deferral of meaning or transference between languages, which happens in time.[16] *Différance*, on the one hand, provides the conditions under which something is possible or constructed, and on other hand, it provides the conditions of its impossibility or destructibility. Therefore, what *différance* proposes is the possibility as well as the impossibility of a positive, metaphysical or onto-theo-logical language that affirms the presence of God. *Différance* neither proves nor disproves the existence of God, but only sets limits for discourse in making ontological claims by presenting the complexity and insufficiency of language without destroying the meaning of language entirely. This indeterminacy that surfaces *différance* is interpreted as theistic as well as atheistic. The

[14] Derrida's most famous statement: *iln'y a pa de hors-texte* (there is nothing outside the text). Jacques Derrida, *Of Grammatology*, trans. Gayatri Spivak, Baltimore: Johns Hopkins University Press, 1974, 158.

[15] Ward, "Deconstructive Theology," 80.

[16] John D. Caputo, ed., *Questioning God* (Bloomington: Indiana University Press, 2001), 14-15. This is from the roundtable discussion at Villanova University in 1999.

theistic camp considers the binaries as mutually exclusive and opposite. For them, Derrida is an atheist and *différance* is a-theological as having no relevance for theology. For the theistic camp, the binaries are quasi-transcendental, and therefore, significant for theology. Even though Derrida's theological intent cannot be overstated, his fascination with negative theology is due to its strategy of speaking about the unspeakable, without speaking through hyper terms. To the question of whether deconstruction is similar to negative theology, Derrida's answer is yes and no: "It is and it is not." Différance cannot be identified with God; it is not even the God of negative theology.[17] However, John D. Caputo has interpreted Derrida in more of a theistic line.[18]According to him, deconstruction has close connections with negative theology, not only in the way that denial forms the starting point, but also in the way that both

[17] Derrida speaks about the similarity and dissimilarity between negative theology and *difference*: "So much so that the detours, locutions, and syntax in which I will often have to take recourse will resemble those of negative theology, occasionally even to the point of being indistinguishable from negative theology. Already we have had to *delineate that difference is not*, does not exist, is not a present-being (*on*) in any form; and we will be led to delineate everything *that* it *is not*, that is, everything; and consequently that it has neither existence nor essence. It derives from no category of being, whether present or absent. And yet those aspects of *différance* which are thereby delineated are not theological, not even in the order of the most negative of negative theologies, which are always concerned with disengaging a super-essentiality beyond the finite categories of essence and existence, that is, of presence, and always hastening to recall that God is refused the predicate of existence, only in order to acknowledge his superior, inconceivable, and ineffable mode of being [...]. *Différance* is not only irreducible to any ontological or theological – ontotheological- reappropriation, but as the very opening of the space in which ontotheology-philosophy- produces its system and its history, it includes ontotheology, inscribing it and exceeding it without return." Jacques Derrida, *Margins of Philosophy*, trans. Alan Bass, Chicago: University of Chicago Press, 1982, 6.

[18] Caputo, *The Prayers and Tears of Jacques Derrida*, 2. In this book Caputo challenges the critics who consider Derrida's deconstruction as anti-religious, exploring the deep messianic, apocalyptic, and prophetic tones underlying his writings. He interprets Derrida as a man of faith or a religious thinker whose writings operate as a bridge builder between the Christian and Jewish traditions. For a discussion on the disputed relationship between deconstruction and Derrida in response to Caputo's book, see James H. Olthuis, ed., *Religion With/out Religion,* London/New York: Routledge, 2002.

of them desire the same thing, in desiring the impossible.[19] He argues that in the desire for the *tout autre*, the wholly other, deconstruction finds itself in a similar position as negative theology, because deconstruction does not know how not to speak of it. In imagining the mystery or the Wholly Other, we are waiting for a call that comes to us, whether or not we call it theology. Caputo argues that in his later years, Derrida advanced in affirming his relationship with negative theology.

Even though the close relationship existing between deconstruction and negative theology cannot be ruled out, the theistic interpretation of the wholly other seems somewhat arbitrary.[20] Strictly speaking, Derrida's retrieval of negative theology is not theological, but philosophical, as compared with the tradition of faith as practiced by Dionysius. Derrida is concerned with the presence of meaning which is not the presence as understood theologically. He never considers presence as grace, as it is in the Christian theological tradition.[21] He admires negative theology as a discursive source of language, but he is far off when negative theology turns into a higher form of representing the hyper-essence of the divine who is beyond designation and naming. Without having recourse to metaphysical discourse, negative theology comes to an affirmation, perhaps more radical than the former, without language or predication, to the experience of oneness with the God that is present at the heart of every being. Although the resemblance between negative theology and deconstruction is so compelling that one would find différance indistinguishable from negative theology, deconstruction is still not identical with negative theology. The difference is that negative theology is a higher form of affirming God's existence and reality beyond being, affirmation and naming. While upholding the differences existing between negative theology and deconstruction, one must be cautious to interpret deconstruction as anti-theological or atheistic. In this connection, as compared to Derrida, Jean-Luc Marion's

[19] Caputo, *The Prayers and Tears of Jacques Derrida*, 3.

[20] In this regard, Graham Ward takes a moderate position in freeing Derrida of nihilistic charges denying a total rejection of meaning. There is a deferral of meaning, without erasing the meaning. The foremost idea running through the deconstructionist operation is indeterminacy. Ward, "Deconstructive Theology," 86.

[21] Ward, "Deconstructive Theology," 89.

phenomenological project is more on par with negative theology in terms of the purpose it serves.

2. Sacramental Presence and Negative Theology

Marion's interest in Dionysius must be understood in the context of his radical re-construction of God in the trajectory of the postmodern quest for a non-onto-theological God. He found Dionysius as a valuable resource in the development of his theology. In this section we will examine some key notions of Marion's theological project that incorporate insights from mystical theology.

2.1. The Quest for a God Beyond Being

A major concern for both Marion and Dionysius is to uphold God's transcendence and to overcome the conceptual idolatry by conceiving of God as beyond being.[22] He achieves this by extending the horizon of phenomenology to God-talk. Marion develops a phenomenology which considers givenness as the essence of phenomenality. He employs his phenomenology to interpret the phenomenon of revelation in terms of givenness. Thus, he opens the way to think about God as revealed in Christ. Within the phenomenology of givenness, God has the freedom to reveal himself. Having argued that Givenness is constitutive of phenomenality, he goes on to describe the possibility of a phenomenon that is governed by excess/surplus rather than limited by the intentionality of the subject. The excess of the phenomenon over-fulfills intentional consciousness by saturating it. Marion argues for the possibility of such a phenomenon that gives itself in excess according to maximum phenomenality, which he calls "the saturated phenomenon."[23] Such a phenomenon may be impossible to know. Nevertheless, the impossibility of knowledge of the phenomenon arises not because of the lack of intuition, but because

---

[22] Jean-Luc Marion, *God Without Being*, trans. Thomas A. Carlson, Chicago, London: The University of Chicago Press, 1991.

[23] Jean-Luc Marion, *Being Given: Toward a Phenomenology of Givenness*, trans. Jeffrey L. Kosky (Stanford, California: Stanford University Press, 2002), 24-25, 225-228. His concept of the 'saturated phenomenon' generated a great deal of criticism. For example, see John D. Caputo, "Apostles of the Impossible: On God and the Gift in Derrida and Marion," in *God, the Gift and Postmodernism*, ed. John D. Caputo and Michael J. Scanlon, Bloomington: Indiana University Press, 1999, 185-222.

of its *excess* that surpasses all conceptual horizons.[24] Marion holds that the Christian God can be thought of only in relation to an "excess" or "saturation" which is beyond the notion of God as Being. Thus, the essence of God is not being, but rather an excess of Givenness. Marion situates the revelation of Christ within phenomenality, presenting it as the highest form of saturated phenomenon. It is in this sense that he understands the revelation of Christ as "the saturation par excellence" or "saturation of saturation."[25] This is the biblical figure of God who is Givenness, having been freed from the language of metaphysics that subjects God to Being.

Marion's exposition of God other than being, in terms of givenness, draws very much on the theology of Dionysius' God (Good) beyond being. He uses language which is similar to that of the mystical mode of theology that goes beyond the apophatic and kataphatic moments, that of negation and affirmation, to that of excess. In the vein of Dionysius, the binary or alternative categories of affirmation and negation are overcome by the phenomenological notion of excess in which God's unconditional and total giving is thought of according to his name, *agape*. The significance of Marion's project consists in its theological intent as well as its postmodern approach in thinking of God outside of the categories of Being, which Marion himself would call a "relief for theology."[26]

---

[24] Jean-Luc Marion, *In Excess: Studies of Saturated Phenomena*, ed. John D. Caputo, trans. Robyn Horner and Vincent Berraud, Perspectives in Continental Philosophy, New York: Fordham University Press, 2002, 159.

[25] For Marion, admitting the revelation of God as a genuine phenomenological possibility implies freeing phenomenality from the confines of objectivity (Husserl) and of Being (Heidegger). See *Being Given*, 242. For this reason, Marion has been criticized for crossing the limits of phenomenology, because phenomenality in its radical forms is only possible through intentionality.

[26] Jean-Luc Marion, "Metaphysics and Phenomenology: A Relief for Theology," *Critical Inquiry* 20 (1994).

2.2. Givenness and Mystery

Marion uses the two contrasting "categories" of the idol and the icon in order to distinguish between the different ways of conceiving God.[27] They are two basic orientations of the human subject, which we may call iconic and idolatrous gazes. An idol is created when we attempt to conceptually circumscribe God according to the human gaze. The idol that is created by measuring God by human understanding is actually the creation of human conceptuality. Therefore, the idol becomes an invisible mirror that reflects the represented image of the human gaze. The image of the divinity is equated with the consciousness of the constituting subject. Therefore, God is reduced to the limits of human conceptual consciousness. This is metaphysical idolatry. The icon allows one's gaze to move beyond the icon to the mystery which is invisible. The icon draws the viewer from what is seen to what is unseen beyond the represented image. In contrast to the idol, the icon refers to the invisible and brings the invisible to visibility without representing or resembling it *as such* but instead as an opening onto it. In contrast to the idol, which tends to reinforce the identity of the *ego*, the icon empties the *ego*, thereby liberating us from the metaphysical tendency of the subject to master, grasp, and controls everything.[28] Much of Christian theology, especially since the Middle Ages, has fallen prey to this metaphysical tendency. Marion contends that God's way of revealing Godself is through the icon. In the iconic way of revelation, the perceiver, who perceives, is also already being perceived. As such, intentionality can be said to be reversed, in the sense that the human subject consigns himself/herself and remains open to the mystery which is already gazing at him/her and is given maximally and without limit. In order to embrace the iconic gaze we must abandon the idolatrous gaze or any attempt to measure God by our own human gaze. Applied to the divine, the idol consists in the naming of or defining God, which is obviously equating God with the concepts of subjective intentionality. Looking at God idolatrously

---

27 A few examples are: Marion, *God Without Being*; *The Idol and Distance*; *Being Given*; Jean-Luc Marion, *Prolegomena to Charity*, trans. Stephen Lewis, New York: Fordham University Press, 2002.

28 Robyn Horner, *Jean-Luc Marion: A Theological Introduction*, Aldershot, U.K., Burlington, USA: Ashgate Publishing Company, 2005, 64.

means thinking of God as in philosophical theology, or as *causa sui*. Marion takes us away from the conceptual idolatry of metaphysics to a non-metaphysical route of love in which God is thought of as love, revealed in the person of Christ. Thinking of God iconically means considering God as the God of the Bible, who was revealed in Jesus as love. The icon provides the condition (simultaneously its non-condition) for the crossing out of the conceptual idol of God, making room for the crossed out God to appear, whose name is YHWH (Ex 3:4, 14),[29] or *Agape*. According to Marion, the name YHWH is a paradox, and says nothing about the essence of the divine. God escapes every concept and definition, which he illustrates based on Dionysius' theology of Divine Names.[30] In a way, even in revealing God's name, YHWH remains beyond names, because God's name (I AM WHO AM) is a name which is not a name.

The theological significance of the icon is found in its ability to make it possible to think about God through the mystical route of love, without falling into the idolatry of metaphysics that is based on being. In fact, in his attempt to provide an iconic perspective to God-talk, he is reinstalling the mystical tradition of Christian theology which was lost by the insurgence of metaphysics into theology. What unites both Dionysius and Marion is conceiving transcendence in terms of mystery. For both Marion and Dionysius, there is no concept that adequately captures God, who is beyond being. Marion's categories of the icon and the idol are akin to Dionysius's emphasis on the positive value of symbols that manifest the unmanifest. In the iconic scheme of representation, like in the Dionysian scheme, visibility is not by resemblance, but dissemblance. The destruction of all conceptual idols of God opens the space for "negative theophany" where the invisible is encountered in the visible. For Marion the icon is the theological space where this crossing of the visible and the invisible takes place as manifested in the iconic figure of Christ. Christ becomes the icon of the invisible God (Col 1:15; see also Rom 1:20) in his disfigured humanity, forfeiting event the least trace of his glory. Therefore, Christ becomes the icon of God's love whereby God's giving expresses itself in maximum phenomenality, as

[29] Marion, *God Without Being*, 73ff.

[30] Marion, *God Without Being*, 76ff.

the saturated phenomenon par excellence, or paradox of paradoxes, not by resembling but by dissembling the image, and in distance. The excess of the phenomenon assumes the mode of absence as exemplified in the iconic figure of Christ. This has implications in reimagining sacramental excess in a non-metaphysical way.

3. Traces of Mysticism in Sacramental Theology

Postmodern critique of the "metaphysics of presence" challenges a sacramental theology founded on classical metaphysics to find its own basis for interpreting sacramental presence. Theology's response to this challenge assumes a mystical mode by reimagining God's insistent and abiding presence, paradoxically, in terms of apparent withdrawal, distance, or absence.

3.1. Beyond Metaphysics of Presence and Negative Theology

The non-metaphysical way of conceiving transcendence helps Marion to develop a non-metaphysical concept of presence according to the post-modern sensibility. Employing Pseudo-Dionysius' notion of God as beyond affirmation and negation, he ascribes presence, the full capacity to appear or give itself in excess, in the icon. The disavowal of the ultimacy of Being and human conceptuality has discredited the metaphysical understanding of presence. Nevertheless, presence cannot be reduced to mere absence either. In this regard, Marion opens the means for overcoming the two traditional ways of explaining presence, namely, the language of affirmation (*kataphasis*) and negation (*apophasis*), which according to Marion, fall under the impasse created by the metaphysics of presence, assigning full capacity to the notion of the icon. Accordingly, the category of the icon (in contrast to the idol) opens up the possibility of a third way (the way of not-naming or de-nomination), within which sacramental presence can be thought of as beyond affirmation and negation.[31] Marion contends that the critique

---

[31] Jean-Luc Marion, "In the Name: How to Avoid Speaking of 'Negative Theology'," in *God, the Gift, and Postmodernism*, ed. John D. Caputo and Michael. J. Scanlon (Bloomington and Indianapolis: Indiana University Press, 1999), 24-42. See also Nathan D. Mitchell, *Meeting Mystery* (New York: Orbis Books, 2006), 271; Mitchell, *Meeting Mystery*, 271. Marion rejects the general proposition of identifying Dionysius with an *apophatic* theology. According to him, Dionysius does not make a choice

of the metaphysical concept of presence is actually not the rejection of the presence of God, but rather, a corrective to a totalitarian concept of presence. According to him, the death of the idolatrous concept of God makes an "empty space of a new presence."[32] Therefore, the abyss created by the disfigured figure of Christ is not mere emptiness, but an empty space which is saturated with presence, whose visibility opens up to an absence. The self-giving God gives himself in maximum phenomenality in the abyss of the Cross and the Resurrection. Thus, what Marion advocates is a pragmatic theology of absence. Therefore, presence can no longer be subjected to metaphysical idolatry, nor can it be left to be informed by a negative theology. By the pragmatic theology of absence, Marion does not attempt to establish the non-presence of God, but rather, to protect God from the metaphysics of presence. As he puts it, "[b]y theology of absence [...] we mean, not the non-presence of God, but the fact that the name that God is given, the name which gives God, which is given as God [...] *serves to shield God from presence*...and offers him precisely as an exception to presence."[33] Marion continues, "the Name does not name God as an essence; it designates what passes beyond every name. The Name designates what one does not name and

---

between *apophatic* and *kataphatic* theologies, but rather, opts for a "third way" which understands God as beyond Being. Marion writes, "De-nomination [...] does not end up in a 'metaphysics of presence' that does not call itself as such. Rather, it ends up as a pragmatic theology of absence – where the name is given as having no name, as not giving the essence, and having nothing but this absence to make manifest; a theology where hearing happens." Marion, *In Excess*, 155. Marion says, "the paradox or paradoxes [the saturated phenomenon/phenomenon of revelation] does not have to choose between [c]ataphasis and apophasis any more than between saturation and shortage of intuition; it uses them all in order to push to its end the phenomenality of what shows itself only insofar as it gives itself." Marion, *Being Given*, 245.

[32] Marion, *The Idol and Distance*, 36. In this sense, Marion interprets the "death of God" of Nietzsche as the death of the idolatrous concept of God. He writes, "What the last (or next-to-last) metaphysical word calls the "death of God" does not signify that God passes out of play, but indicates the *modern* face of his insistent and eternal fidelity." "[N]o "death of God" goes as far as the desertion of Christ by the Father on Good Friday; and from the bottom of the inferal abyss that opened at the very heart of our history, once and for all, there issues the insurpassable filiation that eternally confesses the paternity of the Father." Marion, *The Idol and Distance*, xxxv.

[33] Marion, "In the Name," 37. See also Marion, *In Excess*, 156.

says that one does not name it."[34] Therefore, the function of Name is no longer to incarnate God into predicative language, but by naming, the believing subjects are inscribed in the very horizon of God, according to Marion, as it happens at baptism.[35] The manner of presence that Jesus guarantees to the Church is the one that gives itself in absence, in the mode of the icon and in distance as we will see now.

3.2. Eucharistic Present and Presence

According to Marion, Easter becomes the innovative site for developing the real presence, without yielding to the metaphysical concept of being and causality. As he understands it, it is Easter that "innovates," and the innovation of Easter motivates us to conceive of the "real presence" without confining it to an empirical place.[36] Thus, Easter becomes the vantage point for the reinterpretation of the understanding of sacramental presence. As Marion points out, even after the Resurrection, the disciples of Jesus were moved by the overwhelming desire to "see" and "touch" his corpse. They are urged not to touch him (Jn 20:17). Thomas was boggled to touch him, although Christ condescends due his lack of faith (Jn 20:27). What we see after all is the absence: the void of the tomb (Jn 20:2) and his disappearance after the recognition of the (sacramental) sign at Emmaus (Lk 24:30-31). Jesus becomes non-visible to them in the void of the "cloud" (Acts 1:9) and a heaven (Lk 24:51). Thus, it becomes evident that in the post-resurrected age, between the already and the not-yet, presence is maintained and radicalized in absence.

Nevertheless, the presence of God that overrides ordinary modes of presence (touch, sight) is still overshadowed by the scandal of the body. The presence in absence is the present (gift) given in the corporality of the Eucharist and of the community.[37] Eucharistic presence is Christ's presence in the present (gifts of bread and wine), here and now. In other

[34] Marion, "In the Name," 157.

[35] Marion, "In the Name," 157.

[36] Jean-Luc Marion, *Prolegomena to Charity* (New York: Fordham University Press, 2002), 124.

[37] Marion illustrates this idea. He establishes a link between *blessing* and *presence*, *recognition* and *gift*, in his theological exegesis of the Emmaus story (Lk 24:13-35) and the story of ascension in the gospel of Luke (24:50-53). See Marion, *God Without Being*; *Prolegomena to Charity*, 127-137.

words, presence cannot be identified with the present (the gift given). As Mitchell Nathan puts it, "[s]acraments are situations in which Christ's mode of presence is perceived as "absence," since, by their nature, sacramental signs are self-effacing, kenotic; they draw us beyond themselves to a reality they may embody, but never exhaust."[38] Only the givenness opens up the way to the reception of sacramental excess, acknowledging the mystery in the given (gifts) that realizes the past (memory), present and the future (eschaton) in its excess, abundance, and incomprehensibility. As Marion observes, the manner of presence does not pertain to the present (here and now) alone, but rather, "*of the present, that is to say of the gift*."[39] Thus, in articulating presence, starting from the gift realizes presence in the present in the gift given as mystery (hidden).

In the Eucharist, Christ gives himself paradoxically, as in the paradoxical figure of Christ on the Cross. The way in which the Eucharist gives itself, in the "anteriority, exteriority, and materiality of the sacrament" is exposed to idolatry.[40] Indeed, the Eucharist, understood iconically, as the visible of the invisible, reinforces the irreducibility of God's presence, Christ's presence to one's own horizons, because Eucharistic presence is fundamentally marked by an absence in the mode of the icon. Jesus' appearance and apparent disappearance invites us to move toward a mode of presence marked by absence (not emptiness), to a belief without seeing (Jn 20:29), and to a concept of real presence without confining presence to an empirical space (localized) and to the visible alone (thing). Christ's presence after Easter supersedes ordinary modes of presence (touch, sight). God's gracious gift of the Eucharist discloses itself while concealing it, retaining the radical difference and otherness of God. The presence of Jesus is mediated in and through the visible and tangible (bread and wine). Nevertheless, it can neither be reduced to a simple thing (object) nor to its essence. Paradoxically, the gracious gift of the Eucharist discloses itself while at the same

---

[38] Nathan D. Mitchell, "'But, Only Say the Word,'" *Worship* 80 (2006): 455.

[39] Marion, *God Without Being*, 171.

[40] Luis-Marie Chauvet, *Symbol and Sacrament: A Sacramental Reinterpretation of Christian Existence*, trans. Patrick Medigan and Madeleine Beaumont (Collegeville, Minnesota: The Liturgical Press, 1995), 402.

time concealing itself under the species of bread and wine. As Chauvet explains, the Eucharistic presence is not the "simple *esse* of a mere thing," but Christ's "*coming-into-presence*" in the Eucharist under the mode of the *absence* of the *sacramentum* of the bread and wine, in the emptiness of the broken bread.[41] Thus, the Eucharist is the "*paradigmatic figure of the presence-of-the absence of God.*"[42] In the Eucharist, the gracious gift of God is received in the species of bread and wine. What is given in the present, here and now, is given by the past and the future. In other words, Eucharistic presence is a gift given in the present (gift/time) in terms of the past (memorial) as well as the future (eschaton).[43]In the celebration of the Eucharist, we encounter Jesus who 'says' the words about himself (liturgy of the word) and gives himself in excess in the breaking of the bread (liturgy of the Eucharist), unceasingly, without measure, until he comes again (acclamation)!

Conclusion

To sum up, in this article, we have attempted to explore the recent reception of Dionysius in postmodern philosophy and theology. Even though one cannot ignore the incipient theistic leaning of Derridean thought, a radical retrieval of negative theology can be found only in Jean-Luc Marion. Marion's recovery of Dionysius goes beyond mere linguistic or epistemological implications of his thought to the level of theology (mysticism). In harmony with postmodern sensibilities, Marion's theological and phenomenological projects attempt to liberate theology's God (and phenomenology's phenomenon) from the limits and preconditions of human thought and language. Dionysius' influence is crucial in his project. It is self-evident that the Dionysian God or Good beyond being appears as the God without being in the phenomenological theology of Marion. Marion employs the Dionysian notion of God as beyond both affirmation (metaphysics of presence)

[41] Chauvet, *Symbol and Sacrament*, 404-408. The emptiness that enthralls the broken bread can be understood as *kenosis*. See Lambert J. Leijssen, *With the Silent Glimmer of God's Spirit: A Postmodern Look at the Sacraments*, trans. Marie Baird, New York/ Mahwah, NJ: Paulist Press, 2006, 26, 28.

[42] Chauvet, *Symbol and Sacrament*, 405.

[43] For a detailed interpretation of Eucharistic presence in terms of the past and the future, see Marion, *God Without Being*, 161-182.

and negation (negative theology), in order to open up the possibility of a "third way" in which he understands God as beyond being, or as excess through givenness. Thus the "third way" of Dionysius underlies the notion of excess and the saturated phenomenon. A radical reproach to causality can be found both in Dionysius and Marion. Dionysius overcomes causality by the notion of the call or summons, whereas Marion achieves it by the notion of *a priori* givenness. One might also find the theme of the call appearing in Marion's *l'adonné* (the gifted one) which is beyond the purview of the present essay. More importantly, Marion draws heavily on the rhetoric of negative theology in introducing excess in the mode of absence, withdrawal and distance. The retrieval of Dionysius' theology by Marion embodies the re-emergence of mysticism in postmodern theology by reimagining God's insistent and abiding presence, paradoxically, in terms of apparent withdrawal, distance, or absence.

Bibliography

1. Balthasar, Hans Urs von, *The Glory of the Lord: A Theological Aesthetics*, trans. Erasmo Leiva-Merikakis, Vol. 1. 2 ed. San Francisco: Ignatius Press, 1982.
2. Caputo, John D., *The Prayers and Tears of Jacques Derrida: Religion without Religion*, Bloomington/Indianapolis: Indiana University Press, 1997.
3. Caputo, John D., "Apostles of the Impossible: On God and the Gift in Derrida and Marion," in *God, the Gift and Postmodernism*, ed. John D. Caputo and Michael J. Scanlon, 185-222, Bloomington: Indiana University Press, 1999.
4. Caputo, John D., ed., *Questioning God*, Bloomington: Indiana University Press, 2001.
5. Chauvet, Luis-Marie, *Symbol and Sacrament: A Sacramental Reinterpretation of Christian Existence*, trans. Patrick Medigan and Madeleine Beaumont, Collegeville, Minnesota: The Liturgical Press, 1995.
6. Derrida, Jacques, *Of Grammatology*, trans. Gayatri Spivak, Baltimore: Johns Hopkins University Press, 1974.
7. Derrida, Jacques, "Violence and Metaphysics," in *Writing and Difference*, ed. Alan Bass, 79-153, Chicago: University of Chicago, 1978.
8. Derrida, Jacques, *Margins of Philosophy*, trans. Alan Bass, Chicago: University of Chicago Press, 1982.
9. Horner, Robyn, *Rethinking God as Gift: Marion, Derrida, and the Limits of Phenomenology*, New York: Fordham University Press, 2001.
10. Horner, Robyn, *Jean-Luc Marion: A Theological Introduction*, Aldershot, U. K., Burlington, USA: Ashgate Publishing Company, 2005.

11. Janicaud, Dominique, Le tournant théologique de la phénoménologie française, Vol. Tiré à part, Paris: éditions de l'éclat, 1990.
12. Janicaud, Dominiqueet al,"Phenomenology and the 'Theological Turn': *The French Debate Perspectives in Continental Philosophy,* ed. John D. Caputo, New York: Fordham University Press, 2000.
13. Jones, John D., "An Absolutely Simple God? Frameworks for Reading Pseudo-Dionysius the Areopagite," *The Thomist* 69 (2005): 371-406.
14. Kosky, Jeffrey L., "Contemporary Encounters with Apophatic Theology: The Case of Emmanuel Levinas," *Journal for Cultural and Religious Theory*, no. 1.3 (2000). http://www.jcrt.org/archives/01.3/kosky.shtml [accessed December 2010].
15. Leijssen, Lambert J., *With the Silent Glimmer of God's Spirit: A Postmodern Look at the Sacraments*, trans. Marie Baird, New York/Mahwah, NJ: Paulist Press, 2006.
16. Marion, Jean-Luc, *God Without Being*, trans. Thomas A. Carlson, Chicago, London: The University of Chicago Press, 1991.
17. Marion, Jean-Luc, "Metaphysics and Phenomenology: A Relief for Theology," *Critical Inquiry* 20 (1994): 572-591.
18. Marion, Jean-Luc, "In the Name: How to Avoid Speaking of 'Negative Theology'," in *God, the Gift, and Postmodernism*, ed. John D. Caputo and Michael. J. Scanlon, 784-800, Bloomington and Indianapolis: Indiana University Press, 1999.
19. Marion, Jean-Luc, *The Idol and Distance*, trans. Thomas A. Carlson, New York: Fordham University Press, 2001.
20. Marion, Jean-Luc, *Being Given: Toward a Phenomenology of Givenness*, trans. Jeffrey L. Kosky, Stanford, California: Stanford University Press, 2002.
21. Marion, Jean-Luc, *In Excess: Studies of Saturated Phenomena*, trans. Robyn Horner and Vincent Berraud, *Perspectives in Continental Philosophy*, ed. John D. Caputo, New York: Fordham University Press, 2002.
22. Marion, Jean-Luc, *Prolegomena to Charity*, trans. Stephen Lewis, New York: Fordham University Press, 2002.
23. Marion, Jean-Luc, *The Crossing of the Visible*, trans. James K. A. Smith, Stanford, California: 24. Stanford University Press, 2004.
24. McGinn, Bernard, *The Foundations of Mysticism*, New York: Crossroad Press, 1992.
25. Mitchell, Nathan D., *Meeting Mystery*, New York: Orbis Books, 2006.
26. Olthuis, James H., ed. Religion With/out Religion: The Prayers and Tears of John D. Caputo. London/New York: Routledge, 2002.
27. Pseudo-Dionysius, *Psuedo-Dionysius: The Complete Works*, trans. Colm Luibheid, New York/Manwah: Paulist Press, 1987.

28. Rosemann, Philipp Wolfram, "Postmodern Philosophy and J.-L. Marion's Eucharistic Realism," in *The Mystery of Faith: Reflections on the Encyclical Ecclesia de Eucharistia*, ed. James McEvoy and Maurice Hogan, 224-244, Dublin: The Columba Press, 2005.
29. Ward, Graham, "Deconstructive Theology," in *The Cambridge Companion to Postmodern Theology*, ed. Kevin J. Vanhoozer, 76-91, Cambridge, UK: Cambridge University Press, 2003.

14

Contributors

Dr. Bernard McGinn is the Naomi Shenstone Donnelley Professor Emeritus of Historical Theology and of the History of Christianity in the Divinity School and the Committees on Medieval Studies and on General Studies, the University of Chicago, USA. His specialized areas of study and research are the history of Christianity and the history of Christian thought, primarily in the medieval period. Dr. McGinn has written extensively in the areas of the history of apocalyptic thought and, most recently, in the areas of spirituality and mysticism. His current long-range project is a five-volume history of Christian Mysticism in the West under the general title *The Presence of God*, four volumes of which have appeared: *The Origins of Mysticism*; *The Growth of Mysticism*; *The Flowering of Mysticism*; and *The Harvest of Mysticism in Medieval Germany*.

Dr. Antoon Vandevelde is a full Professor at the Centre for Economics and Ethics, and dean of the Institute of Philosophy of K.U. Leuven, Belgium. He graduated in 1986 with a PhD on *Exchange and Recognition*. Formerly he was teaching at the universities of Antwerp and Rotterdam, and has served as a guest professor at the universities of Tilburg and Nijmegen (The Netherlands), Bandung (Indonesia), Stellenbosch (South Africa) and at the Université Nationale du Rwanda. He has published many articles, mainly in the field of economic ethics and political philosophy, for instance, philosophy of social security, migration policy, responsibility for future generations, altruism and the logic of the gift, and communitarianism. Together with G. Erreygers, he edited a book on

Is Inheritance Legitimate? – Ethical and Economic Aspects of Wealth Transfers (Springer, 1997), and another book is on *Gifts and Interests* (Peeters, 2000). Recently, he published together with Thomas Nijs en Yvonne Denier a book on *Autonomy and paternalism – Reflections on the Theory and Practice of Health Care*, (Peeters, 2007).

Dr. Roy Varghese Palatty studied at the Centre for Ethics, Social and Political Philosophy, Institute of Philosophy, K.U. Leuven, Belgium. Recently, he defended his dissertation on the political theories of Amartya Sen's and Ronald Dworkin, under the guidance of Prof. Dr. Antoon Vandevelde. His research interests are ethics, religion, social, and political philosophy. He has published a book, *Cathedrals of Development: A Critique on the Developmental Modal of Amartya Sen* (Bangalore: Christ University Publications, 2009) and several articles. He serves as the General Editor of *Sunday Shalom*, a Christian Weekly Newspaper from Kerala, India.

Dr. Una Agnew is currently Associate Professor Emeritain the Faculty of Theology at Milltown-Institute, Dublin, Ireland. She completed her doctoral study on the spirituality of Patrick Kavanagh's work in 1991 at University College Dublin under the direction of the late Professor Augustine Martin. She has published *The Mystical Imagination of Patrick Kavanagh: A Buttonhole in Heaven*(Dublin, 1998) and edited, with Dr. Bernadette Flanagan and Greg Heylin, *With Wisdom Seeking God: The Academic Study of Spirituality*, Supplement 15, *Studies in Spirituality* (Leuven, 2008). Celtic Spirituality, Mysticism, Local history and the interface between Literature and Spirituality are her research interests. Dr. Agnew is a Founder Member of AISGA (All Ireland Spiritual Guidance Association) and Founding Member of its Board of Directors.

Dr. Paul Moyaert is Professor of Philosophy at the Institute of Philosophy, Katholieke Universiteit Leuven, Belgium, Catholic University of Louvain-la-Neuve, and Catholic University of Paris, France. He is a trained psychoanalyst in the Belgian School for Psychoanalysis, teaching subjects like moral philosophy, psychology and philosophical anthropology. He is the author of several monographs on psychoanalysis and the philosophy of religion. His latest monograph is on the theological and psychological relevance of icons: *Iconen en beeldverering. Godsdienst als symbolische praktijk* (Amsterdam, Boom, 2007). He is preparing a monograph on Lacan and moral philosophy *Pushing Lacan into Moral philosophy.*

Dr. Jonathan Weidenbaum is an instructor of Liberal Arts at Berkeley College, in New York City. He received his Ph.D. in Philosophy at the University at Buffalo (2003). He is a specialist in the philosophy of religion, and has a strong interest in phenomenology and the philosophy of perception, and he recently discovered the relevance of classical American philosophy, and draws upon the ideas of William James, John Dewey, and Alfred North Whitehead. He has published several essays in *The Global Spiral*, *The Journal of Liberal Religion*, *The Journal of Media and Religion*, *Glimpse*, and *Transcendent Philosophy*. Dr Weidenbaum has delivered papers at conferences in Spain, Poland, Mexico, Canada, and various cities throughout the United States.

Dr. Roger Burggraeve, an Emeritus Professor of the Katholieke Universiteit Leuven, Belgium, has taught at the Faculties of Theology, Pharmacy, Philosophy and Medicine, courses of Fundamental Theological Ethics; Sexual and Relational Ethics; Faith, Biblical Thought, and Ethics; Faith, Values, and Emmanuel Levinas' Ethical and Metaphysical Thinking. He also served as a Visiting Professor at the International Institute, "Lumen Vitae" (Brussels), Dharmaram College (Bangalore, India), in Congo, Kenya, and Canada. He has developed an ethical model of growth for education, social welfare, and pastoral work. He is a member of several Ethical Committees (Caritas Catholica Flanders, Ethical Committee for Mentally Disabled People). He has published more than 365 books, articles and contributions in English, Dutch, French, Italian, and Japanese on: Emmanuel Levinas; relational, sexual and marriage ethics; Bible and ethics; education, pastoral guidance, social welfare and ethics.

Dr. Joseph Pathrapankal CMI, Professor Emeritus of Theology, holds a Th.D from Pontifical Gregorian University, Rome, and an Honorary PhD in Theology from the University of Uppsala, Sweden. He was a member of the Pontifical Biblical Commission, Rome, Vice President of the Conference of Catholic Theological Institutions (COCTI, and President of Dharmaram Vidya Kshetram, Bangalore, India. He has served as President of Theological Publications in India. He has published several books and numerous scholarly papers in national and international journals. Some of his books include *Christian Life: New Testament Perspectives*, *Critical and Creative*, *Text and Context*, *Dimensions of the Word*, *Time and History*, and *The Christian Programme*.

Dr. Patrick Menneteau is Professor of British literature and the History of Ideas in the Enlightenment, Faculty of Arts, University of Toulon, France. He obtained his Ph.D. from the université de la Sorbonne-nouvelle-Paris III. He has served several times as Head of the Department of English (Mulhouse, Toulon), and Dean of the Faculty of Arts in the University of Toulon (2000-2003). Dr. Menneteau is the author of 45 scientific papers on William Blake, John Locke, David Hume, Robert Fergusson, James Hogg, Robert-Louis Stevenson, and 18th century literature and ideas, and the book, *La poésie de William Blake* (Paris, 1999). His main interests are William Blake's mysticism and Carl Gustav Jung's psychology and its application in literary criticism.

Late **Dr. Thomas Manikkam CMI**, Professor Emeritus of Philosophy, was the Head of the Department of Philosophy at the Faculty of St. John Vianney Seminary, Pretoria, South Africa. He obtained his Ph.D. in Comparative Philosophy from Banaras Hindu University, Varanasi, India; a Post-doctoral Diploma in Comparative Theology from K.U. Leuven, Belgium, and a second Post-Doctoral Diploma in Comparative Religion from UCSB, USA. His areas of Specialization were Theology of Inter-religious Dialogue, Theology of World Religions, Judeo-Christian Ethics vis-à-vis Hindu Ethics, Buddhist-Christian Dialogical Encounter, Eco- Spirituality, and Eco-Mysticism. Besides his doctoral thesis, *Dharma according to Manu and Moses* (Bangalore, 1977) Dr. Manikkam has published over 168 research papers in a number of international and national journals. He was the Chief Editor of *Journal of Dharma*, published by the CSWR, DVK, Bangalore. At the time of his sad demise, he had been editing for publication his dissertation of UCSB, *Concept of Divine Revelation in World Religions*.

Dr. Lieven Boeve is Professor of Fundamental Theology at the Faculty of Theology and Religious Studies, KU Leuven, Belgium. He had been the Dean of the Faculty of Theology and the President of the European Society for Catholic Theology. Currently, he serves as the Director-General of the Flemish Office for Catholic Education (VSKO). He founded the Research Group Theology in a Postmodern Context, in which research is conducted regarding theological epistemology, theology and continental philosophy, etc. Apart from more than 50 articles in international journals and 60 contributions to collected volumes, he is the author of *Interrupting Tradition. An Essay on Christian Faith in a Postmodern Context* (Leuven, 2003), *God Interrupts History. Theology in a Time of Upheaval* (New York, 2007; and *Lyotard and Theology: Beyond the Christian Master Narrative of Love* (London, 2014).

Dr. Peter Mark Tyler is the Director of the Pastoral Theology Programme at St Mary's University College, Twickenham, London. He completed his Doctorate at Durham University on the 'mystical strategies' of St Teresa of Avila from a Wittgensteinian perspective. This work is published as *The Return of the Mystical: Wittgenstein, Teresa of Avila and the Christian Mystical Tradition* by Continuum (London) in 2011. Dr. Tyler has published *The Way of Ecstasy: Praying with St Teresa of Avila* (Canterbury, 1997), *St John of the Cross: Outstanding Christian Thinker* (Continuum, 2010) and *Sources of Transformation: Revitalizing Christian Spirituality* (with Edward Howells and Bernard McGinn, Continuum, 2010) as well as numerous articles and papers on the relevance of the mystical tradition.

Dr. Sebastian Madathummuriyil, MCBS, is Assistant Professor of the Duquesne University, Pittsburgh, USA. He holds a Doctor's Degree (Ph.D.) in Theology from the Faculty of Theology, Katholieke Universiteit Leuven, Belgium. His areas of research are Pneumatology and Grace, Theological Views of the Person and Classical and Contemporary Theology. His recent publications include *Toward a Sacramental Hermeneutics of Givenness* (Leuven, 2010). He has also published several research papers in national and international journals.

15

Index of Subjects

Absence 11, 78, 80, 83, 119, 168, 177, 259-264
Absolute 4, 8, 75, 77, 81-82, 85-87, 89-93, 107, 119, 124, 147, 201, 247
Absolute dependence 4
Aesthetic beauty 50
Affective 4, 10, 226-229, 241-242
Affirmation 10, 67, 120-121, 124, 137, 179, 202, 217, 246-247, 254, 256, 259, 263
Alchemy 9, 158, 163, 168-169
All-encompassing 87
Altruism 39, 148
Amor amicitiae 79-80, 83, 85, 96
Amor concupiscientiae 83-84
Animation 127-130
Anthropocentrism 197
Antithetical 5
Anxiety 75, 89
Apophaticism 10, 201, 206, 209-210, 213-216, 219
Apostle 141, 144, 150, 255, 264
Archetypal 35, 155, 157-158, 163
Archetypes 162-163, 170-172, 175
Arguments 3, 23, 33, 106, 110, 161, 192, 226, 232
Art forms 1, 5-6
Asceticism 33, 61
Asymmetrical 62, 78
Atheism 119-121, 123, 205, 213
Atomistic individualism 41
Attitude 4, 33, 51, 59, 76, 80, 90, 113, 148, 191, 193-195, 198, 214, 239
Attractive force 76
Attractive power 87
Authorization 144
Awakening 36, 99, 123, 130-132, 139, 189
Awareness 1, 6-7, 9, 11, 18, 51-52, 66, 70, 108, 181, 197, 217-218

Baptism 150, 261
Being 8, 113-114, 123, 185, 204, 255, 257-258, 260-263, 265
Being-for-the-other 129, 138
Benevolence 43, 78, 80-81, 83-84
Benevolent 66, 83-84
Bhakti 142, 146-148, 150
Biblical 9, 78, 131, 133, 136, 141, 184, 186, 225, 256
Biology 1, 103, 112, 127, 212
Body 15, 35-36, 45, 53, 61, 67, 90, 104, 106, 109, 128-129, 179, 188, 197, 229, 261

Body of Christ 15
Boundaries 5-6, 11, 51, 62, 68, 71, 117, 171, 199
Buddha-nature 103
Buddhism 1, 3, 43, 99
Buddhist meditation 3
Business 32-34, 37, 41-42, 46-48, 51-52, 55, 229, 231, 233

Care-holder 32, 52
Celestial 32
Celtic 7-8, 57-64, 66, 68-69, 71, 73
Challenges 10, 152, 191, 201, 203, 216, 218, 226, 253, 259
Character 33, 36, 39, 43, 52, 67, 78, 100, 106, 109, 119, 154, 176, 195, 251
Charity 48, 85, 257, 261, 265
Children of God 188, 190
Chrematistics 52-53
Christendom 17
Christianity 1, 7, 10, 15-16, 19, 32, 57-61, 63-66, 68, 73, 77, 89, 138, 206, 208-212, 214, 219
Christo-Centrism 145
Christological 25, 137, 217
Church 15-17, 28, 38-39, 55, 69, 73, 76, 111, 141, 143, 170, 223, 225, 240-241, 261
Cognitive 2, 4, 77, 107
Collective self 41
Commitment/s 7, 15, 39, 43, 45, 48, 82, 143, 145-150, 152
Common good 37, 41, 43, 47, 50-51, 53-54
Communication 6, 36
Communion 1, 6, 85, 96, 146, 185-186, 196, 238
Community 31, 33, 38-39, 46, 53-54, 61-62, 69, 78-80, 83, 85, 127, 180, 193, 230-231, 252, 261
Complementarity 4-5
Conative 4
Concealment 250
Conscience 34, 47-48, 52, 163-165, 168, 171, 173-176
Consciousness 1-2, 4-6, 9, 14, 35, 41, 63, 68, 70, 72-74, 100-101, 103, 105-106, 108-109, 123, 126, 128, 131-133, 181-182, 189, 191, 195, 197, 200, 204, 207, 210, 214, 216, 218, 255, 257
Consumerism 45, 73, 193
Contemplatio mystica 14
Contemplation 19, 40-41, 88-90, 154, 187, 224
Contemptus mundi 87
Contradiction 10, 122, 171, 232, 242
Convergence 5-6, 24, 118
Conversion 7, 36, 65
Conviction 3, 16, 75, 108, 143-145, 148, 152, 157, 167
Corporality 15, 261
Corporate 31, 41, 46, 51
Corporate ashram 32, 51
Corporation 42-43, 47, 51
Cosmology 9, 19, 179
Cosmos 180-181, 186, 199, 249
Cosmo-theandric 9, 179, 185-186, 190, 197-199
Creation 7, 17, 19, 21, 26, 32, 57-59, 61-62, 64, 66-67, 73, 78, 97, 122, 135-136, 138, 176, 180, 185-188, 194, 196, 199, 202, 249-250, 257
Creator 19, 46, 120, 123, 135, 137, 174, 186, 189
Creature 26, 46, 92, 109, 122, 129, 137, 153, 185, 187, 234
Cultural 1, 10, 16, 18, 196, 203, 206, 208-210, 213-217, 219, 265

Dance 1, 6, 68, 156, 191
Deconstruction 204-205, 209, 228, 242, 245-246, 252-254
Deconstructive 10, 241, 251-252, 254, 266
Deity 7
Deliberation 40
Democratization 17
Depths of life 6
Designer 9, 179, 188
Despair 75, 93, 95-97, 171
Destiny 17, 20, 32, 133, 251
Detachment 22, 32-33, 45, 169, 198
Detraditionalisation 206-208, 214
Development 7, 15-16, 31, 33, 38, 47, 52, 55, 64, 170, 174, 177, 192-193, 206, 219, 255
Devotees 141
Dharma 34, 41-42, 146, 187
Dialectic 22
Dialogue 8, 18, 72, 118, 143, 177
Différance 204
Dignity 26, 47, 50, 121
Discourse 159, 165, 169, 171, 173, 204-205, 216-217, 228-229, 231-232, 248, 251-252, 254
Discrimination 40, 97, 150
Disenchantment 207
Disorientation 10, 235, 242
Distance 11, 81-83, 90, 119, 167-168, 259, 261, 264-265
Distress 8, 75, 80, 232, 238
Diversity 6, 208, 210-211, 214-215, 252
Divine 6, 8, 14, 18-19, 24-25, 27, 32, 60, 64, 67-68, 71-73, 77-79, 83, 86-88, 93, 98, 108, 114, 117-120, 122, 124, 130-138, 141-143, 146, 149, 154-155, 169, 184-188, 193, 196, 198, 202, 208, 210, 217, 240, 247-249, 251, 254, 257-258
Divine love 78-79, 83, 86, 135-138
Divine presence 14, 60, 117
Divine Providence 134
Divinity 1, 73, 121-122, 124, 185, 189, 257
Doctrinal 18
Dualism/s 105, 107

Ecological 9, 37, 43, 52-53, 72, 104-105, 112, 180, 195
Ecological psychology 104-105, 112
Economic 7, 31-33, 37-39, 41-42, 46, 48-49, 51-53, 55, 169, 176, 194
Eco-spirituality 51, 188
Ecstatic 86-88, 90-91, 93, 99, 109
Ecumenism 32
Ego-centeredness 42
Ego-transcending 5
Empirical 3, 87, 100, 157, 159, 261-262
Empiricism 9, 105, 112, 126, 159, 161, 167
Employee 47
Employer 44, 48-49
Encompassing 117, 135, 196, 210
Encounter 7, 14-15, 24, 113, 126, 144, 146, 149, 151, 248, 263
Energies 64, 89, 182, 190
Enlightenment 3, 17, 35, 51, 99, 124, 164, 167, 170
Enthusiasm 8, 90-91, 93, 113-120, 123-125, 129-130, 133-134, 139, 144, 167, 192
Epiphany 67, 73-74, 125-126, 182
Epistemic chauvinism 4
Epistemological 5, 107, 206, 210, 217, 263
Epistemology 6, 104, 211
Equanimity 32, 60, 80, 88
Erotic 84

Eternal 14-15, 20-21, 23, 34, 50, 67, 154, 172, 198
Eternity 14, 20-26, 34, 50, 69-70, 177
Ethical 37-38, 51, 54, 113, 123-133, 136-138, 169, 181, 193
Ethical values 37-38
Ethics 3-4, 40, 43-44, 52, 54-55, 126, 137-138, 176, 194, 196
Ethics of belief 3-4
Eucharistic 261-263, 266
Evidence 3-4, 8, 18, 111, 165
Evil 38, 47, 61-62, 85, 198, 224
Evolution 15-16, 65, 110, 132, 173-174, 181, 183, 185, 196, 212
Experience 1, 3-5, 8-11, 20, 32, 34, 46, 49-50, 72, 77, 93, 95, 100-112, 115, 117-119, 123, 133, 135, 141-142, 144, 146, 149-154, 157-160, 166-169, 171, 175, 185-188, 195, 202-203, 206-214, 216, 218-219, 223, 227, 231, 238, 254
External 22, 35, 39-40, 42, 101-103, 105, 109-110, 117, 137, 221, 223

Faith 14, 16, 73, 75, 89, 108, 110-112, 142, 146, 148-150, 194, 203, 207, 209, 212-216, 219, 223, 226, 243, 254, 261, 266
Falling in love 39, 80-81, 91
Fanaticism 165, 168
Feeling 4, 81, 117-118, 158-159, 161, 163, 165-166, 176, 228, 231, 240
Fertility 60, 65, 68, 71
Fidelity 34
Forms of love 76, 79
Foundational 7, 64, 184, 190

Gaelic 57-59, 62
Givenness 255-257, 262, 264-265
Glory of God 32, 195
God 1, 4, 6-10, 14-18, 20-28, 32, 34, 45, 47, 49, 51, 57-64, 66-70, 72-79, 85-91, 93-97, 100-102, 107, 111-112, 115, 117, 119-123, 125, 131-139, 141-143, 145-146, 149-151, 153, 165-166, 169-172, 175, 177, 179-182, 184-191, 193-195, 199, 201-203, 205-207, 212-217, 219, 223, 227-229, 231-235, 245-264
God-experience 11, 185
Godhead 25, 64, 117
God-intoxication 7, 59, 73
Gratuitous love 3

Happiness 23, 33, 40-41, 95, 97, 148, 208
Harmony 10, 41, 47, 109, 180, 185-188, 190, 192, 196, 208, 210-213, 263
Hasidism 115-116
Hassidic 115, 133
Heart 4, 24, 32-33, 35, 59, 62, 70-71, 136, 139, 163, 187-188, 199, 254
Heaven 5, 20-21, 50, 59, 74, 92, 97, 112, 185, 230, 261
Hedonistic 40
Helplessness 75
Hermeneutics 204, 206, 213, 217-218, 251-252
Heteronomy 128
Highest Good 33, 41
Hinduism 1
Historical 7, 15-16, 28, 137, 205-206, 211, 215
Holiness 62, 69, 121, 124-125, 227
Holistic vision 63, 180, 186
Homo *mysticus* 52
Homoo *economicus* 52
Honesty 38
Human faculties 4

Human icons 6
Human immortality 101, 108, 112
Human nature 17, 75-77, 94, 99, 156, 159, 164, 177
Human predicament 44
Human response 4, 211
Human thought 10, 263
Humanism 53, 121, 123, 232
Humanities 1
Humility 10, 137, 197, 232, 235, 239-240, 242
Humour 10, 236, 238-240, 242

Icon 6, 257-259, 261-262
Identity 1, 17, 41, 119, 127, 129, 143, 208, 257
Identity with God 17
Image of God 131, 133-135
Imagination/s 6, 48, 62, 67, 73, 75-76, 87, 89, 159, 162, 164, 208, 238
Immanence 26, 61, 128, 130, 136, 249
Incantation/s 60, 64
Independence 22, 118-121, 123, 135-136, 149
Individual 9, 20, 41, 43-44, 46, 76, 79, 86, 96-97, 101, 142, 156, 169, 176, 181
Individuation 168-169, 171, 175-177
Indwelling 184-186, 196
Infinity 8, 13, 21, 26, 50, 113-114, 122, 124-125, 131, 138
Infra-human 40
Inner life 106, 172
Inner reality 5, 36
Inquisition 224-225, 230
Insight 1, 24, 43, 61, 77, 160, 187, 196, 230
Insight/s 9, 18-19, 151, 213-215, 255
Inspiration 65, 67, 72, 77, 127-129, 134, 138, 156, 190, 222
Integrated 40, 63, 73, 181
Integrity 39-40, 47
Interconnectedness 43, 182
Interconnections 183
Interdependence 5, 188, 190
Interdisciplinarity 5-6
Interiorisation 138
Internal 17, 102, 105, 137, 221
Interpretation 9, 28, 32, 112, 123, 135, 141, 155, 158, 176, 213, 215-216, 251, 254
Interreligious 10, 18, 203, 214, 218
Intersection 13, 15-16, 18-19, 21, 25, 27
Intrinsic value 9, 36, 179
Intuition 1, 40, 106, 109, 158, 165-166, 175, 182, 207-208, 255
Inward turn 77
Islam 1, 224

Jnana 142, 146-148, 150
Joy 8, 20, 23, 34, 44, 75-76, 80, 87, 89-90, 97, 142, 172, 188, 208, 232
Judaism 1, 114-116, 142, 144, 147
Justification 37

Karma 32, 34, 142, 147-148, 150
Kataphatic 217, 247, 256
Know thyself 168-169
Knowledge 3, 6, 28, 48, 52, 70, 75, 101, 111, 116, 124, 128, 146-147, 153, 155, 159, 161-163, 165-166, 172, 202, 214-215, 246-247, 255

Language 9-10, 17, 20, 49, 53, 58-59, 62, 104, 109, 128, 142, 147, 153, 157, 191, 201-202, 205-206, 209-210, 213-214, 216-219, 226,

234, 239-241, 246-248, 251-252, 254, 256, 259, 261, 263
Leader/ship 34-35, 43-44, 46, 52, 54, 69
Liberation 3, 109, 188, 209
Life-transforming 14
Limitations of knowledge 6
Linguistic 85, 168, 205, 232-233, 251-252, 263
Locution 10, 230, 242
Logic 1, 38, 45, 49, 51, 53
Loneliness 75
Longing 20, 25, 32-33, 45, 82-84, 86, 92, 96, 132, 188, 207-210, 250
Loss of self 118
Love-affair 75-98
Love-object 78, 80

Mammon 45
Management 42, 46, 52-55
Manager/s 37, 42, 47
Manifestation 54, 81, 85, 155-156, 163, 171-172, 174, 176, 186, 249-250
Marriage with God 8, 85
Material prosperity 42
Materialism 8, 34, 60, 72-73, 99, 106, 169, 175-176
Medical Materialism 8, 99, 106
Meditation 3, 13, 26, 35, 88-90, 151
Mendicants 17
Messianic 204-205
Metaphysical 78, 124-125, 161, 166, 169, 182, 246, 252, 254, 257-261
Methodology 4
Mind 4, 10, 23, 32, 34-36, 81, 84-85, 95, 101, 103, 105, 107-109, 112, 123, 142, 155, 158-159, 161, 164-165, 167, 177, 180, 181-183, 191, 199-200, 231, 240, 243
Models of religion 5
Monasticism 16, 61, 69, 73
Money and wealth 43
Monotheism 116, 120-121
Moral consideration/s 37-38
Morality 38, 52
Motivation/s 31-32, 37-38, 40, 42, 44, 49, 54, 76
Multiplicity 6, 21-22, 123, 175
Music 1, 6, 161
Mystic union 9, 87, 142
Mystical enthusiasm 8, 113-114, 123-125, 134
Mystical prayer 10, 63, 73, 86, 90, 241
Mystical strategy 10, 241-242
Mystical teachings 5, 93
Mystical utterances 5
Mystical vision 9, 134, 165, 195
Mysticism 1-3, 5-11, 13-19, 23, 27-28, 33-34, 68, 76-77, 85-86, 88-89, 99, 106, 113, 115, 122-125, 127, 130, 133-134, 136, 138, 141, 153, 155, 157-158, 164, 166-167, 169-171, 175-177, 179, 181-182, 190, 196, 201-203, 214-215, 218-219, 243, 246-247, 259, 263-265
Mythology 9, 107, 158

Naming 201-202, 214, 216, 247, 254, 257, 261
Narrativity 10, 204-206, 213, 217, 219
Naturalism 101
Nature 6, 8, 17-18, 21, 33, 36, 38, 40-41, 44, 49-51, 55, 70, 73, 75-79, 83, 94, 99-100, 103, 105, 109-110, 114, 121, 126, 128, 156, 159, 163-164, 166, 173-174, 176-177, 180-181, 183, 188-193, 195-199, 202, 206, 219, 223, 247, 251, 262
Negative 10, 20, 42, 60, 75-76, 123, 193, 201-206, 210, 212-219, 245-249, 251, 253-255, 258-260, 263-264

Negative theology 10, 201-207, 210, 212-214, 216-219, 245-249, 251, 253-255, 259-260, 263-265

Neurological 8, 107-108, 212-213, 219

Neuroscience 1, 101, 104

Neurotheology 99-102, 106-107, 109, 111-112, 213

Nexus 21, 41

Nihilism 207

Nirvana 3, 109

Non-violence 190-193

Normative 16, 183

Nothingness 26, 95, 153-155

Novelty 84

Numinosity 73, 166

Numinous experiences 165, 168

Obedience 34

Objectification 52

Objectivity 4, 159, 163, 168

Occultism 9

Oikonomia 32, 52-53

Okologics 32

Omnipresence 49, 62, 115, 122

Ontology 6, 126, 250

Orthodox 136, 207

Otherness 124-125, 202, 206, 215, 219, 262

Paradigms 32, 51

Paradoxical 8, 21, 42, 81, 94, 113, 128, 134, 153, 173, 217, 262

Parental love 78-79, 83

Participation 115, 117, 119-122, 180, 186, 197

Particle/s 25, 173, 182, 184

Particularity 10, 15, 22, 204-206, 213-219

Passionate love 8, 81-86, 91

Passive 89, 95, 127, 129

Passivity 128, 131, 138

Path 24, 27, 86, 117, 120, 210, 222

Patristic 202, 240

Pauline 22, 150, 234

Perfection 3, 23, 80, 87-89, 93-94, 122-123, 151, 172, 187-189

Persecuting 145

Personality 39-40, 146, 175, 191

Phenomenology 6, 9, 55, 105, 109, 124, 159, 168, 170-171, 177, 245

Phenomenon 1, 3, 6-7, 10, 14-15, 34, 55, 58-59, 66, 68, 71, 81, 161, 165, 167, 174, 207, 255-256, 259, 263-264

Philosophy 1-2, 4, 8, 18, 31, 36, 38, 44, 54, 75, 81, 100, 102, 123, 143, 159-161, 177, 179, 203-204, 251, 263-266

Philosophy of religion 4, 8

Physics 1, 5, 9, 104, 180-182, 188, 199-200

Pilgrim 19-21

Planet 9, 33, 43, 52, 170, 173, 179-181, 185, 189, 192, 195, 198

Pleasures 41-42, 84, 91, 227

Poetry 1, 6, 9, 28, 69, 73, 92, 161, 175

Positive 20, 44, 60, 68, 76, 113, 125, 191, 193, 206, 247, 252, 258

Prayer 7, 10, 25, 32, 58-63, 66, 73, 85-91, 96-97, 115, 204, 206, 212, 222-224, 227-228, 231

Presence 10-11, 14, 28, 50, 58-60, 67, 69-70, 80-84, 87, 90-91, 96-97, 117, 179, 184-186, 195, 199, 216, 228-229, 245-246, 252, 254-255, 259-264

Primordial 7, 64, 195

Primum mobile 21

Process 7, 9, 14-16, 18, 35, 94, 109, 111, 121, 134, 142, 147, 162, 168-169,

171-172, 175, 177, 180-181, 183, 186-188, 202, 207, 211, 218, 224
Profit 33, 37, 43, 52, 75, 111
Projection/s 118, 155-156, 171, 175-176, 180
Proof 3-4, 139, 148, 174
Protestantism 17
Proximity 83-84, 125, 127, 132, 238
Psychological 9, 46-47, 77, 155, 157, 164-165, 167, 171, 174, 191
Psychology 1, 9, 18, 77, 104-105, 112, 153, 157, 164, 170-171, 175-176
Purification 88, 92, 94, 121

Quantum physics 5, 9, 180, 188
Quietistism 17

Rabbi 115-116, 133, 144, 147
Rapture 87-88, 93, 95, 117, 238
Rationality 4, 37, 39, 46, 50, 54, 207
Realization 3, 7, 48, 142
Rebirth 17
Reciprocity 48-49, 52, 78-81, 83, 85, 136
Re-emergence 11, 264
Reflection/s 8-9, 16, 23, 90, 123, 133, 136, 149-151, 158, 170, 174, 181, 201-202, 205, 215, 266
Reification 108, 110-111
Relation 4, 7, 23, 39-40, 46, 72, 75-77, 79, 81, 85-86, 96, 127, 195, 203-205, 217, 256
Relationship 9, 25-26, 41, 52, 76, 79, 82, 96-97, 101, 105-107, 120-121, 124-125, 132, 134, 150, 152, 166, 180, 187-190, 194, 198-199, 201-202, 206, 210, 214, 218, 238, 245-246, 249-251, 254
Religion 4-5, 7-8, 10, 14, 18, 45, 64, 66, 75-76, 86, 101-102, 106, 108, 111, 115, 120-121, 123, 142, 144, 146, 148, 166, 177, 203-208, 210-214, 218-219, 240, 252, 264-265
Religious experience 4, 100-101, 103, 106-107, 109, 111-112, 118, 123, 141, 146, 149, 151, 209, 211-212, 223
Religious subjectivism 4
Remuneration 37
Renunciation 94, 193-194
Responsibility 32, 34, 43, 46, 49, 52, 55, 113, 124-127, 133-134, 136, 138, 207
Restlessness 84
Revelation 24-25, 70, 119-120, 144-145, 186-187, 215, 217, 250, 255-257
Reverence 7, 58, 66, 69, 180, 234
Rituals 1, 6, 64, 68, 110, 209, 215
Roman Catholicism 17
Romanticism 165

Sacramental 73, 223, 246, 255, 259, 261-262, 264
Sacred 6-7, 32, 51, 57, 60, 66, 68, 72, 108, 119, 121, 135, 182, 184, 247
Sacred stories 6
Sacredness 7
Sacrifice 34, 39, 52, 65, 71
Salvation 3, 19, 134-135, 142
Sanctity 193, 242
Sanity 193
Satisfaction 82-85, 92, 143, 145, 148, 229, 232
Satori 100
Saturation 247, 256
Science and religion 4-5
Sciences 1, 5-6, 9, 102, 158, 177, 188
Scientific cosmology 9, 179
Scripture 7, 16, 62, 115, 184, 223, 235, 247

Secularization 17
Seeking God 24-25, 89
Self-abandonment 42
Self-development 42
Self-emptying 137
Self-esteem 47
Selfhood 179
Self-interest 32-33, 36-39, 41, 54, 236
Selfless love 34
Selflessness 13
Self-mortification 94-95
Self-subsistent 21
Self-surrender 13
Sense perception 4
Sensibility 70, 129, 214, 216, 259
Sensus mysticus 14
Service 23, 36-37, 39, 46, 138
Solidarity 33, 130
Soul 22, 25, 35-36, 45, 61-62, 77, 83-98, 107, 118, 126, 128, 131-134, 138, 162, 169, 227, 229, 232, 236, 240
Speech 10, 148, 217, 231, 236, 239, 241-242, 247-248
Spiritual 1, 7, 31-36, 38-40, 42-43, 45-46, 51-54, 60, 62, 65, 69, 71, 73, 76-77, 85, 88-89, 91, 93-96, 99-101, 103, 109-111, 115-117, 134, 141, 148, 154, 157, 165, 171, 175-176, 182, 187, 189, 193, 198, 200, 211, 221-222, 225-226, 233-234, 236, 238
Spiritual legacy 73
Spirituality 1, 5-8, 10, 15, 27-29, 31-36, 40-41, 43, 48-49, 52-55, 58-59, 62, 66, 69, 73, 93-94, 100, 111-112, 115, 118, 138-139, 145, 187-188, 190, 193-194, 203-204, 208, 210-211, 215, 218, 221, 225-226, 229, 238
Stakeholder/s 43, 52
Strategies 10, 212, 221, 226, 228-229, 233, 242
Subconscious 9, 155-156, 158, 163, 166, 168, 171, 175-177
Subjectification 52
Subjectivity 127, 158, 165, 168
Substance 91, 105, 168, 211
Suffering love 84
Supernatural 101, 108, 110
Sustainable 33, 42, 54, 193
Symbolic 6, 62-63, 72, 85, 137, 155, 166, 202, 211, 249
Sympathy 38
Synthesis 132, 187

Taoism 1
Technology 50, 212
Temporal dimension 7, 14-15
The wholly Other 124-125, 246, 251, 254
Theologia mystica 10, 14, 20, 222, 225-226, 228, 230, 232, 235-236, 239-241
Theology 1-2, 10-11, 16, 18, 26, 28-29, 45, 54, 75, 77, 111-113, 136, 150, 153, 166, 200-207, 210, 212-219, 228-229, 233, 236, 240, 243, 245-266
Theophany 61, 258
Theosophical 157, 165
Third way 10, 246-248, 259, 264
Timeless 13-16, 18-19, 21, 27, 199
Torah-Centrism 145
Totality 8, 105, 113-114, 122, 124-125, 135
Tradition 2-3, 5, 7, 10, 14-16, 18-19, 32, 35, 41-42, 58, 61, 68, 72, 115, 133, 136, 142, 164, 203, 207, 209, 215-216, 224, 226, 230, 241, 243, 246, 254, 258

Tranquillity 95
Transcendence 6-7, 26, 31, 39-40, 42, 73, 121-123, 125, 128, 130, 132, 134, 136, 202, 215, 249, 255, 258-259
Transcendent 7, 39, 44, 46, 51, 53, 67, 96, 120-121, 125, 131, 135, 206, 210-211, 219, 249-250
Transformation 8, 27, 36, 66, 86-87, 94-95, 97, 163, 206-207, 209-210
Trinitarian 21, 58, 65, 74
Truth 1, 3, 14, 18-19, 22-24, 34, 41, 75, 83-84, 86, 90, 137, 159-161, 163, 165-166, 169-170, 176, 185, 187, 195-197, 199, 202, 205-206, 210, 214, 216-218, 231

Ultimate Realty 1, 10, 107, 153, 165, 182, 184
Unconditional 78, 147, 256
Unification 86, 88, 187
Unity 6, 11, 21, 39, 42, 64, 84, 95, 97-98, 165, 171, 181-182, 185-186, 188, 190, 199, 210, 213
Unity of humanity 6
Unity of self 11, 42
Universal 14, 19, 38, 164-165, 170, 176, 181, 204, 211, 214
Universe 7, 9, 21, 36, 49, 59, 64, 66, 106, 133, 142, 171, 173, 179-190, 194-196, 198-200, 249-250
Unknowing 10, 24-26, 28, 205, 229-230, 238

Valuational 3
Value 2-3, 9, 36, 39, 42, 44-45, 53, 92, 105, 119, 121, 132, 165, 176, 179, 258
Vernacularization 17
View of life 5, 32, 43, 48
Vision 5, 20, 24, 26, 47, 51, 55, 63, 70, 134, 155, 164-165, 173, 176, 180, 182-183, 185-186, 188, 193-195, 197-199, 222, 243
Visionary 24, 59
Visual arts 1, 6
Vocal prayer 227

Wakefulness 123, 130, 132
Wealth 31-33, 37-38, 40-46, 55, 184, 189, 194
Welfare of all 6
Well-being 33, 42, 127, 130
Willingness 22, 94
Withdrawal 11, 122, 224, 259, 264
Witness/ing 91, 139, 148, 215, 217
Work 3, 6-8, 17, 32, 34, 36, 42-44, 48-50, 52-54, 57, 67, 69, 100, 105, 110, 112-114, 123-125, 148, 196, 206, 213, 216, 219, 222-223, 226-229, 231, 233, 237, 240
World community 38
World spirituality 15
World-transcending 5
Worldview 6, 195

Yoga 9, 141-142, 150

16

Index of Authors

Agnew, Una 2, 7, 57-73
Ahlgren, Gillian 223, 225-226
Alan of Lille 27
Albrecht, Carl 3
Alper, Matthew 102
Alston, William 4
Alvarez, T. 242
Aquinas, Thomas 27, 85
Aristotle 36, 39-41, 44-45, 51-53, 87, 136
Augustine, Saint 76, 83-84
Aurobindo, Sri 36

Bataillon, M. 223-224, 242
Bateson, G 9, 181
Ben Eliëzer, Israel 115
Blake, William 9, 50, 153, 156-157, 159, 163-165, 171-172, 175, 177
Boehme, Jacob 153, 155, 157, 164, 169, 172, 176-177
Boeve, Lieven 2, 10, 201-219
Bohm, David 183
Borgman, Erik 209
Bouckaert, Luk 33, 54
Bouyer, Louis 14, 27
Bruemmer, Vincent 5
Burggraeve, Roger 8, 113-139

Calhoun, Cheshire 40, 54
Cannato, Judy 199
Capra, Fritjof 181
Caputo, John D. 203-204, 253
Carabine, D. 202
Carmichael, Alexander 59
Carnap, Rudolph 160, 177
Cazenave, Michel 177
Chakraborty, S. K. 35, 54
Chauvet, Luis-Marie 262-264
Clifford, W. 3-4
Cobb, John B. 53
Cousins, Ewert H. 15
Couwenberg, S. W. 207
Coyne, George V. 199

D'Auili, Eugene 112
Dalferth, I. 201
Daly, Herman E. 53
Dante Aligheri 20, 27
Davies, Glyn 54
Davis, Carmel Brendon 26-27
Dawkins, Richard 182, 212
De Boeck, E. 213
de Bujanda, J. 225
de Chardin, Teilhard 15, 180, 185

de Dios, Efrén de la Madre 242
de Leon, Fray Luis 230
de Medina, Bartolomé 233
de Osuna, Francisco 225-226
de Rougemont, D. 83
Deane, John F. 62
Delio, Ilia 200
Dennett, Daniel 212
Derrida, Jacques 203, 246
Desmond, William 50, 54
Dewey, John 99, 101-102, 105
Dhómnaill, Nuala Ní 72
Dionysius 10, 201, 245-251, 254-256, 258, 263-264
Donohue, John O. 73
Douglas, Mary 48, 54
Drucker, Peter F. 46, 54
Duinn, Seán O. 7, 63

Eckhart, Meister 5, 18-19, 22, 103
Egan, Harvey D. 34, 54
Einstein, Albert 9, 179
Eliade, Mircea 73
Eliot, T.S. 13

Flasche, H. 232
Frankfurt, Harry 40
Freud, Sigmund 155

Gale, Richard M. 108
Gandhi, M. K. 45-46, 52-54, 191
Garon, Henry A. 200
Gerson 235-236
Gildroy, Doreen 72
Gimello 3
Goodchild, Philip 45
Gregory of Nyssa 202

Hamilton, A. 223, 225, 243
Harris, Samuel 212
Hayyim of Volozhin, Rabbi 133
Heaney, Seamus 70
Hederman, Mark Patrick 69
Heft, Harry 105
Hegel, W. 100, 251
Heidegger, Martin 73
Hick, John 210
Hodgson, Phyllis 25
Horner, Robyn 256-257, 264-265
Hudry, Françoise 27, 28
Hume, David 158-159, 164, 168, 177
Husserl, Edmund 126, 177
Huston, Phil 11
Huxley, Aldous 99

James, William 99-102, 105
Janicaud, Dominiqueet 55, 245, 265
Jantisch, Eric 181-182
John of the Cross, Saint 86, 91, 93, 230
Jones, John D. 246, 265
Joyce, Timothy 61
Julian of Norwich 24-25
Jung, Carl G. 9, 155-156, 171, 174

Kachappilly, Kurian 1-11
Kant, Immanuel 50, 54
Kautilya 42
Kavanagh, Patrick 67
Kavanaugh, K. 242
Kearney, Richard 203
Kierkegaard, Soren 3, 137
Knitter, Paul 210
Kosky, Jeffrey L. 249
Kramer, Kenneth Paul 13, 28

Lambert, Y. 207-208
Lardreau, Guy 154, 159
Laredo 235
Lassalle, H. M. E. 3
Leijssen, Lambert J. 263-265
Levinas, Emmanuel 114, 123, 246, 249, 251, 265
Locke, John 161, 164, 167, 178
Losoncz, Alpar 42, 54
Luria 122

Macquarrie, John 59
Madathummuriyil, Sebastian 10, 245-265
Mahnke, Dietrich 27-28
Maisonneuve, Roland 26, 28
Malthète, J. F. 116
Manikkam, Thomas 9, 179-199
Marcos, Antonio 241
Marion, Jean-Luc 10, 203, 245, 254, 263
Márquez, A. 223-224
Martin, Andrés 224
Martínez, Llamas 229
Mathews, Freya 179
Mauss, Marcel 48, 54
McGinn, Bernard 2, 6-7, 13-29, 249
Melanson, Steve 169
Menéndez, Pidal R. 231-232
Menneteau, Patrick 9, 153-177
Merrigan, Terry 217
Mieth, Dietmar 23, 28
Mitchell, Nathan D. 262
Moevs, Christian 21
Monod, Jacques 163
Moses, Greg 2, 50, 54
Moyaert, Paul 2, 8, 75-97
Muller, Sylvie 60
Murray, Patrick 67
Murray, Paul 13, 28
Murthy, N. R., Narayana 46
Myers, Kimberly R. 72

Nadler, A. 116
Naess, Arne 180
Nandram, Sharda S. 34, 55
Newberg, A. B. 212
Newberg, Andrew 103, 107, 112
Nicholas of Cusa 27
Nietzsche, F. 160, 251
Nikhilanda, Swami 55

O'Murchu, Darmuid 200
O'Rourke, F. 202
Olivetti, M. 204
Olthuis, James H. 205, 253, 265
Omizzolo, Alessandro 199

Painadath, Sebastian 211
Palatty, Roy Varghese 7, 31-55
Panikkar, Raimundo 185-186
Pathrapankal, Joseph 8, 141-151
Paul, Saint 85, 180, 185, 187-188
Peers, Allison E. 239-240, 242
Persinger, Michael A. 111
Plato 118, 132, 164-165
Plotinus 5, 108
Pollefeyt, D. 213
Pseudo-Dionysius 18, 245-246, 259

Rahner, Karl 34
Ratzinger, Joseph Cardinal 38, 55
Rause, Vince 112
Raynauld, Isabelle 112
Reeves, Hubert 173
Richard of St. Victor 91
Ricoeur, Paul 49

Rivers, Elias 240
Rodriguez, O. 242
Rogers, Perry M. 5
Rosemann, Philipp Wolfram 266
Rowling, A. K. 61

Schleiermacher, W. 4
Schmid, K. 201
Schoenborn, Christoph Cardinal 200
Scholem, Gershom 19
Schrijvers, J. 203
Schumacher, E. F. 42
Schürmann, Reiner 23, 28
Sen, Amartya 44, 55
Silesius, Angelus 172
Smith, Adam 38, 44, 47
Socrates 164
Spencer, Michael 13, 28
Steggink, Otger 242
Stephen, Saint 60
Stoellger, P. 201
Stueckelberger, Christoph 50, 55

Tagore, Rabindranath 32
Talbot, Michael 182
Teresa of Avila, Saint 10, 77, 86, 221-242
Thomas Kinsella, Thomas 64
Thomas, R. S. 70
Tillich, Paul 211
Tobin, Frank 29
Turner, D. 202
Tyler, Peter 2, 10

Urs von Balthasar, Hans 248

Van der Leeuw, Gerardus 6
van der Ven, J. A. 209
van Harskamp, A. 208
Vandevelde, Antoon 2, 7, 31-55
Vattimo, G. 204
von Balthasar, Hans Urs 248
Wahl, Jean 124, 126
Wald, George 182
Waldman, Mark Robert 112
Walsh, James 25, 28
Ward, Graham 25, 254, 266
Watson, Nicholas 26, 28
Weber, A. 234-235, 237
Weidenbaum, Jonathan 8, 99-111
Weinberg, S. 183
Wells, Harold 200
Windstosser, M. 153, 172, 178
Wittgenstein, Ludwig 225, 243, 251
Wolpert, L. 173, 178
Yeats, W. B. 65, 67